The Digital Edge

*How Black and Latino Youth
Navigate Digital Inequality*

S. Craig Watkins

with Andres Lombana-Bermudez

Alexander Cho

Vivian Shaw

Jacqueline Ryan Vickery

Lauren Weinzimmer

NEW YORK UNIVERSITY PRESS

New York

NEW YORK UNIVERSITY PRESS
New York
www.nyupress.org

References to Internet websites (URLs) were accurate at the time of writing. Neither the author nor New York University Press is responsible for URLs that may have expired or changed since the manuscript was prepared.

Library of Congress Cataloging-in-Publication Data
Names: Watkins, S. Craig (Samuel Craig), author.
Title: The digital edge : how Black and Latino youth navigate digital inequality /
    S. Craig Watkins [and five others].
Description: New York, NY : New York University Press, [2018] |
    Series: Connected youth and digital futures | Includes bibliographical references and index.
Identifiers: LCCN 2018021509| ISBN 9781479854110 (cl : alk. paper) |
    ISBN 9781479849857 (pb : alk. paper)
Subjects: LCSH: Digital divide—United States. | Internet and youth—United States. |
    African American youth—Social conditions. | Hispanic American youth—Social
    conditions. | Low income high school students—United States. | Equality—United States.
Classification: LCC HN90.I56 W38 2018 | DDC 303.48/33—dc23
LC record available at https://lccn.loc.gov/2018021509

New York University Press books are printed on acid-free paper, and their binding materials are chosen for strength and durability. We strive to use environmentally responsible suppliers and materials to the greatest extent possible in publishing our books.

Manufactured in the United States of America

10 9 8 7 6 5 4 3 2 1

Also available as an ebook

The Digital Edge

CONNECTED YOUTH AND DIGITAL FUTURES

Series Editor: Julian Sefton-Green

This series explores young people's day-to-day lives and futures. The volumes consider changes at the intersection of civil and political reform, transformations in employment and education, and the growing presence of digital technologies in all aspects of social, cultural, and political life. The John D. and Catherine T. MacArthur Foundation's Digital Media and Learning (DML) Initiative has supported two research networks that have helped launch this series: the Youth and Participatory Politics Research Network and the Connected Learning Research Network. The DML Initiative and the DML Hub at the University of California, Irvine, also support production and open access for this series.

connectedyouth.nyupress.org

By Any Media Necessary: The New Activism of American Youth
Henry Jenkins, Sangita Shresthova, Liana Gamber-Thompson,
Neta Kligler-Vilenchik, and Arely Zimmerman

The Class: Living and Learning in the Digital Age
Sonia Livingstone and Julian Sefton-Green

The Digital Edge: How Black and Latino Youth Navigate Digital Inequality
S. Craig Watkins with Andres Lombana-Bermudez, Alexander Cho, Jacqueline Ryan Vickery, Vivian Shaw, and Lauren Weinzimmer

This book is dedicated to the students, teachers, parents, and guardians who welcomed us into their classrooms, homes, and lives.

Contents

Preface

S. Craig Watkins

In 2010, just a year into Barack Obama's first term as president, the President's Council of Advisors on Science and Technology submitted an ambitious 142-page report that outlined the challenges and opportunities related to revitalizing science, technology, engineering, and math (STEM) education in the United States. The council operated from the widely accepted premise that the nation must redesign education for a world that is undergoing steady and profound social, economic, and technological change.

As president of the United States, Mr. Obama led several high-profile initiatives that were intended to bolster America's technological and economic future by improving the quality of STEM education. The president consistently used his bully pulpit to rally educators, tech enthusiasts, industry leaders, and community activists around the movement to prepare the next generation of leaders in STEM.

Composed of leaders from tech giants such as Google and Microsoft, vice presidents from the National Academy of Sciences and the National Academy of Engineering, and university presidents, researchers, and scientists, the President's Council of Advisors on Science and Technology identified what it believed were the essential challenges to creating the educational strategy and school system the nation needed in a tech- and knowledge-driven economy. In its report to the president, the council wrote that "to meet our needs for a STEM-capable citizenry, a STEM-proficient workforce, and future STEM experts the nation must focus on two complimentary goals: preparation and inspiration."[1]

Many of the council members were intimately familiar with the rise and impact of intelligent machines and the increasing demand for highly skilled labor in the global economy and the U.S. workforce. The president had also emphasized the need to not only build the tech workforce of the future but ensure that it was inclusive and diverse.

Accordingly, the council was attentive to the equity challenges in STEM and the startling lack of gender, racial, and ethnic diversity in the innovation economy. The report added, "We must prepare all students, including girls and minorities who are underrepresented in these fields, to be proficient in STEM subjects."[2] The council wrote that the nation must "inspire all students to learn STEM and, in the process, motivate many of them to pursue STEM careers."

Among other things, the extensive report addressed the federal role in K–12 STEM education, the need for improved standards and assessments, the importance of a well-trained corps of teachers, advances in educational technology, students, and school systems. Buoyed by a team of respected experts, data, and insights, the explanation of the problems prohibiting the creation and implementation of a more robust STEM curriculum was largely unassailable. However, among the thousands of sentences in the report, this one is especially peculiar: "Despite its transformative role across the global economy, technology has not played a major role in K–12 education to date."[3] The statement is peculiar largely because you could make a strong case that nothing has influenced public education more over the last thirty years than technological transformation. The tools and applications that have flowed into the classroom—computers, smart boards, the Internet, mobile devices, tablets, social media, and advanced software—influence how we deliver and even define education today. Since at least the 1990s there has been a persistent and largely uncontested view that every school must have computers and the Internet and that students should learn to use them.

The technological capacity of U.S. public schools underwent a profound transformation between 1994 and 2005. In 1994, a student attending a lower-income school was unlikely to see a computer in her classroom. Only 3 percent of U.S. instructional classrooms offered access to computers. Roughly ten years later, in 2005, a student attending a lower-income school was almost as likely as her more affluent counterpart to see a computer in her classroom. By 2005, 94 percent of the instructional classrooms in the United States had computers.

In recent years the Internet, mobile platforms, massive data-based networks, and a new generation of software applications have nudged education toward a new but uncertain future. The big tech companies, led by Google and Apple, are engaged in an epic battle to exert wide influence in U.S. classrooms. In other words, technology plays a major role in our schools, just not the one that many believe it should be playing.

A more penetrating statement might be that technology has not adequately addressed the equity issues that continue to produce unequal opportunities to learn in our nation's schools. In fact, some argue that technology has actually made the educational and economic disparities in the United States worse. Technology, from this view, has primarily served to more deeply entrench the social, educational, and economic advantages of the privileged classes. And this is all true despite the fact that black, Latino, and poor students are today just about as likely as their white and more affluent counterparts to attend schools that offer access to computers and the Internet.

For more than five decades a variety of experts including economists, sociologists, and futurists have been predicting the coming of a new society and a new economy. Much of the forecasting has been influenced by technological innovation and related economic transformation. But even as smart machines, robots, and artificial intelligence grab considerable attention, the most important skills of the twenty-first century are turning out to be thinking skills rather than technical skills. Computational thinking, design thinking, critical thinking, and expert thinking, for example, are vital assets in our innovation economy. The challenge, as some researchers have pointed out, is not that black, Latino, and lower-income students do not have access to technology. The real challenge is that they often lack access to the instructional expertise and curricula resources that develop the cognitive skills that drive our knowledge-based economy.

Students from more affluent households not only benefit from superior educational opportunities—opportunities to grow their human capital. They also benefit from more diverse social ties—opportunities to grow their social capital. Schools that are rich in human *and* social capital offer their students extraordinary advantages compared with schools that struggle to cultivate these assets.

As part of an ethnographic study our research team conducted in a high school located on the suburban fringes of Austin, Texas, we witnessed the social and educational disparities that lower-income students face. We were in the high school just as a number of President Obama's efforts to scale up the initiatives to remake STEM education began to take form. The president and his team worked diligently to bring the ethos of the innovation economy—experimentation, a bias toward action, failing fast, rapid prototyping, and creative problem solving—to the staid world of education. Our fieldwork also coincided with the rising call to make skills like coding and design thinking central components of our nation's educational curriculum.

Much of the debate about STEM, education, and equity is shaped by a number of problematic claims. No claim may be more imprudent than the view that black, Latino, and poor students and their families undervalue education in general and STEM education more specifically. During our research we observed a community of black, Latino, and lower-income students who were heavily interested in STEM. Moreover, they invested in a variety of creative practices to pursue their educational and aspirational interests in the domain, even though school resources were limited.

These students, as you will learn in the following pages, did not suffer from a lack of interest in STEM. Rather, they suffered from a lack of opportunities to learn STEM skills in the classes available to them.

The parents that we met also ran counter to type. Though many of them struggled with low-skill, low-paying, low-status jobs, they understood the value of education and STEM. Many of them labored hard and made personal sacrifices to provide their children access to computers, smartphones, and the Internet. These parents knew better than anyone what it meant to try to make a life for a family in today's world without the vital education and skills that are closely linked to economic opportunity and social mobility.

The story that we tell is one of the first attempts to see up close how the debates about technology, equity, and the future of learning take shape in the real world. It is one thing to theorize about the future of learning. It is one thing to prepare reports that envision a more robust STEM education system. It is another to be charged with building that future in a community and a school bereft of crucial resources. In the world that we observed, students, families, and schools faced a string of hard choices. For example, we personally witnessed classrooms that had the resources to purchase technology but not to develop the instruction, curricula and learning opportunities that prepare students for a rapidly evolving society and economy. We also observed parents in working poor families make sacrifices to afford computers and Internet access even as they typically lacked the financial resources to expose their kids to the out-of-school enrichment activities that are routinely available to children in more affluent households.

But the story that we tell in this book is also influenced by students who in the face of unprecedented challenges and widening disparities struggled earnestly and creatively to find their pathways to better futures. Many of the students that we got to know worked hard to make school a more relevant place by transforming their classrooms, after-school life, and social relations into a vibrant ecosystem for exploring, tinkering, and learning with technology. We believe that if the president, tech leaders, high-powered councils, and policy makers could meet the students that we met, they would see the challenges in education through a different lens. Rather than labeling black, Latino, and lower-income students as disinterested in learning STEM—lacking inspiration—they would come to appreciate how the most diverse student body in U.S. history is eager to participate in building tomorrow's world.

Our research team did not know it, but the site for our fieldwork— the school, the city, and the state—emerged as a powerfully emblematic place to think about many of the challenges and (missed) opportunities in STEM education addressed by the President's Council of Advisors on Science and Technology. Many of the issues that are connected to the crisis in our schools (the lack of educational opportunity) and the crisis in the tech industry (the lack of diversity) were on vivid display throughout our fieldwork. The school that we were fortunate enough to gain access to placed us on the front lines of the future—a future marked by increasing diversity, uncertainty, and complexity.

This is the world that we share with you in the following pages.

Acknowledgments

A book like this does not happen without the support and contributions of a number of people. There are far too many to mention by name here so a special thanks to the many people, organizations, and universities that contributed to this project in some way.

I owe a special thanks to the Digital Edge team, which helped to design the study and collect and analyze the data that informs this book. The core team members over the life of this project were Andres Lombana-Bermudez, Jacqueline Vickery, Alexander Cho, Vivian Shaw, Lauren Weinzimmer, Adam Williams, Jennifer Noble, and Bailey Cool.

This project was also influenced by my colleagues from the Connected Learning Research Network, a team of extraordinarily generous scholars who offered expertise, feedback, and rich perspectives over the life of this work. This group includes, Mimi Ito, Sonia Livinstone, Kris Gutiérrez, Juliet Schor, Jean Rhodes, Bill Penuel, Vera Michalchik, and Dalton Conley. Also, advisors to the CLRN that influenced this project include Julian Sefton-Green, Ben Kirshner, Richard Arum, Katie Salen Tekinbaş, Nichole Pinkard, Daniel Schwartz, and Kylie Peppler.

A lot of this work was also supported by the fantastic team at the Digital Media and Learning Hub at the University of California at Irvine, including David Theo Goldberg, Claudia Caro Sullivan, Amanda Wortman, Mimi Ko Cruz, Anita Centeno, and Jeff Brazil.

Several of my colleagues at the University of Texas at Austin also provided intellectual support and encouragement, including Sharon Strover and the UT|Portugal Collaboration, Wenhong Chen, Tom Schatz, Joseph Straubhaar, Kathleen Tyner, and two Deans, Rod Hart and Jay Bernhart.

The Digital Edge team and CLRN were the beneficiaries of generous and forward thinking funding from the MacArthur Foundation and the Digital Media and Learning—DML—initiative. DML anticipated the digital revolution in the lives of young people and funded both research, policy, and the prototyping of new learning futures. During her stewardship of the DML effort, Connie Yowell was a significant advocate of the work that I and my CLRN colleagues conducted. There are so many people to thank at the Foundation including, Jennifer Humke and the current President, Julie M. Stasch.

Family provide more than they ever know when taking on a project of this scope. Thus, I'd like to thank my beautiful wife and daughter, Angela Hall Watkins and Cameron Grace Watkins. I shared many insightful conversations about this project with Sherry Watkins and Karen Munson, two people who have been a constant source of inspiration in my life.

Finally, this book was made possible by members of the Freeway High School community—teachers, administrators, district leaders, parents, and students—who gave us incredible access to their lives. We could not have asked for more and hope that we represent you in a fair, respectful, and appreciative light.

Introduction

The Digital Edge

S. Craig Watkins

In a 2013 cover story for *Time* magazine titled "Why Texas Is Our Future," economist Tyler Cowen explains why a growing number of Americans are moving to Texas. Cowen writes, "More than any other state, Texas looks like the future . . . offering a glimpse of what's to come for the country at large in the decades ahead."[1] One data point about Texas and what it implies about the nation's future from the most recent U.S. Census is especially revealing: between 2000 and 2010 the number of under-eighteen-year-olds in the United States increased by about two million. Roughly half of the nation's increase occurred in one state: Texas.[2] Moreover, fully 95 percent of the growth in Texas was by Latino children.

Freeway High School is emblematic of the changes that are shaping the future of American demography, geography, and opportunity. Like many things in Texas, Freeway is big. The cavernous school is broad, tall, and home to more than 2,200 students. Located in the suburban fringes of Austin, Freeway is tucked far away from the entrepreneurial energy and affluence that are commonly associated with Austin's technology- and university-driven innovation economy.[3] The school building is surrounded by many of the familiar landmarks of a suburban geography characterized by nondistinct architecture, big-box stores, fast-food chains, immigrant-owned mini-markets, and arterial roads that are built, in theory, to aid the navigation of Austin's sprawling metropolis.

Freeway was also the home of our research team for nearly two years and provided an opportunity to examine the many challenges that confront our schools in a time of epic change. If, as Cowen claims, Texas is a microcosm of our future, then Freeway presents a unique opportunity to see that future up close.

Ostensibly, the goal of our research was to gain an on-the-ground perspective of the role that digital media play in the formal and informal learning environments of teens from resource-constrained schools and households. We were aware of the many studies that suggested that Latino, African American, and lower-income youth were adopters of social and mobile media.[4] In fact, their adoption of social and mobile media has prompted some to argue that smartphones, the poor's primary platform for Internet access, have accomplished what many well-intentioned policy makers, philanthropists, and educators have failed to do—bridge the nation's stubborn digital divide. Even before beginning our fieldwork at Freeway we knew that the story was more complex than that narrative suggested.

Freeway presented an opportunity to develop a more detailed and textured understanding of the media practices forming in the daily lives of black and Latino teens. Additionally, we wanted to explore the implications of this evolving digital media ecology for learning, opportunity, and social mobility. More specifically, we explore in detail what we call the *digital edge*.

The digital edge is a reference to the institutions, practices, and social relations that make up the daily and mediated lives of black, Latino, and lower-income youth. Our notion of the digital edge is informed by an essential conflict that is woven throughout the chapters in this book: even though a greater diversity of children and teens are using Internet technologies than ever before, not all forms of technology adoption are equal. The digital media practices of black, Latino, and lower-income youth are influenced by broader social and economic currents that give rise to distinct practices, techno-dispositions, and opportunities for participation in the digital world.

In the technology world, "edge" usually connotes something positive and even forward oriented. Being on the "cutting edge" of technology usually references innovation in either the design of technology (e.g., building a new platform) or the creative use of technology (e.g., finding inventive ways to use technology). Our use of the term "edge" is meant to highlight the contradictory contours that mark the digital media lives of black and Latino teens.

For example, the "digital edge" acknowledges the marginalized position that black and Latino teens navigate as they participate in the digital world. Black and Latino youth often live in homes with intermittent access to broadband Internet, confront outdated hardware and software, and learn in poor curriculum classrooms. In this context, "edge" is equated with being on the margins of the tech economy, tech rich households, and high quality schooling.

But the "digital edge" also acknowledges the innovative position that black and Latino teens occupy in the digital world. As we reflected on our fieldwork it became clear that so much of the literature focuses on what we might call the *deficit narrative*—that is, an almost exclusive examination of what black, Latino, and lower-income youth do not have in relation to a rapidly evolving tech landscape. While we understand that black and Latino teens are often bereft of key resources, what they do have is an important part of the story too. We call this the *asset narrative*. For example, black and Latino teens bring a number of assets to their engagement with technology, including innovative techno-dispositions and practices that have led to important modes of digital expression and community like Black Twitter and social media enhanced movements like Black Lives Matter. Media practices like these highlights the degree to which diverse users of digital media expand what is possible in the connected world.

Three specific dimensions of the digital edge inform our efforts to understand the educational environments and the technology and creative practices that we observed during our fieldwork. These dimensions are the new geography of inequality, persistent racial achievement gaps in education, and evolving trends in the adoption of media technologies. Though distinct from each other, these three elements intersect in complex ways to give an uneven shape and urgency to the making of the digital edge and the lives and futures of young people coming of age in the social and economic margins.

Income inequality in the United States is rising.[5] Although some progress has been made in closing the academic achievement gaps in U.S. schools, racial and class disparities persist at the primary, secondary, and postsecondary levels. And then there are the complex shifts that mark the diffusion of technological innovation. For example, even as black and Latino teens are just as likely as their white and Asian counterparts to use the Internet, they are also more likely to grow up in homes that do not provide access to broadband, a crucial gateway to more capital-enriching forms of digital participation.

The New Geography of Inequality

A key dimension of the digital edge is the changing geography of inequality. Despite living in a hyperconnected world where physical distance is often characterized as immaterial, geography—or more precisely, where people live—still matters.[6] The neighborhood that a person lives in and the resources (knowledge, schools, and people) available in that neighborhood profoundly shape his or her life chances and access to opportunity. Freeway students lived figuratively and literally on the edges of Austin and its rapidly evolving innovation and tech-driven economy.[7]

During our fieldwork and subsequent analysis, other insights underscored the significance of geography and its relationship to opportunity and social mobility in the United States. For example, the research of Raj Chetty and colleagues on geography and the dynamics of intergenerational mobility informed our work.[8] In their analysis of administrative records on the incomes of more than forty million children and their parents, the researchers argue that specific geographic attributes, and not simply growing up in a poor neighborhood, shape the prospects for a child to rise out of poverty.

The geographical variation in intergenerational mobility detected by Chetty and his colleagues is correlated with factors such as segregation, school quality, and social capital. Upward income mobility, for example, is significantly lower in areas with large and segregated African American populations. Proxies for the quality of K–12 education include things such as test scores, dropout rates, and class sizes. Further, children growing up in communities that rank high in social capital—things like religious affiliation, greater participation in local civic organizations, low crime rates—tend to do better in terms of social mobility measures.[9] Neighborhoods in which students perform well across these measures tend to have higher rates of upward mobility.[10]

Further, the geography of inequality in Austin reflects what Brookings Institution researchers Elizabeth Kneebone and Alan Berube identify as the "suburbanization of poverty."[11] Whereas living in a U.S. suburb was once synonymous with white flight, affluence, and upward social mobility, the story is more complex today. The trend toward greater suburban poverty accelerated during the 2000s. Between 2000 and 2010, suburbs in the nation's largest metropolitan areas saw their poor population grow by 53 percent. Poverty in metro suburbs grew at a rate that was more than five times that of primary cities. According to Kneebone and Berube, "By 2010, the suburban poor population exceeded that in cities by 2.6 million residents."[12]

Between 2000 and 2011 the suburban city that was home to Freeway tripled in size.[13] In 2000, white residents made up 77 percent of the suburban population. By 2010 that percentage had decreased to 64 percent. Conversely, Latinos made up 16.7 percent of the population in 2000 compared with 27.7 percent in 2010. African Americans made up 9.5 percent of the population in 2000 and 15.5 percent in 2010. Whereas Asians were less than 1 percent (0.01 percent) of the population in 2000, that percentage climbed to 7.4 percent by 2010. The proportion of foreign-born residents living in this particular suburb increased substantially, too, growing from 6.4 percent in 2000 to 13.3 percent in 2011. By 2010, this suburban area had become what demographers refer to as a "majority-minority city."[14] The population changes did more than remake the demographics of the suburb; they also remade the public schools and educational opportunities that were available to students.

During the first decade of the new millennium, student enrollment in the Austin Metro Area School District (MASD) increased 64 percent and was driven primarily by the enrollment of Latino, black, Asian, immigrant, and lower-income students.[15] From 2000 to 2010, the district reported a 115 percent increase in Asian/Pacific Islander students, a 118 percent increase in black students, and a 177 percent increase in Latino students. White student enrollment during the period decreased by 9 percent. The demographic shifts inside the city limits of Austin were considerably different during this period and reflect the racial and class dynamics of population flows in the Austin metropolitan area.[16]

The rise of Austin's innovation economy has led to sharp cost of living increases that are driving families, especially working poor and poor families, to the periphery of the city. A study by University of Texas researcher Eric Tang found that Austin was unique in one important way among the nation's fastest-growing locales: it was the only one to have a net loss of African Americans.[17]

Social class and economics also marked the student population shifts. During this period, the MASD reported a 194 percent increase among students receiving free lunch and a 376 percent increase in students demonstrating limited English proficiency. Like the district as a whole, Freeway experienced a sharp rise among students from lower-income households. In 1997, 13 percent of Freeway students were designated as economically disadvantaged compared with 60 percent by 2011.

Finally, 45 percent of Freeway students were identified as "at risk" of dropping out of school during our time in the field.[18] Labels like these are value laden and generally have implications for how teen bodies are perceived and schooled.[19] In the context of education, for example, these labels impact how students are sorted and tracked into specific curricula and courses, which has significant implications for their opportunity to cultivate the social and academic skills that support either the school-to-work or the school-to-postsecondary-education transition.

The school district that we encountered while conducting our fieldwork was undergoing a dramatic transformation. Between the 1990s and the close of the first decade of the 2000s, the MASD transformed from a predominantly white and middle-income school district to a high minority and immigrant and lower-income district. Life at Freeway reflected these changes and the challenges that ensued for the school, students, and their families. These big demographic shifts were visible in our fieldwork and illuminate the social, economic, and educational disparities that are central features of the digital edge.

The Resegregation of Schools and Learning

One of the defining characteristics of U.S. schools is sharp racial segregation. Because most schools are neighborhood schools, this is a reflection of the legacy of residential segregation along racial, ethnic, and economic lines.[20] Freeway, however, was a multiracial, multiethnic, and multilingual school. During our fieldwork, the Freeway student population was predominantly Latino (48 percent) and African

American (24 percent), but Asian (13 percent) and white (11 percent) students were also represented among the student body. English language learners represented 11 percent of the student population.

If the racial and ethnic diversity at Freeway ran against the norm, the racial academic achievement gaps at Freeway were consistent with long-standing patterns. One of the ironies of racially diverse schools is that they end up being racially segregated within, especially along academic lines and perceived academic ability. White and Asian American students, for instance, are much more likely to be represented in the high track, Advanced Placement (AP), college prep, and gifted courses.[21] By contrast, black and Latino students are typically underrepresented in those classes, thus leading to some racially inflected notions about race, learning, and ability. Some researchers refer to this as second-generation segregation, a reference to a post–civil rights era of schooling that reproduces many of the disparities in educational opportunity associated with previous formations of racially segregated schools. Data compiled by the Texas Education Agency highlights clear racial achievement disparities at Freeway.

For example, Asian (57 percent) and white (43 percent) students were more than twice as likely as Latino (20 percent) or black (15 percent) students to have taken at least one AP or International Baccalaureate examination. White (71 percent) and Asian (66 percent) students were substantially more likely than Latino (39 percent) or black (38 percent) students to be college ready in English language arts and mathematics, two cornerstone academic subjects. English language learner (71 percent), Latino (83 percent), and black (88 percent) students were less likely to complete high school in four years than their Asian (93 percent) and white (91 percent) counterparts. Moreover, Latino and English language learners were the most likely to leave high school without a diploma in hand. The academic disparities at Freeway are consistent with national educational trends in which black and Latinos, compared to white and Asian students, score much lower on educational tests and are also less likely to be enrolled in advanced academic courses.[22]

These achievement gaps explain, in part, why white and Asian students were much more likely to earn a postsecondary degree within six years of high school graduation than their black and Latino counterparts.[23] Many of the students that we met did not see college as an option in their future. As we discuss in the book's conclusion, students who do not earn a postsecondary credential are especially vulnerable in an economy that privileges higher-educated and higher-skill persons.

The Shifting Contours of the Digital Divide

Our examination of the digital edge was also shaped by another important development—the remaking of the digital divide. Even in a school in which 65 percent of the students were designated as economically disadvantaged, we routinely witnessed students using the Internet and social and mobile media technologies. For example, students used digital cameras, computers, and editing software to produce videos and graphic art in technology courses. Students also used game-authoring software to design simple games in their game design class. At Freeway, technology was incorporated in some of the classes, but the most creative uses took place in the after-school hours. During that time we observed students codesigning digital media and learning environments to support extracurricular activities and media projects that were peer driven, creative, and tech savvy.

Freeway was not a technology-poor school. In fact, the use of technology by the students in our study illuminates how widely the adoption of the Internet, for example, has spread across U.S. schools. In 2000 low-income students attended schools that offered limited access to computers and the Internet, if they offered it all.[24] By 2005, schools emerged as one of the more reliable places for lower-income students to access computers and the Internet.[25]

As recently as the early 2000s, young blacks and Latinos barely figured in the conversations about technology adoption and use. At best, they were considered laggards or late adopters. This gave rise to the digital divide concept, a narrative that largely viewed blacks and Latinos as marginal to the digital world.[26] The data since the middle 2000s strongly suggest that black and Latino teens have become increasingly central in the making of the teen-driven social media and digital world.[27] The adoption of the mobile web and social media by African American and Latino teens has been decisive and also turns the theories about the digital divide and diffusion of innovation on their heads.

No one would have predicted that black and Latino youth would be trendsetters when it came to the early adoption of the mobile Internet. No one would have predicted that by the close of the first decade of the new millennium black and Latino teens would be spending more time online than their white and Asian American counterparts.[28] But their reasons for the adoption of the mobile Internet are complex. Their use of mobile platforms, especially smartphones, suggests early adopter status, on the one hand, while also illuminating the lack of reliable access to home broadband connections, on the other. In chapter two we refer to this as the "mobile paradox."

Black and Latino youth are extraordinarily active when it comes to using their mobile phones to connect with peers, play games, listen to music, and watch videos.[29] Still, very little is known about the creative and media production practices that are also a part of their social and media ecologies. When Steve Jobs introduced the iPad to the world in 2010, he repeatedly stated that the tablet "was like holding the Internet in your hand." Our fieldwork suggests that black and Latino teens had already been holding the Internet in their hands via mobile phones. Throughout this book we consider two questions. First, what kind of Internet are black and Latino teens holding? Second, what are the social and educational implications of the Internet they hold? Researchers must develop a sharper portrait of the rapidly evolving media ecologies of black and Latino teens to learn what, if anything, is distinct about their use of media and Internet technologies.

Some of the more interesting questions regarding the media practices of black and Latino teens are sociological. How is their media ecology evolving with the adoption of social and mobile platforms? How does their embrace of the mobile phone as the hub of their social, informational, and cultural life rewrite the digital divide narrative? What distinct skills, assets, and dispositions do they bring to their adoption of smart technologies? Likewise, how does their adoption of mobile reproduce concerns about digital access, participation, and literacy that have been long-standing themes in the digital divide narrative? What are the social, educational, and civic implications of their engagement with media technologies? We address these and other questions in the following pages.

Black and Latino teens go online often and from a variety of places—school, libraries, community tech centers, home, and via mobile devices. Their adoption of media technologies has provoked some researchers to shift from studying the "access gap" to studying what is characterized as the "participation gap" or "digital literacy gap."[30] This shift acknowledges that as more diverse populations join the digital world, analysts must delineate the different environments, genres of use, and skills that produce diverse media environments, practices, and modes of participation in digital media culture.

Many of the chapters in the book illuminate how the technology practices of black and Latino teens are remaking the digital divide. Thus, rather than frame their use of digital media in the *context of deficits*, we frame their media behaviors in the *context of assets, too*. In other words, rather than thinking only about what black and Latino teens lack when engaged in the digital world, we also consider what they bring to their engagement. Importantly, the chapters also consider how social and economic inequalities continue to influence the digital practices and educational opportunities of African American and Latino teens even as their participation in the digital world expands.

As knowledge about the multifaceted aspects of digital inequality (i.e., access gaps, participation gaps, literacy gaps) continues to evolve, research and policy interventions must also evolve. We view the digital divide as not simply a matter of access to technology but also access to the social, human, and learning resources that support more capital-enhancing modes of adoption and participation.[31] Moreover, we maintain that schools and other youth-serving entities invested in preparing young people for the world of tomorrow must help them develop the skills and the disposition to use technology to intervene in the world around them. Access to technology, we argue, is no longer a sufficient measure of success, better learning futures, or digital equity. Rather, those on the ground—parents, educators—or designing policy to enrich the lives of young people must seek to create spaces, resources, and learning opportunities that empower young people to participate in the making of new social, civic, and economic futures.

Much of the debate about technology in the education of teens in the digital edge pivots around workforce development or preparing them for jobs that are steadily being erased by automation and globalization. The career-ready discourse, as we discuss in the conclusion, misses the critical opportunity to design schools and curricula that prepare students for a society and economy marked by complexity, uncertainty, and diversity. As a result of our fieldwork at Freeway, we pose a different challenge: rather than preparing students for today's jobs (career readiness), why not support their preparation for the social, civic, and economic uncertainties of tomorrow (future readiness).

The three factors noted above—the new geography of inequality, the resegregation of school and learning, and shifts in the digital divide—contribute in unique ways to the making of the digital edge and the prospects for opportunity and mobility among Freeway students. Schools do not live in a vacuum. In fact, schools are a prominent reflection of society's racial formations and social and economic inequalities.[32] As we began to analyze the data from our fieldwork, we found ourselves striving to understand how the social and economic currents that were happening outside the walls of Freeway influenced what we observed inside the school.

Doing School in the Digital Edge

The demographic and academic achievement data cited above offer insight into the world that we encountered at Freeway. But these data do not tell the whole story. In fact, only looking at these data obscures the practices and social relations that present a more nuanced portrait of Freeway. Thus, our analysis is attentive to the diverse ways Freeway students "do school." In her investigation of a group of high-achieving high school students, Denise Clark Pope identifies a number of ways that they craftily manage the stress of high-demand courses, hypercompetitive extracurricular schedules, and parental expectations that they gain admission to a select college.[33] During our fieldwork at Freeway we considered this question: How do students in resource poor and underperforming school settings do school?

Much of the research to date has been influenced by the view that low-performing black students, for example, foster an oppositional culture that negates academic achievement.[34] This claim essentially states that black students do school by trying to fail. In recent years, however, researchers have challenged the oppositional culture perspective.

For example, Prudence Carter suggests that black students' struggles in school may have less to do with an opposition to learning and more to do with an opposition to authority and a disciplinary apparatus that subjects them to harsher punishment and cultural misunderstandings over their sartorial styles, language, and sources of cultural capital.[35] Karolyn Tyson argues that the academic experiences of low-achieving students may be shaped by the practice of resegregation, especially in the form of being sorted into low-ability classes that often establish extremely low expectations.[36] Angel Harris compiled an impressive array of data to demonstrate that "kids don't want to fail" in school.[37] Harris maintains that most black students value school and want to achieve but that they may not know how.

In our case studies, students "do school" in a variety of ways. In chapter three Jacqueline Ryan Vickery and Vivian Shaw explain how students do school by resisting and revising the often antiquated district policies that restrict their ability to be more creative with the technology that they have access to in school. As Alexander Cho, Vivian Shaw, and S. Craig Watkins discuss in chapter seven, some of the students in our study enrolled in AP courses and strategically pursued extracurricular activities to establish a competitive academic profile for college. But most of the students in our study employed more nonconventional tactics in the ways that they did school.

In chapter five, for example, Watkins discusses how a group of students formed their own quasi studio to turn their game design class into a more collaborative and dynamic learning experience. Watkins, Andres Lombana-Bermudez, and Lauren Weinzimmer describe in chapter six how some Freeway students transformed the after-school hours into a lively lab for creativity, collaboration, and content creation. In these last two examples, students were less interested in building a competitive profile for college than they were in building opportunities and social relations that simply made school a more interesting and relevant place to be.

Many of these activities were not academic in a traditional manner. But rather than describe them as deviant or oppositional to learning and achievement, we pursue a different analytic track. More precisely, these forms of learning and media production highlight how students do school in ways that are inventive, engaged, and achievement oriented.

This study is also informed by the Connected Learning framework, an approach to learning and youth practice that has been developed by a series of research and design initiatives supported by the MacArthur Foundation.[38] The Connected Learning model is as much a vision of learning as it is a theory of learning. More generally, connected learning posits that when learning is linked across multiple spheres—school, after school, peers, home, and online—it is likely to be more powerful and more meaningful.

From a Connected Learning perspective, learning should be networked, experiential, production centered, and marked by a shared purpose between students and adults.[39] Unfortunately, the bulk of learning in America's schools runs counter to these principles and is, instead, typically cut off from the networked world, routinized, test centered, and individualized. In a connected learning world, students are expected to actively produce and apply knowledge. In most schools, students are generally required to passively consume and memorize information.

Not surprisingly, it is much more likely that students from resource-abundant schools and communities will have greater access to connected learning opportunities than their resource-constrained counterparts. In addition to richer opportunities to learn in school, students from affluent households benefit from richer out-of-school learning opportunities.[40] Still, even when schools and the adults who run them organize learning in more traditional ways, students occasionally find opportunities to redesign learning in ways that counter established conventions and reflect some of the principles of connected learning. The clever ways in which some Freeway students do school underscore this point.

Technology Is Not a Solution

Our fieldwork was an opportunity to see up close how the social, digital, and educational lives of black, Latino, and lower-income teens are evolving. This is a fact: teens from lower-income families are more likely to have access to Internet-enabled technologies today than they were a decade ago.[41] As we discuss in chapter one, access to Internet media comes in a variety of forms, including more affordable computers and smartphones. Similarly, access to Internet media comes from a variety of places, including schools, after-school settings, and home. While access to the Internet and media technologies is improving for young people, access to dynamic educational (i.e., formal curricula) and social (i.e., informal knowledge networks) resources that sustain more capital-enhancing forms of digital participation remains tenuous for teens in resource-constrained settings.

In our fieldwork we tracked two classes—a game design course and a video and technology applications course—to better understand the challenges and opportunities associated with efforts to design and implement digital media and learning in the formal classroom. These were the two main Career and Technology Education courses at Freeway. Consequently, the teachers of these classes were charged with orienting students toward information, technology, and creative careers. Both classes were burdened by the legacy problems associated with vocational education in the United States.[42] More specifically, the classes were oriented toward "tools literacy" rather than more academic and design-oriented literacies.[43] Tools literacy skills such as learning how to use basic software applications like Word or PowerPoint are foundational. By contrast, academic oriented skills such as coding and design thinking are transformational. In the chapters that follow we fully consider the limits of vocational technical education and the implication for learning and future opportunity.

Additionally, we spent tens of hours observing the activities in the after-school spaces that were devoted to the digital media arts, including, for example, video and film production, social media, graphic design, and game development. The students involved in these activities devoted substantial amounts of time and energy to pursuing creative activities, social relations, and learning experiences that often exceeded what was available during the school day to grow their skills and aspirations as digital media content creators.

Like their counterparts in many schools, Freeway teachers and administrators believed that the mere use of technology in the classroom was a source of achievement. We dispute this view in our analysis but also maintain that Freeway was the most important node in the digital media ecology of students from lower-income households for two main reasons. First, Freeway was the most reliable source for them to access computers, the Internet, and the software applications that supported sustained engagement in production-centered digital media practices.

Similar to national trends, home broadband Internet adoption was irregular and intermittent for many in our study.[44] Second, some of the classes and after-school settings offered access to the kinds of social milieus and creative spaces that support deeper engagement in the production of digital media content.[45] While access to technology—hardware and software—is commonly recognized as important to enabling robust participation in the digital world, access to vibrant social spaces, knowledge-rich peer networks, and supportive communities is often overlooked.

We entered this study excited about the opportunity to see up close the use of technology in a school populated by teens from black, Latino, immigrant, and lower-income households. Freeway had just launched a game development track that aspired to enhance the STEM literacies of students and prepare them for entry into a knowledge-driven economy. The technology applications course intended to expose students to media production, digital storytelling, and elements of design. Finally, we were intrigued to learn about the digital media club, an extracurricular activity that created a space and a community for the school's most passionate digital media makers. These were all indicators of a school that appeared to embrace new learning futures that included technology-rich courses, STEM education, and extracurricular activities that spark the development of what are often characterized as twenty-first-century skills and new media literacies.[46]

But as our time in the school grew so did the questions that we felt obligated to ask. What is the role of education in a knowledge-driven economy? What kinds of curricular resources should schools cultivate to provide rich digital media and learning opportunities? What kinds of skills—social, cognitive, technological—should schools be cultivating among their students? Moreover, why do school officials put more faith in the acquisition of technology than in the development of rich curriculum and instruction?

We engaged these questions through long, deep, and up close observation. The world that we became intimate with at Freeway—the world of formal schooling and learning—is remarkably complex. As we contend in the following pages, studying Freeway provided us with a detailed glimpse of one of the most pivotal challenges our country faces—preparing the nation's most diverse student population in history for a rapidly evolving society and economy. The teachers, administrators, students, and parents that we discuss in the book opened up their world to us. They gave us access to their classrooms, extracurricular activities, home life, and more. In addition, they participated in candid, in-depth conversations about many issues. Without their generosity this book would not be possible.

As researchers we are obligated to document and analyze what we observed as fairly and rigorously as we possibly can. This means being critical of people we came to know and respect. If you have ever spent time in a U.S. public school, you know that it consists mainly of noble people striving to do the good work of education. In a time of growing economic uncertainty and societal change, the work of education may be tougher than ever. Schools are trying valiantly to remain relevant even as they appear to be losing ground in the face of historical changes and mounting pressure. It is an epic struggle and one that produces stunning disparities in the quality of education that black, Latino, and lower-income students receive.

We discuss these and other outcomes not to be critical of the school and teachers that invited us in but rather to be as forthcoming as we can about the challenges our nation faces. Only through persistent documentation and analysis can we design schools that are capable of building better futures. For all of the shortcomings that we observed at Freeway, one thing was strikingly clear: the school was the last, best chance for many of the students in our study to find their unique pathway to opportunity.

Freeway was the only place students could reliably pursue both formal and informal learning opportunities that were connected to their interest in digital media. Also, Freeway was the only place students could access the hardware and software that enabled them to join in robust forms of digital media learning and participatory cultures. Freeway, moreover, was a crucial source of community, offering access to peers, teachers, mentors, and a cluster of media makers that helped students transform the school into a place that, at times, was relevant and inspiring. In short, Freeway was a source of human capital, techno-capital, and social capital for many students.

The teachers that we met at Freeway struggled to design and implement a curriculum that supported deep learning. Some even taught courses that they were not qualified to teach. Still, teachers like the ones that you meet in the book—Mr. Warren and Mr. Lopez—gave students more than we could ever credit them for in this book. In addition to sharing their knowledge with students, they shared their time and their social ties. Mr. Warren and Mr. Lopez stayed late after school to share their classrooms and the technology they supervised, allowing students to take laptops, software, and digital cameras home to work on a variety of creative projects such as films, games, music, and graphic art. In the face of diminishing resources, the teachers empowered several of the students and their extraordinary struggle to make school matter.

Ethnographic accounts of schools provide a glimpse into the practices, experiences, and social relations that are fluid and messy but also vital to understanding schools as complex social systems. In theory, schools are places where students go for academic-oriented learning. In addition, schools are supposed to prepare students for the transition to young adulthood, including work or postsecondary education. Still, it is common knowledge that some schools are better resourced to prepare their students for life's transitions than others. Not surprisingly, the economic and population shifts that remade the student body at Freeway severely challenged the school's ability to build and sustain high-quality instructional environments and viable future-oriented pathways.

The chapters draw from our extensive fieldwork to share our insights regarding the challenges that schools face in preparing students for the world of tomorrow. Even as technology has spread to more schools, disparities in academic achievement, economic opportunity, and social mobility persist. This suggests two things: first, that a technology-driven solution to the education crisis is a solution that is certain to fail; and second, that a substantive remake of education requires engagement with broader social and economic forces. In short, the challenges that schools like Freeway face are far more severe than any technology or in-school-only solution can adequately resolve.

1

How Black and Latino Youth
Are Remaking the Digital Divide

S. Craig Watkins

One of the factors that attracted our team to Freeway was the abundance of technology in the school. From the mobile devices that students owned to some relatively technology-rich classrooms, Freeway was living proof that the United States has entered a new era in the spread of media and Internet technologies. The often resilient and creative media practices of black and Latino teens are not only dramatically remaking the digital divide but also disrupting decades-old assumptions about race, technology, and participation in the digital world. As you will learn in this and several other chapters in this volume, the students at Freeway did not always suffer from a lack of technology. Still, they constantly found themselves in situations that required them to be creative in the face of the constant barriers—familial, financial, educational—that threatened to block their participation in the digital media cultures shaped and coveted by teens.

When more conventional or middle-class paths of access to and participation in digital media cultures were not available (e.g., home broadband, computer ownership), teens worked around social and economic barriers to pursue their creative investments in digital media. Within our research team we often referred to these activities as a form of *social hacking*.

The social hacking that we frequently observed differs from *technical hacking* but is no less ingenuous. Whereas technical hacking involves reprogramming or reengineering technology to do something that it was not originally designed to do, social hacking involves reengineering social situations to do something that one was not originally in a position to do, such as creating digital media content. The forms of social hacking that are profiled throughout this book are customary features of life in the digital edge and a pivotal reminder that many black and

Latino youth face persistent barriers to cultivating more substantive and sustained participation in digital media cultures.

Moreover, these practices compel a reconsideration of how the contours of the digital divide are shifting largely as a result of the inventive ways black and Latino youth are making distinct media practices. Despite the persistence of economic challenges—for example, lack of home broadband, outdated computers, data caps—many of the students in our sample found ways to get their hands on digital media. But the story does not end there. Black and Latino youth have done more than simply find ways to access social and mobile media. To the surprise of many, they emerged as early adopters and trendsetters in the social media space, leading the migration to the mobile Internet and driving the rise, for example, of Black Twitter a force in both pop culture and political life. In the case of black and Latino teens, their early adopter and trendsetter status has occurred in spite of the fact that they are not the beneficiaries of economic privilege or members of the tech elite, attributes that are typically associated with early adopter status in the consumer technology economy.

Several quantitative studies suggest that black and Latino teens are quite active when it comes to the use of, for example, social and mobile media.[1] Still, we know very little about the intricacies of black and Latino teens' engagement with these technologies. Our qualitative study is designed, in part, to fill in some of the knowledge gaps related to the rapidly changing dynamics of black and Latino teen participation in the digital media world. Whereas quantitative data can tell us how much time black and Latino teens spend on social media on a given day, qualitative data can tell us what they do when using social media. Furthermore, qualitative approaches can offer more in-depth perspective on the context and conditions in which black and Latino teens are using technology. This last point is especially crucial because the settings in which teens use technology—in school, at home, with peers—are in constant flux and situate different opportunities for engagement.

But even as access to the Internet for black and Latino teens has improved over the years, this does not mean that all forms of access are equal. Young people's Internet-related activities continue to be influenced, for example, by race and ethnicity, parental education, and the quality of schools they attend. Black and Latino youth are much more likely than their white and Asian counterparts to grow up in homes without access to broadband Internet. Parental education often influences, for example, the kinds of social ties and support systems their children have access to. Black and Latino youth are also more likely to attend schools that offer limited access to classes, instructors, and learning opportunities that develop the technical and cognitive skills that align with a rapidly evolving knowledge economy. It is also true that black and Latino youth carve out their own distinct spaces for identity and community in the digital spaces that are transforming youth culture and everyday life. In this chapter we offer a framework for understanding the agency that Latino and black youth assert in the making of their social and mobile media lives but in relation to structural conditions that are not of their own making.

In the United States (and around the world) we are witnessing a social transformation as a greater diversity of youth than ever before are using Internet-based technologies and networks. Today, black and Latino youth spend more time using social and mobile media than their white counterparts, a fact that no one would have dared to predict just a few years ago.[2] Still, access to technology does not necessarily lead to greater digital media literacy or, as we discuss throughout this book, social and economic opportunity. Similarly, access to media technology does not guarantee access to the forms of capital—social and cultural—that are the crucial gateway to educational achievement, economic development, and political engagement.

Immersion in the everyday schooling and learning lives of black and Latino teens confirmed that poor and low-income families are significantly more likely to have access to Internet-based platforms than they were ten years ago. However, access to social and digital media technologies remains tenuous for young people growing up in resource-constrained homes, communities, and schools. Lose a phone and one could go several weeks or months before getting a replacement. Rapid changes in hardware and software can often leave members in modest-income households stuck with outdated devices, defunct applications, and limited computing and network capacity. Faced with the choice of providing food for the family or having Internet access, a working parent makes the obvious choice, which means that Internet service at home is disrupted. These are the everyday struggles that the families and teens in the digital edge had to contend with. And while economic constraints did not completely stall the desires of black and Latino teens to participate in digital media culture, they certainly shaped them.

Remapping the Digital Divide

The digital divide is made up of many distinct components. Much has changed from the period when the digital divide was largely understood as a matter of access to computers.[3] The need for a more meticulous mapping of ongoing digital disparities is driven by technological and sociological change. First, the sheer pace and intensity of technological change necessitate new questions and analytical frameworks. For example, the platforms for participating in digital media cultures are evolving at a fierce pace. Smarter, smaller, and more affordable technologies (e.g., mobile devices) are radically expanding who participates in the digital world. Second, the divide is being remade as a result of significant social changes, characterized by new modes of adoption and participation, creative activity, civic imaginations, and entrepreneurial energy. Populations that were once figured as disconnected from the digital world are rendering such claims inadequate as they assert their own vision of life in the digital age.

The assorted ways in which Freeway students accessed and used media technologies complicate conventional theorizations of the digital divide, especially the notion of monolithic practices, impacts, and outcomes. There was substantial variation in the social and mobile media practices among the largely Latino, African American, and English-language-learning student body that populated the classrooms at Freeway. These differences make any reference to a single digital divide experience unsatisfactory. As our knowledge about life in the digital edge continues to evolve, it is clear that multiple dimensions of the digital divide exist. In this chapter and throughout the book we focus on three distinct yet interlocking aspects of digital inequality: the access gap, the participation gap, and the digital literacy or skills gap.

Internet Access

The issue of access to computers and the Internet has grown more complex over the years. Internet access is no longer simply a matter of whether a teen, for instance, has access to a computer and an Internet connection. Access varies in terms of the type of connection, including broadband, mobile, and high- or low-capacity networks. Lower-income families are much more likely than their higher-income counterparts to have mobile-only access to the Internet.[4] And while mobile has accelerated the pace of Internet access for lower-income populations, a reliance only on mobile for Internet connectivity poses many challenges. More specifically, the challenges are not necessarily related to access but rather quality of access and opportunities for diverse forms of participation.

Additionally, there is the question of not only *how* we access the Internet but *where* we access the Internet. Interestingly enough, the social and physical spaces of Internet connectivity significantly influence the quality of the experience and the kinds of opportunities a person is likely to have. In our study, access to the Internet came in the two primary spaces teens spend their time, home and school. The main advantage of home broadband connections is the opportunity to pursue interests and creative practices in a more deliberate fashion. Teens who grow up in broadband households are more likely than teens who do not to do a wider range of things online, develop richer forms of online social capital, and be producers rather than mere consumers of digital content.

Public settings like libraries, for instance, often restrict how much time teens can spend on computers as well as the kinds of creative activities they can pursue. In the Austin metropolitan area suburb that was the setting for our study, public libraries or community technology centers were essentially off-limits due to transportation and quality of service issues. Inadequate public transit options in poor suburbs make it difficult to get around.[5]

Many of the students that expressed an interest in digital media desired a place that allowed them to tinker, play, and collaborate with peers. Libraries and community technology centers often restrict opportunities for more social creative digital media practices. For most of the students in our in-depth cases, school—and more specifically, after-school time—emerged as a fertile space and opportunity to gain access to not only hardware and software but also a social and creative milieu that supported deeper forms of digital engagement, media production, and peer collaboration. These latter elements underscore what we might call *network effects*, that is, the importance of having access to a diverse and dynamic set of social ties that support deep learning, thinking, and making with digital media.

Participation

When teens gain access to the Internet, the all-important question, How do they use it? comes to the forefront. Even as access to the Internet is spreading, not all forms of access and participation are equal. Researchers are beginning to map the various modes of Internet engagement that identify the subtle characteristics of teen social media behaviors. An ethnographic study of young people's digital media practices by Ito et al. identifies two primary genres of participation: friendship-driven and interest-driven.[6] Friendship-driven practices refer to the dynamic ways teens use Internet technologies to interact with their peers through the use of smartphones and social media channels like Snapchat and Instagram. The ability to use technology to connect with peers and create what is, in effect, a social space with little adult intrusion or authority has been an enduring feature of teenagers' adoption of computer and Internet-based technologies from instant messaging to social networking.[7]

Interest-driven practices highlight the fact that some teens are drawn to the Internet to pursue specific domains of interest. The teens in our study developed a wide variety of interests including music, games, film, design, and fashion. In virtually all of these cases the Internet was a go-to tool, learning resource, and community to further develop their expertise and engagement in an interest-driven activity.

There are certainly other modes of participation, including pop culture and civic. Later in this chapter I discuss some of the ways pop culture figures into the digital media repertoire of black and Latino teens. And while our study did not find students devoting substantial time and energy to civic genres of participation, this particular sphere of activity continues to evolve in ways that deserve additional inquiry and analysis.[8] Students received practically all of their news and information about the civic and political sphere from the Internet. In a 2018 study, Vicky Rideout and S. Craig Watkins find that black and Latino youth are actually more likely than their white counterparts to use social media, for example, as a resource for civic expression and participation.[9]

Whether it is to hang out with friends, pursue specific interests, or partake in new modes of civic and political activity, what teens do with the Internet is inextricably linked to the social, educational, and economic currents that are always at work in their lives. How do issues of equity influence teen engagement with the Internet and the connected world? Are some youth more likely, for example, to pursue interest-driven or civic-driven activities than others? If so, why? Moreover, how do these different forms of participation influence the future aspirations and trajectories of young people?

Digital Literacy

In an age of rapid technological change a main requisite is the cultivation of the skills and competencies to use networked technologies in relevant, dynamic, and capital-enhancing ways. It is no longer simply enough to provide young people access to computers and the Internet; they also need access to the resources—social and educational—and opportunities that develop the skills and dispositions that are associated with more dynamic forms of tech adoption and engagement. In this study we ask, what skills and dispositions do teens bring to their engagement with Internet-based technologies? More important, how and where do young people develop the skills that lead to more diverse and dynamic forms of participation in a knowledge-driven society and economy?

The question of digital literacy and its relationship to the digital divide consists of many distinct, yet connected components that span a continuum of skills and dispositions. For example, there is the matter of what Kathleen Tyner refers to as "tool literacy."[10] This is a reference to the foundational skills that are required to participate in our technology-driven world and includes everything from learning how to use a tracking pad to operating a smartphone. The design of mobile interfaces or social software assumes certain skills and a general facility with smart technologies. A move along the skills continuum includes the ability to use general computer software such as word processing, spreadsheet, and email applications. As one climbs the technical skills ladder the ability to master more complex software involving media creation, analytics, and coding emerges. These are all features of digital media literacy.

All of the students that we met at Freeway had developed many of the rudimentary skills that allowed them to use the Internet with little or no difficulties. For example, they could operate computers to conduct searches, create documents, download content, and send and receive emails. Literacy in general is not static and typically shifts in relation to technological and social transformations.[11] In short, what it means to be literate in an ever-evolving and technology-driven society is constantly changing.

Digital literacy is not simply about "technical competency" but also about developing important social and critical thinking competencies. For example, a teen may be able to conduct a search to find information related to a task that she is trying to complete. But she must also execute a series of other more nuanced cognitive tasks. For instance, she must be able to critically evaluate search results and make discerning choices regarding the quality, relevance, and usefulness of the information accessed. We might call this mastering the skills of information literacy.[12] Further, she must be able to take information from her search and engage in comparison and contrast, dissection, critique, and critical thinking. This is where critical thinking and analytical skills are prominent.

Transforming the information that she has evaluated into something tangible and in the form of an expressed artifact or representation—a graphic, game, report, or piece of code—is yet another dimension of digital literacy. These practices are related to design and production literacies. Schools devote most of their resources to teaching students technical skills with varying degrees of success. However, a more dynamic approach to digital literacy must also help students cultivate a questioning disposition that employs technology to practice innovation and problem solving.

Virtually all of the students that we met at Freeway were aware of and used a mix of platforms to search for information—Google, Wikipedia, and YouTube. However, the skills and the disposition to use that information in responsive and innovative ways were not nearly as prevalent. Skills related to tool literacy and basic computing like searching and downloading represent lower-order thinking skills, or skills that are not cognitively demanding. Skills related to evaluation, critique, design, and creation represent higher-order thinking skills, or skills that are more likely to demonstrate cognitive rigor and nuance. Whereas lower-order skills are fundamental to participating in a digital and knowledge-driven economy, higher-order skills are essential to thriving. If the students in our study are any indication, schools do relatively well at developing lower-order skills but struggle to cultivate higher-order skills.

Finally, schools must also develop curricula that empower students to practice greater data literacy. The revelations in 2016 that social media platforms like Facebook and Twitter had been used in the presidential election to deliberately spread false information or what has become known as "fake news" through online social networks provokes a discussion about what role schools can play in building a more informed citizenry. The Facebook scandal involving the political consulting firm Cambridge Analytica further exposed the dangers of the connected world. Developments like these highlight the urgent need for schools to assume a greater role in helping young people understand the economics and politics of the Internet. Regarding the former, young people must cultivate a better understanding of how virtually everything they do online from posting pictures, to liking a video, to searching for a product is data that can be used to profile them and monetize their digital identities and practices. Regarding the latter, young people must cultivate a better understanding of how their online activities can expose them to political communication that is deliberately misleading and undermines the core principles of democracy. Whereas the former—the economics of the Internet—raise concerns about the monetization of data the latter—the politics of the Internet—raise concerns about the weaponization of data. Consequently, schools should not only be teaching students how to search, design, or code. Schools should also be teaching students how to think critically about how the algorithms built by coders shape our digital media practices specifically and our lives more generally.

Issues like these expand how schools and society should be thinking about what it means to be literate and high functioning in the digital world. Tool literacy involves learning how to use computers and software. Information literacy includes learning how to manage and navigate the flurry of information available in a connected world. Design literacy highlights the need to be able to make tech tools and information actionable. Critical literacy points to the need to comprehend the functions and implications of a rapidly evolving digital economy and society. And data literacy includes the preparation of citizens who better understand the data-driven policies of tech companies and how they affect society. These components are distinct and mark an increasingly complex spectrum of digital literacies.

The Changing Landscape of Internet Access

Among the students in our in-depth study, access to the Internet ranged from the conventional to the nonconventional. A small fraction of the families were technology rich and maintained reliable access to broadband. For example, in Jasmine's lower-middle-class African American household, she and other family members—mother, father, and younger brother—each owned an Internet-enabled mobile device. There were several computers in the household. In addition to her laptop, Jasmine owned a smartphone and went online regularly from home. Jack, one of the few white students in our sample, also lived in a tech-rich environment. Compared with the majority of students in our in-depth case studies, Jack lived in an affluent household. Jack's mother and father worked in professional occupations. Although his parents were divorced they provided him with abundant technology. Jack was the only student who owned an iPad in our sample. He used the tablet to play games, though he did download a couple of textbooks for school. He also owned a smartphone and used it frequently at school to Facebook with friends, play games, and go online.

Many of the families in our study resided on the opposite end of the technology ownership and broadband access spectrum. Take Kyle and his family, for instance. They were poor and constantly on the move. During our year in Freeway the family was hit hard by a devastating fire, which made their meager financial circumstances especially dire. When we met Kyle, his family had resettled in a multigenerational household where he shared a sofa bed with his thirty-two-year-old uncle. There was only one computer in the household, and it was an outdated PC. The phone that Kyle owned was limited to texting. In this familial environment, broadband Internet was a luxury that simply could not be considered. Kyle's home environment was similar to that of a number of students in our study, in that it did not afford the opportunity to cultivate the online social and digital capital that fuel deeper and more diverse forms of engagement in digital media and participatory cultures.

Amina faced similar challenges. She and her mother moved frequently. Amina grew up in Rochester, New York, and moved to Austin in her junior year. She spent her sophomore year in Ethiopia living with an aunt. Her family is ethnically Ethiopian and Amina spoke Amharic. During our yearlong fieldwork at Freeway, a conflict with her mother forced Amina to move in with a friend's family for a brief period of time. Her mother went back to school, determined to shore up her postsecondary credentials and opportunities for more meaningful employment. As a result, Amina became a breadwinner as income from her job as a restaurant worker helped support basic household expenses. From time to time she also had to provide childcare for her two-year-old sibling. Through all of this Amina took AP courses and maintained aspirations for college.

By the end of the school year she moved into an apartment with a female acquaintance, starting her transition to young adulthood much earlier than most people her age (eighteen). They both worked in low-wage service occupations, and the struggle to make rent, utilities, and other necessary expenses made broadband Internet a luxury. In cases like Amina's, a mobile data plan was the most reliable form of Internet access. But as we discuss below and in chapter two, mobile-only access limits the range of activities and kinds of media and production literacy skills that young people develop.

Parental Persistence

During our time in the school the economic recovery from the Great Recession was plodding along slowly for lower-income households. Faced with limited prospects for meaningful employment, many of the families experienced periodic disruptions in their home Internet access. Still, most families managed to offer some degree of access to computers and the Internet at home. Diego's family experience was not atypical among our study participants.

Diego was a senior, smart, and deep into games. (In chapter six we discuss his games-based interests and activities in detail.) He and his younger brother lived in a Spanish-language-dominant household. They spent weekdays with their mother and weekends with their father.

When it was a struggle to keep up with rent and utilities, Diego's mother would opt to overlook the monthly payment for Internet service. Diego described the times without home Internet as frustrating, "because you feel disconnected from the world," he told one of our researchers.

Most of the parents in our study worked in lower-wage, lower-status service occupations. Still, nearly all of them placed substantial value on digital media and made sacrifices to ensure greater access to computers, the Internet, and mobile devices in their home. Parents overwhelmingly viewed the Internet as a necessary bridge to educational enrichment and better future opportunities. As one mother told us, "You have to know how to use computers in today's world. If you don't it's really hard to find a good job."

Diego's mother illustrates the parental sacrifices that we observed. She spoke very little English and worked in a middle school cafeteria. Though it was a constant struggle she insisted on trying to keep up with the monthly payments for home Internet access. Diego often joked about how little his mother used technology. "She has no idea how to use Facebook," he noted during a conversation with one of our researchers. Further, she did not use a mobile phone. Still, she had a full appreciation of how important technology was in the lives of her two sons and worked diligently to provide them access to a computer and the Internet at home. She patiently saved money and was able to surprise Diego with a brand new iPhone for Christmas. When he showed one of our researchers the phone after the holiday break, his eyes still sparkled from the elation the unexpected gift stirred.

One aspect of life in the digital edge that is little noticed is the extraordinary effort that some parents display to secure a richer technology and literacy environment for their children. No one needs to tell these parents that technology is important in education and the paid labor force. They understand better than most how low educational attainment or a lack of knowledge about computers and the digital economy limits your prospects for higher-wage, higher-status employment and social mobility. How these parents persist to create a more favorable media, technology, and literacy environment for their children deserves more detailed attention than even we give to the matter. Faced with limited financial resources, these parents make important investments in the lives of their children even as they face extraordinarily challenging odds.

Why the Home Broadband Internet Gap Matters

As the discussion above explains, several families in our study struggled to sustain access to home broadband Internet. The presence of broadband in the home is associated with a number of important outcomes related to young people's participation in the digital world. During the period of our fieldwork, 73 percent of U.S. households adopted broadband Internet, according to the National Telecommunications and Information Administration (NTIA).[13] Adoption varied along some predictable categories. For example, the lowest-family-income households (48 percent) were less likely to have access to home broadband than the highest-family-income households (95 percent). Similarly, white households (77 percent) were more likely than black (61 percent) or Latino (63 percent) households to have home broadband.[14]

About 28 percent of the 122 million households represented in the NTIA's study did not use broadband at home. The NTIA identified several reasons why some households were nonadopters of broadband Internet. The main reason given for nonadoption was "don't need it, not interested." We saw no evidence of this viewpoint in our study. This is likely due to one main fact: the presence of school-aged children in all of the households in our fieldwork. A child in the home has long been a good predictor of whether technologies like computers, gaming platforms, or the Internet will be available in the home. As we noted above, all of the parents that we met understood the basic benefits of computers and the Internet.

The second reason cited by the NTIA—broadband is too expensive—was a common refrain among the households in our study that were nonadopters of broadband. Among the families in our study, economic difficulties were a constant barrier to the acquisition of nonessential household-related goods and services. Another reason cited by the NTIA—the presence of an inadequate computer—consistently appeared in our conversations with students. Many of the Freeway students in our study had home access to computers and mobile phones. However, as these devices aged, an upgrade to a new computer or phone was not a certainty. As we discuss in chapter two, for instance, students often had to make do with dilapidated mobile devices and household computers;

thus, their home access to a more robust Internet experience was severely limited.

The broadband gap in the United States matters for several reasons. Students who have broadband access only at school or in public spaces like a library may not have sufficient time to tinker, play, or develop the repertoire of digital skills and social capital that are often associated with more dynamic digital media practices. Additionally, young people who lack access to high-capacity digital networks are more likely to be only consumers rather than producers of digital media content. Home broadband users are much more likely than nonusers to create and share content, two key features in the participatory cultures that are a significant aspect of the networked world. This has implications for the quality of young people's engagement with media as well as their prospects for cultivating more advanced thinking and digital making skills.

The absence of home broadband has serious educational implications too. Students who do not have reliable access to broadband Internet face serious limitations in their academic endeavors and preparation for a knowledge economy. Whether it is in school or out of school, we live in a world that takes for granted the ability to collaborate with others, work with networked documents, and use mobile and cloud-based platforms.

Living in homes and attending schools that are short on financial and technological resources requires one to be creative and flexible. Freeway students were constantly adapting their Internet use to changing or uncertain circumstances—a lost or broken mobile device, social media filters at school, or no Internet connection at home. Students who did not have Internet access at home or via their own mobile device mined other options, including computers at school, public Wi-Fi, and the devices of friends. This last method—relying on devices from friends— was especially interesting and reflects the creation of what we call an informal sharing economy.

The student-powered "sharing economy" that we detected was marked by a series of practices that involved trading, co-owning, and partnering with peers to use handheld mobile devices like smartphones and iPods. The swapping and sharing of mobile handhelds created a distinct community of trust while also providing access to the media content coveted by many teens. The decision to share devices and passwords embodies the resilience that characterizes how students navigated the daily realities of life in the digital edge. We discuss this informal sharing economy in greater detail in chapter two.

Further, students became experts at finding Wi-Fi hotspots when they could not afford mobile data plans. Some students even acknowledged that they figured out ways to use neighboring Wi-Fi connections even when they were not open to the public. A few students turned the computers at Freeway into their personal platform during the after-school hours. And others leveraged good relations with teachers to earn weekend borrowing privileges that allowed them to use laptops and digital editing software at home. In other words, even when access to a robust Internet experience or opportunity to produce digital media seemed unlikely as a result of social and economic barriers, students designed their own social hack to pursue their interests and creative aspirations in the digital world.

A Case Study of Creative Resilience: Miguel and Marcus

Miguel and Marcus, twins who lived in a trailer park community with their immigrant parents, are excellent examples of the tenacity many students displayed to ensure their meaningful participation in the digital world. All of our interactions and conversations with the twin brothers and their parents strongly suggest that the family were undocumented Mexican immigrants. Like many of the students from immigrant households, Miguel and Marcus began their schooling in the United States in an English language learner class. They mastered that curriculum relatively early in their academic career and transitioned seamlessly to an English-language curriculum. The twins were in the ninth grade, well adjusted, and enrolled in two pre-AP classes when we met them.

The media practices of the twins took shape in a home environment that offered a modicum of access to the social and gaming media they coveted. There was a computer and two televisions in the home. The computer was a PC that was shared among four siblings and two adults. Moreover, the PC was an aging machine with a temperamental graphics card, which made it unsuitable for the gaming adventures and social media that the twins enjoyed. The Internet connection was not broadband but it was functional. No one in the household owned a smartphone. Miguel, however, did own a Nintendo DS—a handheld gaming platform that was steadily losing market share to the Apple products during our fieldwork.

In the cramped bedroom that the twins shared was a Wii game console and television set. The Wii, according to Miguel, was hooked up to an old television. "It's a small old TV like the one that releases all that static," he said during one of our many interviews with him. Due to the PC's limited performance capacity, the twins opted to use their Wii gaming console whenever they logged into Facebook at home.

Occasionally, Miguel used his DS to connect with peers. "The DS has a browser and you can connect to Facebook Mobile," he explained. He used the social network to "personal message" friends, but it was a much slower form of communication. "Most people have phones and they text each other," Miguel said. When asked what else he did with the DS, Miguel said, "I can put music on it. There are programs and games. There is a notebook thing that I can write down memos and meetings." He also had a few games on the device. Miguel expressed frustration that the DS could not connect to the Wi-Fi at school. He noted that Apple products like the iPhone and iPod connected with no problems.

In addition to connecting with his peers from school on Facebook, Miguel used the social network to connect with people he had met through *Perfect World*, a popular multiplayer online role-playing game. *Perfect World* is a 3D adventure and fantasy virtual world based on Chinese mythology. As with *World of Warcraft*, it took the commitment of seemingly endless hours to develop both the technical proficiency and the social currency necessary to build a more compelling experience in *Perfect World*. He played every night for two hours when he arrived home from school. He acknowledged that he would have played much longer, but "my parents only give me two hours of computer time a night." His commitment to playing also led to the creation of some fruitful social relationships within the game.

Jason, a fifteen-year-old from Florida, was someone that Miguel met in the virtual gaming world. "I was a noob [newbie] and had a quest that needed to be done and he decided to help," Miguel told us. During the quest they entered a dungeon and killed the boss. Shortly after that they became in-game friends and connected with each other outside of the game through Facebook.

Another colleague in the game also came to his rescue in a time of need. "I had this other friend that invited me to his faction because my old faction was full of a-holes," Miguel said. He needed another quest to complete a level, and the leader of the other guild helped him achieve his mission. They started chatting after that. The leader of that guild was twenty-four years old and lived in New York. Miguel was fourteen. He also befriended a couple based in Brooklyn. He chatted with them three or four times a week via Skype's voice service.

Needless to say, the strategic play, social ties, and skills that Miguel developed through participation in *Perfect World* intrigued us. This was a whole different person. In school Miguel was reserved, quiet, and un-assuming. Out of school he was actively involved in a virtual gaming world that required him to collaborate with strangers to problem solve and that also led to meaningful social interactions outside of the game.

The challenging computing conditions that they faced at home made after-school time especially appealing to Miguel and Marcus. Like a core group of students in our study, the twins stayed after school to access the Internet. When the school day ended, their social gaming and computing lives began. The twins were tinkerers and fond of experimenting with new online gaming platforms, forms of play, and communities.

As a result of their curiosity, the twins introduced *Minecraft* into their peer group's informal gaming ecology. Somebody (it was never revealed who) took the time to secretly download *Minecraft* on all of the computers in Mr. Warren's Game Lab. This act of bravado turned the classroom into a quasi-*Minecraft* studio for a brief period of time. In addition to playing the game, several students shared their perspectives and knowledge about the open and innovative world the *Minecraft* platform has sparked.

While Marcus, Miguel, and some of the other students played the game recreationally after school, Mr. Warren, the advanced game design instructor, was exposed to *Minecraft* and its merits as a learning engine. The following summer Marcus and Miguel were among a small cadre of students who received an invitation to work on a *Minecraft*-based project with geologists from a local university. The informal gameplay enriched the formal learning opportunities for the twins and some of their peers.

Critics typically decry engagement in gaming worlds, but the assorted skills—social, tactical, and communication—that some pick up can be useful beyond the game world.[15] The twins were among the few students in our sample who played in this particular sandbox of digital and participatory culture. In many ways, their play was socially networked and reciprocal—that is, connected to other gamers who helped them execute various quests, level up, and attain skills and in-game assets that raised their status and capabilities within *Perfect World*. These are precisely the kinds of skills—leveraging networks to achieve mastery, greater competency, and social mobility—that are growing increasingly valuable in a knowledge-driven and networked world.

Even in a home environment that required four siblings to share an outdated PC, Miguel actively participated in a connected gaming community. Moreover, Miguel and Marcus's discovery of *Minecraft* contributed to the making of a rich, informal learning and gaming ecology at Freeway. Their openness to new gaming platforms and experiences led to important learning opportunities for them and their peers and also embodies the creative resilience that is a vital but seldom noticed feature of life in the digital edge.

Shifting Contexts of Internet Engagement

In addition to learning about their access to Internet media, we were interested in learning more about the contexts in which black, Latino, and low-income youth use media technologies. Their widespread use of social and mobile media can be attributed to many factors, including a rapidly evolving media environment. In this section we focus on two features of this changing environment. First, we consider the widespread adoption of the Internet in schools. Second, we discuss how the diffusion of Internet-enabled handheld devices has profoundly reshaped the technology landscape and practices of black, Latino, and lower-income youth.

The Internet Goes to School

Since the mid-1990s, public schools in the United States have made steady progress in expanding Internet access. In 1994, 3 percent of U.S. schools had Internet access in instructional rooms.[16] By 2005, nearly all (94 percent) public schools had Internet access in instructional rooms.[17]

Predictably, schools with high poverty and black and Latino student populations were less likely than their counterpart schools to provide Internet access. In 1999, about three-quarters, 74 percent, of low-minority schools provided Internet access in instructional classrooms compared with 43 percent of high-minority schools. By 2005 schools with "majority-minority" populations (92 percent) were about as likely as schools with "majority-majority" populations (96 percent) to have access to the Internet in instructional classrooms.[18] The same was true across economic lines. Schools with a majority of students from lower-income households (91 percent) were nearly as likely as schools with a majority of students from higher-income households (96 percent) to provide Internet access in instructional classrooms.[19]

In short, by 2005 most public school students—lower-income/ higher-income, black/white/Latino, primary/secondary—were in classrooms that could provide Internet access.

These data, however, are misleading. Even though virtually all schools in the United States are connected to the Internet, not all connections are equal. First, there are substantial differences in the speed and quality of connections. During our time in the field, only 30 percent of U.S. public schools were meeting the Federal Communications Commission's minimum Internet access goal of one hundred kilobits per second per student, according to a study by the nonprofit EducationSuperHighway.[20] Freeway offered wireless connectivity, but it was spotty and occasionally required patience to use.

While Freeway was a wired school, not every classroom had computers. This was not atypical or inherently problematic. The school did not have sufficient funds for distributing laptops or tablets to each student to create what are commonly called "one-to-one computing environments." A laptop or tablet for every child is more likely to occur in affluent rather than lower-income schools. Freeway's main computer lab consisted of a cluster of desktops in the school's library. The library computers were used on occasion for school-based assignments, but we never observed high traffic or usage. Among the students that we spent the most time with, there was barely any mention of the library computers.

This was in sharp contrast to the two classrooms in which we spent the entire school year—the Game Lab and the Digital Media Lab.

Both of these classrooms were outfitted with Apple iMac computers with large twenty-seven-inch display screens and an impressive suite of software. Students who were enrolled in either the Game Design or the Video and Technology applications elective courses used these computers as a matter of routine to create digital videos, graphics, and even simple games. As we discuss in chapter six, students also used the computers in these two classrooms to pursue more interest-driven projects during the after-school hours. It may have been precisely because the computers in the game and media labs were not marked strictly as "academic" that made them a more desirable destination for students and their "non-academic" creative pursuits.

As recently as 2013, only about 20 percent of U.S. students had access to true high-speed connections in their classrooms.[21] Freeway students frequently complained about the spotty Internet connections when using their own devices. In fact, it was common for Freeway students to express frustration with a school Internet that was also deliberately limited as a result of the school district's decision to block access to social media. In short, even as schools have become a key point of access to the networked world, lower-income students remain hampered by an inadequate technical infrastructure for high-capacity networks, ill-conceived district policies that block access to social media, and limited opportunities to develop more cognitively demanding media and design literacy skills.

The Mobile Breakthrough

No development has impacted the media and connected lives of black and Latino teens more than mobile phones. In fact, mobile technology dramatically altered what is commonly referred to as the digital divide, the formation of the "technology rich" and the "technology poor." In 2012, 55 percent of mobile phone users browsed the web with their phone.[22] But the use of a mobile phone to go online was notably higher among younger and more racially and ethnically diverse populations. Seventy-five percent of mobile phone users aged eighteen to twenty-four years used their phone to go online compared with just 16 percent of those aged sixty-five years and older. Moreover, the Pew Research

Center reported that "roughly two-thirds of black and Latino cell owners go online using their mobile phones, compared with half of whites."[23]

Browsing the web with a mobile device was the norm among Freeway students. Even as educators and policy makers were holding on to a digital divide narrative that described an earlier era (before smartphones), black and Latino teens like those at Freeway were ushering in a new era in the digital world.

To put the adoption of mobile among blacks and Latinos in perspective, consider this: as late as 2011 most Americans were still using a desktop computer to go online.[24] Laptops (61 percent) were a close second. Nearly 40 percent (39 percent) reported using a mobile phone to go online. By contrast, African Americans and Latinos were early adopters of the mobile Internet. Historically, early adopters of innovations in computer and Internet-based technologies have been white, college-educated, affluent, and generally male. This profile flows smoothly with long-standing beliefs about the diffusion of innovations and early adopter characteristics. However, the adoption of mobile phones by African Americans and Latinos to go online turned the typical early adopter narrative on its head.

Furthermore, the adoption of the mobile Internet by blacks and Latinos provoked the popular view that the rapid diffusion of Internet-enabled phones did something that years of policy intervention could not do—bridge the gap between the technology rich and the technology poor. The implications for the adoption of the mobile Internet among black and Latino teens are complicated and obscure some of the challenges they continue to face in securing a more equitable Internet experience. We consider some of the challenges in chapter two.

Social Media: Practices and Participation

Not surprisingly, the social media activities at Freeway were extraordinarily diverse and cut across a wide terrain of interests, identities, and communities. Many of the students that we interviewed were introduced to social media as the transition from MySpace to Facebook was in full swing among teens. While children are exposed to social media at fairly young ages, the use of social media ramps up in the transitions to middle school and high school. Older teens (aged fifteen to seventeen years) are much more likely than younger teens (aged thirteen to four-teen years) to use social network sites.[25] This is due to several factors, including the fact that as teens grow older they actively seek out more autonomous spaces and opportunities to connect with their peers while also crafting interests and identities that are deliberately distinct from the adults in their lives.[26]

Teens, generally speaking, are more likely than any other demo-graphic group to uses multiple social media sites.[27] Moreover, their use of one platform (e.g., Instagram) could vary significantly from how they use another platform (e.g., Twitter). For example, Freeway students used established social media like Facebook to communicate with their friends at school or family members about the more routine aspects of their lives. Some students, however, experimented with sites like Tumblr and Instagram to explore an identity, interest, or creative practice that was not routine.

Gabriella used Tumblr to reflect on her emotional state and deliber-ately kept her profile away from her friends at school and family mem-bers. According to Gabriella, the content that she posted and reposted on Tumblr helped her process her thoughts and emotions. Talking about her involvement with Tumblr, Gabriella says, "I post what I feel. If I get sad then I post what I'm sad about. I have trouble saying things out loud, so I say it on Tumblr." She and her boyfriend also shared a private Tumblr account that was only for them.

Inara was fascinated with the world of fashion and spent a lot of her time online browsing sites like Tumblr and Pinterest to explore design trends. As we discussed above, Miguel and Marcus fashioned a social gaming network that was completely separate from their life and peers at school. After participating in a summer design project Diego devel-oped a fascination with game authoring software and online tutorials related to building gaming computers. In these and other instances, stu-dents adopted social media to cultivate interests and identities that were not rooted in their local peer cultures.

One of the hallmark features of the social media landscape is the for-mation of participatory cultures, defined by Jenkins et al. as "a culture with relatively low barriers to artistic expression . . . strong support for creating and sharing one's creations, and some type of informal mentor-ship whereby what is known by the most experienced is passed along to novices."[28] The Internet has certainly expanded the ways in which affinity groups connect with and engage each other. Digital formations of participatory culture are marked by distributed expertise, collective intelligence, and the creation and circulation of media content. Proponents of participatory culture point to the rise of social and creative milieus in which members believe that their contributions matter and they also feel a connection to one another. Participatory cultures are rich in social capital insofar as they reinforce reciprocity and community.

Throughout our fieldwork we repeatedly encountered instances of students who were reluctant to share their creative work or ideas related to a particular domain of interest in the context of online participatory communities. This is a noteworthy discovery insofar as the sharing of creative content in communities that offer feedback, support, and the opportunity to cultivate a more dynamic online social network is widely regarded as an era-defining feature of today's media and cultural landscape. Why were Freeway students reluctant to circulate their creative work in online participatory cultures? Students offered a mix of reasons.

In some instances, students were uncertain about the quality of their creative work and how it might be received. Students also expressed concern about Internet trolls and mean-spirited comments that can diminish the desire to share creative work. After he posted two videos in which he was playing the guitar, Diego was greeted by a troll who called it "the worst piece of guitar playing s@!t I have ever seen. You should be embarrassed to post this." Diego's response included a couple of expletives of his own. Though not advisable, his retort was certainly understandable. As far as we know he never shared anything else in a context like this again during our time in the school.

We speculate that robust involvement in participatory culture is mediated by the many dimensions of cultural capital such as in-group knowledge, familiarity with community norms and communication styles, and reputation. For instance, in-group knowledge about a specific technology, platform, skill, or interest facilitates entry into and engagement in a participatory community. Moreover, members of participatory cultures develop shared vocabulary and understandings that define community norms and facilitate communication and the exchange of ideas. Finally, engagement in participatory culture is also shaped by reputation and recognition. Effective participation through the sharing of content or feedback establishes an individual's social status and influence within the community.

Participatory cultures certainly foster inclusion and engagement. But participatory cultures also create the conditions for exclusion and disengagement, making it more difficult for some to cultivate the knowledge, cultural fluency, and status that are requisites for effective participation. What are the implications of this exclusion? Owing to their limited engagement in participatory cultures, many Freeway students were unable to expand and diversify their social networks beyond their peers at school, which limited opportunities to deepen their expertise, cultivate cultural fluency and status, and enrich their capacity to circulate their creative work among a wider milieu of content creators. Whatever their reasons for not actively engaging online participatory cultures, the impact was clear: Freeway students were much less likely to benefit from the feedback, support, and network-building capacity that are often generated.

Teens, Social Media, and Pop Culture

Popular culture was also a key driver in the social media practices among Freeway students. While considerable attention has focused on matters like the increase in screen time and media consumption, teen social media practices also enable new modes of identity work and expressive culture.

Freeway students coveted social media and mobile devices because they offer an unfettered path to games, videos, and music. Social and mobile media also offer teens opportunities to explore their creative aspirations and new notions of self. As with previous generations of teens, for example, pop music was a central force in the lives of Freeway students. Music is central to the identities and communities that teens carefully construct and serves many different purposes—social, psychological, political—in their lives.[29] Social media remakes the pop music rituals of teens in a variety of ways. In their engagement with social media, teens make meaningful social and psychological investments in music artists, genres, and narratives that reflect their desires, sensibilities, and aspirations.

No matter where they were in school—in class, in the hallways, hanging out with friends—Freeway students always seemed to be plugged into music via their mobile devices and earbuds. At Freeway, students followed their favorite bands and music artists through social media. Gabriella maintained a separate Twitter account just to coordinate her music interests. She enjoyed getting updates from the bands that she follows and hearing excerpts of their songs. Selena and Amina both posted lyrics they favored on Twitter. Users of Tumblr covered their walls with images and lyrics from their favorite artists. Fans of rap music used social media channels to explore hip hop's digital underground, a creative world bustling with mix tapes (i.e., original rhymes accompanied with elaborate remixes of popular songs and beats), homemade videos, and constant social media chatter about culture, politics, and the mundane aspects of everyday life.[30]

Some students also developed customized media channels to coordinate their personal investments in pop music. In instances like these, teens took to social media to curate their own pop music interests and experiences. Kyle was among a handful of students in our sample who used YouTube as a music media destination. Music-related content on YouTube was a source of creative inspiration for him and the hip hop band that he experimented with. Many aspiring musicians and bands have adopted YouTube as a channel for sharing their music in hopes of connecting directly with audiences.

Sergio also used YouTube as his very own personal music platform. He visited the world's biggest online video site every day, in part, to discover new bands. Sergio subscribed to nearly three hundred music channels, "mainly like independent musicians or bands who are promoting themselves on YouTube," he told us. Students adopted YouTube to watch music videos, follow their favorite music artists, and build a community around their music-based affinities and identities. In 2014, Google moved to convert these kinds of music-driven interests and practices into a formal and more viable music streaming channel and revenue source called YouTube Music Key.[31]

Whereas corporate radio and pop culture brands like MTV were once the undisputed gatekeepers of teen pop music interests and identities, teens are immersed in a steady and fluid stream of social media interactions that are profoundly transforming the traditional flows of power and influence in the pop culture landscape. Corporate media remains powerful, but the intensity of its influence has been subtly and steadily altered by the practices and relationships enabled by social media. Many bands, especially upstart and indie artists, view social media as an opportunity to fashion their creative identity and connect directly with fans. Moreover, fans view social media as an opportunity to connect with each other and fashion their own distinct identities, communities, and sensibilities. Social media channels are just as likely as traditional media channels to influence teen pop music interests, tastes, and consumption. Among other things, shifts like these allow black and Latino teens to assert greater control over which media they consume, thus serving to bring greater diversity to the stories and storytellers they encounter in pop culture.

Pop culture is also a vital terrain of cultural capital for teens. It is a primary resource in the acquisition of in-group prestige and status.[32] Through these and other social media activities, teens are not simply consuming pop music; they are actively fashioning a social identity that affords them a sense of self, status, and recognition among their peers through their engagement with pop music specifically and pop culture more broadly.

We observed similar dynamics in other spheres of pop culture, including gaming. Virtually every student that we met at Freeway played games. Jasmine used social network sites to play *The Sims*. Some preferred casual mobile games like *Angry Birds*. Other students made more intense titles like *Call of Duty* or immersive gaming experiences like *Perfect World* their primary gaming experience.

Students such as Miguel, Marcus, and Diego made substantial social, psychological, and personal investments in games. In years past their deep engagement with games would have easily been dismissed as a distraction from more meaningful uses of their time, especially time spent on academics. But their gaming and media practices challenge traditional concerns about screen time and screen-based media. More specifically, their activities underscore why adults should focus less on the amount of time that teens spend with media and focus more on the repertoire of activities they are engaged in and the kinds of literacies that they develop.

Miguel, Marcus, and Diego spent time playing games, but they also spent time studying the technologies used to create games. Miguel and Marcus did not simply "play" *Minecraft*; they used Facebook to join affinity communities around the platform and turned to YouTube to keep up with *Minecraft* channels that offered tips and tactics for developing a richer gaming, design, and user experience. Diego's experience designing games in a summer enrichment project inspired him to start studying online tutorials during his quest to make games (in school) and build his own gaming computer (out of school). On closer inspection, their gaming activities established pathways to the kinds of literacies (e.g., media, technology, and design) and dispositions (e.g., exploration and experimentation) that schools struggle to develop. In fact, whether it was listening to them describe their gaming practices or observing their practices, it was impossible to discern the difference between playing and learning.

The Hidden Legacy of Social Media

For all of the criticism about the amount of time that teens spend with screens, one fact is undeniable: social media transformed black and Latino teens' relationship with computer-based technologies and the Internet and arguably for the better.

In the 1990s a group of researchers from the University of Texas examined the digital divide in what they called Austin's technopolis.[33] The technopolis was a reference to the elaborate coordination between business interests, city leaders, and university officials to create a vibrant technology and knowledge-driven economy in Austin. One of the group's more secondary findings was that some black and Latino teens, especially males, associated the computer and the Internet with geeks. During this period most African American and Latino teens had limited exposure to people using computers, and the majority of ads did little to dispel the viewpoint that the Internet was a predominantly white and middle-class activity. Thus, the primary image many black and Latino youth had of computer users were geeks whom they interpreted as uncool and unrelated to them. A decade later black and Latino teens' notions of the Internet—who uses it and what it can be used for—had been dramatically altered, in part because of their widespread adoption of social media.

If the early years of computers and Internet use were constructed as predominantly white, male, and middle class, the adoption of social media by black and Latino teens certainly rewrote that narrative. A part of social media's hidden legacy is how it transformed black and Latino teens' relationship with computer-mediated technologies. Through their vigorous adoption of social media platforms like MySpace, Facebook, YouTube, and Twitter, African American and Latino teens, and teens from modest social and economic circumstances began to cultivate a mix of computer-mediated literacies and forms of social capital that had never been associated with them. In other words, they began to develop their own distinct techno-dispositions while also charting very distinct digital media practices.

When Freeway students shared memories of their earliest experiences with social media—MySpace—they consistently spoke about the immense personal satisfaction they gained from building their own personal profiles. Through their engagement with MySpace their notion of what a computer could be used for was greatly expanded. Significantly greater numbers of black, Latino, and low-income teens began using the Internet to communicate, connect, and create content that resonated with their own sense of self and view of the world. In short, playing around with the design of a social media profile or cutting and pasting HTML code dramatically transformed their notion of computers, the Internet, and life in the digital age.

Importantly, black and Latino teens did not simply follow larger social media adoption trends; they became trendsetters. When much of the media was asking why teens were not using Twitter, the percentage of black and Latino teens adopting the platform was steadily rising.[34] Between 2010 and 2012 the percentage of Americans using Twitter doubled. African Americans led the user growth of the micro blogging service among teens.[35] Since at least 2009, African American teen Internet users have been more likely to use Twitter compared with their white counterparts.[36]

During our fieldwork at Freeway we came across repeated references to Twitter. The use of Twitter among Freeway students was primarily driven by peer and pop culture. They used Twitter to experiment with their social identities and new modes of creative expression. Some Freeway students posted song lyrics that reflected their mood. Some posted lines from poems that they or someone else wrote. Twitter was also a way for teens to share their daily thoughts, emotions, and experiences.

When we asked Amina how she used Twitter, she noted that she "updates good news, bad news, what I'm doing, and a song lyric [that] gets in my head." Gabriella stated that Twitter was entertaining, a likely reference to the fact that Twitter has also become a tool used by celebrities to broadcast their lives off-screen. Gabriella went so far as to acknowledge, "I'm addicted to Twitter. I can't stop checking it."

No population in the United States was more poised for the rise of mobile-based social media than young African Americans and Latinos. For a variety of social and economic reasons, practically all of their social media use was via a handheld device. Consequently, black and Latino teens became, in the words of Everett M. Rogers, "early adopters" of mobile social media in the United States.[37] This development, of course, ran counter to the dominant digital divide narrative and long-standing early adopter trends in the tech consumer economy. African American teens were among the first group of American youth to adopt the mobile Internet at scale, a development that has made them extraordinarily influential in the evolution of social media. The rise of Black Twitter, a form of social media engagement that has become a pop culture and political force, is a notable illustration.[38] Black Twitter has become a place to perform blackness, drive pop culture and social media trends, and mobilize political sensibilities that reflect a new era of black youth agency and cultural production.

Social Media and Family Life

Many of the students in our study were members of families that were in constant transit. Consequently, social media was an effective way to keep in touch with distant friends and family. For instance, Marcus used social media to keep up with friends that he left behind in his family's move to an Austin suburb. Michelle used social media to keep up with her family that lived outside the Austin metro area, including her mother, who was divorced from her father. Inara and Carlos used Facebook to stay connected to family members who lived in Mexico.

About 11 percent of the Freeway student population was English language learners, many of them from immigrant households. For these and other students from immigrant families, social media was a way to stay connected to faraway relatives. Some of the students had vague memories of life in Mexico, for example, and social media allowed them to maintain important familial connections through the sharing of pictures and updates posted on Facebook. One of the benefits of social media is that "out of sight" no longer has to mean "out of mind" due to the ambient awareness aspects of social media.[39] In situations like these, Freeway students also served as brokers who helped their parents and guardians navigate the functions of networked technologies to stay connected to family in distant places.

It is common for children to take on a lead role when it comes to the use of new technologies in the home. Researchers have long referred to children as the "technological gurus" in the home. However, children in immigrant households may be called on to display those skills for more family-critical purposes. Latino teens are much more likely than their elders to use the Internet, smartphones, and social media.[40] As a result, children in immigrant households emerge as prime candidates for technology-driven forms of engagement with the outside world. For example, their tech expertise can help Spanish-speaking parents navigate English-only online documents or searches for work and social services.[41] Also, their tech expertise often compels them to serve as the primary bridge in the efforts of teachers to communicate with parents about their academic progress. In other words, children who broker in the context of immigrant families are doing more than playing the role of the typical household tech guru. They are also functioning as intermediaries between their (Spanish language dominant) household and (English language dominant) local institutions.

There is often substantial diversity—social, educational, language—within immigrant households. For example, not all children experience their family's immigrant status the same way. Moreover, not all children develop the same kinds of brokering skills or even the need to take on the brokering role. Older siblings are more likely than younger siblings to assist the family in navigating its relationship with outside social institutions, social media, and correspondence with distant relatives.[42] Many of the students in our study were older teens. Moreover, their exposure to teen and digital media culture meant that they were more likely than their younger siblings to take on the role of brokering in the household.

Our field observations consistently support the data that suggest that black and Latino youths are active in digital media culture. If we had conducted this study in, say 2000, in a school composed of similar students and households, most of them would not have been regular users of the Internet. Despite the many labels—"disadvantaged," "at risk," "low performers," and "English language learners"—Freeway students maintained a robust and diverse repertoire of social, digital, and mobile media activities that illuminate the shifting contours of the digital divide. Further, our research suggests that teens from resource-constrained environments navigate a world in which access to hardware (a computer or smartphone) has improved, but access to the forms of capital (social and cultural) that support more diverse and sustained forms of participation in the digital world remains elusive. Moreover, even as access to technology continues to expand and new modes of participation emerge to shape digital media culture, significant social and economic inequalities persist.

Black, Latino, and lower income teens use social media more than their white or affluent counterparts. On any given day: they spend more time on social media and also post more content on social media.[43] These trends point to a series of enigmas that researchers, including our team, have not fully explored. What are the unintended consequences of black and Latinos teens' valiant efforts to bridge the digital divide? More specifically, what are the perils and the possibilities associated with their greater participation in a digital world that Facebook once described as "more open and more connected?"

2

The Mobile Paradox

Understanding the Mobile Lives of Latino and Black Youth

S. Craig Watkins

Our very first round of interviews with Freeway students occurred one afternoon shortly after they had been released from school. It was a focus group with about seven students from various backgrounds. Amina was a senior whose family had arrived in Austin via New York and before that via Ethiopia. She was bright and articulate, and had a serious side that reflected the serious circumstances that characterized her turbulent home life. Sergio joined us too. Early in our fieldwork we learned that he was generally ambivalent about school but incredibly engaged, active, and driven in the after-school world Freeway offered.

Selena also attended the session. Throughout the school year Selena swayed back and forth, unsure whether she should continue at Freeway and graduate. Many of her friends had dropped out of school, and she had skipped so many classes that she spent as much time in credit recovery as she did in her regular classes. Kyle, always full of energy, joined us. He enjoyed rapping, skateboarding, and playing video games even though his personal and familial life was in serious flux. After losing practically everything in a devastating fire, Kyle, along with his mother and younger sibling, had recently moved in with relatives. Like the majority of students at Freeway, Kyle had no intentions of going to college. Each Friday his father picked him up after school and the two repaired air conditioners together, the trade Kyle decided to pursue after high school.

Cassandra was present and in her typical pleasant mood. But beneath her amiable exterior was grave concern about the changes that were remaking life at home. Her mother and father had recently lost their jobs, creating a great deal of financial strain on the family. Antonio,

Jasmine, and Jada also participated in the group discussion. During part of the school year, Jasmine lived with her grandparents, a loving couple who worked hard to steady her life as she navigated the ups and downs of high school. Jada showed up despite a busy schedule. In addition to working practically every day after school, she also held a spot on the school's dance squad and was a member of the business council. Her parents and siblings had their own phones and computers, making them one of the most tech rich families in our study.

We opened with an icebreaker, a get-to-know-you session that was loosely structured rather than rigidly scripted. To get things started we distributed construction paper, colored pencils, crayons, markers, and provided these simple instructions.

"What we want you to do is draw whatever technology you use the most, right now." Someone blurted out, "Does it have to be electrical?"

"No, your favorite, or what you use the most, right now," a member of our team replied.

Amid the thinking, daydreaming, and drawing one student jokingly suggested a Betamax, which provoked a friendly response from another student, "You took my idea."

As the pictures began to come into form, a clear pattern emerged: most students elected to draw a mobile device.

Jada drew her phone. "I chose my phone because I listen to all my music on there, I get on the Internet, download apps, do everything with my phone." She had owned several phones throughout her teen years, but she described her current phone, an Android, as "the highest technology I've owned." When asked to describe her phone in three words, she chose "awesome," "crap," and "all right." "Because sometime it freezes up on me and I have to turn it off, take out the battery."

"The Android sucks," someone chimed in. Adding, "Even though I have an Android, I think the Android sucks. They have so many problems."

Antonio concurred, "I like it [Android] better than the iPhone, because iPhones cost too much." Cassandra agreed, "That is true." Kyle, in a self-deprecating tone, noted that he was in the stone age, a reference to his small, outdated flip phone. Kyle's device lacked all of the features common in phones today: no camera, no apps, and no ability to email, browse the web, play games, or listen to music.

After noticing Kyle's picture, one interviewer asked, "Did you draw a pager?"

"No. I did my Playstation 2, and an iPod, and my skateboard, because I enjoy listening to music while I skate, and while I play video games, and I pretty much play video games all the time, because that's all I have to do, other than skate." Kyle chose the words "fun," "time-consuming," and "adventurous" to describe his favorite technologies.

Jada drew her phone. "Why is it important to you?" one of our interviewers asked.

"Kind of like the main thing that I use, like, when I come home from work, and stuff, like, sometimes I'm curious, so I get on my phone and like, look, whatever up, you know." She added, "And I talk on the phone forever and I listen to music, mainly so . . . I do practically everything on it." Jada chose the words "beneficial," "convenient," and "interesting" to describe her phone.

Amina drew her iPod Touch, "because it's the only thing I use, pretty much." She uses the iPod to text, go on Facebook, listen to music, and take pictures. Her phone was broke, which forced her to rely heavily on the iPod for social connections and media consumption. Referring to the broken phone she said, "I have to get a new one, but I probably won't." At the time of our focus group she did not have enough money to purchase a new phone. Amina described her iPod as "useful, entertaining, and pretty." Her last adjective, "pretty," reflects the degree to which the social identities of teens are heavily wrapped in the mobile devices they own—that is, mobile phones as a source of status, personal expression, and identity construction.[1]

Sergio produced a picture of his computer because he uses it for everything. "Like, mainly music, because I have some music software on there and I can record my guitar, . . . or I can make different beats, kind of like GarageBand, but better." His aunt purchased the digital music production software for him. The computer, according to Sergio, had been in the family a long time. "My sister got it from her boyfriend." He described the computer as slow. "It's the family computer, so, all these files are bringing it down," he explained. Sergio selected the words "slow," "crap," and "green" (the color of the computer) to describe the laptop.

Cassandra sketched a meticulous picture of her phone.

"Because I use it a lot . . . all the time. It's my only, like, electronic device that's mine," adding, "I use it for texting, calling, my calendar, my notepad, music." She claimed that this must have been her thirteenth phone. "Sometimes they break, and sometimes I break them."

"How would you describe your phone?" an interviewer asked.

"Handy, and slow, and . . . let me think . . . what's a word to describe a good phone that lasts a long time?" she asked. "Dependable," she uttered.

Antonio told the group that his iPod was his favorite device. "I listen to music while playing video games," Antonio said. "I don't play on a computer, because I don't really use it at home, because it's just always being used and I never really get a chance." He explained that the touch screen function was broken on his iPod, "so I can't lock it, or listen to music with it, so I just chose my top five hundred songs of mine and I put them on this [an older iPod Nano]. And now I just listen to those." The three words Antonio chose to describe his iPod were "creative, life, and relaxing."

The pictures that students drew and the stories that accompanied them were a revealing window into the world that we had entered. We strongly suspected that the use of mobile technologies by students, while active, was likely to be structured by complex social, financial, and familial circumstances. The focus group provided some early clues that this hypothesis was not only viable but quite likely in the world that students made at Freeway. While it was clear that the students in our sample used a variety of mobile technologies, it was also clear that the contexts and circumstances—familial flux, economic constraints, and rundown devices—in which they adopted mobile technologies greatly influenced their practices.

Over the course of the year we discovered that mobile media matter in the lives of young people at Freeway in ways that are both obvious and not so obvious. For instance, it was not surprising to learn that mobile devices were the principal gateway to connecting with peers through texting, Facebook, and Twitter. Popular apps like Instagram and Snapchat emerged during the fieldwork and analysis phase of our research. Both Instagram and Snapchat were predicated on the stories that surfaced in the icebreaker exercise described above: teens' interactions with peers and pop culture occur primarily through smartphones. But we also learned that among some students mobile is a crucial node in the informal learning ecologies that they designed and the creative practices that they pursued. In addition to being a lifeline to friends, mobile was a lifeline to learning and creating media.

Teens and Mobile Phone Adoption

One of the major social and technological shifts since the mid-2000s has been the growing number of young children and teens who own their own mobile devices including iPods, tablets, and, of course, smartphones.[2] To gain a fuller view of the central role of mobile in the lives of children and teens, consider the teen mobile adoption studies conducted by the Pew Internet & American Life project.

In 2004, according to Pew, 45 percent of twelve- to seventeen-year-olds owned a mobile phone.[3] By 2015 roughly three in four teens, or 73 percent, owned a smartphone.[4] The mobile phone, in a relatively short period of time, emerged as the central hub of teen life, serving variously as the center for peer interaction and communication, identity work, and media consumption.[5] Moreover, the racial, ethnic, and class dimensions associated with mobile adoption are noteworthy. While young people in general have migrated to mobile devices, black and Latino youths' engagement is especially active compared with that of their white counterparts.

As our fieldwork unfolded, the mobile landscape was shifting. For example, Pew explained that even though teens from higher-income households were slightly more likely to own a mobile phone, "parent income levels do not map as neatly with smartphone ownership among teens."[6] Teens living in the lowest-earning households (under $30,000 per year) were about as likely as teens living in the highest-earning households ($75,000 or more) to own smartphones (39 percent vs. 43 percent).[7] Smartphone ownership among Latino and black teens was higher than that of their white counterparts. Whereas 43 percent and 40 percent, respectively, of Latino and black teens owned a smartphone, only 35 percent of white teens did.[8] The adoption of mobile devices among Latino and African Americans transformed their engagement with the digital world and rewrote the digital divide narrative.

Teens have been a prominent and persistent thread in the study of mobile phones.[9] The implications of mobile platforms for learning, living, connectivity, and opportunity are striking. In this chapter we focus on five themes that emerged from our initial deep dive into the data that we collected related to the mobile lives and practices of Freeway students. The first two themes map some of the broader trends that shape the mobile lives of black and Latino teens. The final three themes offer specific accounts of the mobile practices that we observed during our fieldwork.

First, we consider the *mobile paradox*, a reference to the ironies associated with black and Latino youth adoption of mobile technologies.[10] The mobile media ecologies and practices that we discovered embody the hallmark features of both early adoption and late adoption, a fact that animates the degree to which the use of mobile devices in resource-constrained communities is contradictory and complex. The next section considers the influence of mobile technologies in the rising rates of teen media consumption, most notably among African American and Latino youth. The chapter then addresses the role of mobile in the classroom. Even though the school district adopted strict policies against the use of personal mobile devices in the classroom, the everyday reality at Freeway was that students remained tethered to their handhelds even when they were in class.

In the next section we explore the mobile "learning and creative" ecologies that students established. Even though the school district banned mobile as part of the learning environment, a few students in our study adopted mobile as a key node in their informal learning and creative pursuits. Finally, precarious familial and economic circumstances render access to mobile technologies tenuous for many youth in lower-income households. Financial barriers to handheld devices aside, we discovered a set of creative and improvisational practices that some Freeway students employed to gain access to the devices, media content, and peer connections that make mobile the central artery of teen social life. We refer to this as the making of an informal sharing economy.

The Mobile Paradox

The relationship between social inequality and media adoption is increasingly complex. Lower-income and lower-education households remain somewhat less likely than their higher-income and higher-education counterparts to use the Internet, though that particular gap closed considerably throughout the first decade of the new millennium. However, when you factor in mobile, use of the Internet across categories like household income and education changes as those who are in the lower socioeconomic group are just as likely as, and in some cases more likely than, higher socioeconomic groups to use a mobile phone as the primary gateway to the Internet. We witnessed this trend consistently throughout our fieldwork, which was confirmed by data from the Pew Research Center.

More specifically, Pew measured what it called Internet access *"mostly* on cell phones." African American teens (33 percent) were more likely than white (24 percent) or Latino teens (21 percent) to report that they access the Internet *mostly* on a cell phone.[11] Teens from lower-income households (30 percent) were also more likely than teens from higher-income households (24 percent) to report Internet access *mostly* on a cell phone.[12] The key takeaway here is not that teens from higher-income households were not going online from a mobile phone, but rather that they benefit from a wider set of options when they go online from home, especially in the form of high-capacity network connections.

Americans' use of the Internet via a mobile device began rising sharply after 2007. Roughly one-fifth (24 percent) of Americans used the Internet on a mobile device in 2007.[13] By 2009, nearly a third (33 percent) had done so. Between the end of 2007 and the beginning of 2009, handheld Internet use for the general population on an average day grew by 73 percent.[14] Among African Americans, use of the mobile Internet during this same period was even more pronounced. Handheld Internet use for African Americans grew at twice the rate of the general population, or 141 percent.[15] By 2009 almost half (48 percent) of blacks had used a mobile device at one time to access the Internet.

Higher usage of the mobile Internet notwithstanding, black and Latino teens continue to face significant challenges regarding their engagement with Internet-based media. During our fieldwork, white teens (81 percent) and Latino teens (79 percent) were much more likely than black teens (64 percent) to own a laptop or desktop computer.[16] In our cases the teens that did have home access to a computer typically shared it with other family members. And while studies dating back to the middle and late 1990s have suggested that the presence of a computer in the house corresponds with the presence of a child in that house, sharing a computer can often limit the amount of time young people spend on a home computer, the range of activities they engage in, and, consequently, the kinds of networks, skills, and knowledge that they develop.

Moreover, several students in our cases reported that the computers in their homes often lacked the upgrades, software, or functional capacity to pursue the kinds of online experiences that were of interest to them. Needless to say, a computer that cannot connect to the Internet, stream music or videos, offer game play, or communicate with peers via social media is of little use to most teens. Circumstances like these—sharing a household computer or limited computer functionality—contribute greatly to the increasing use of mobile phones and the mobile Internet in lower-income households.

Meanwhile, as the use of mobile was rising for blacks and Latinos, their access to home broadband Internet lagged behind that of white and Asian households. The uneven distribution of home broadband Internet service is especially noteworthy. In the United States, home broadband Internet adoption continues to be strongly associated with a mix of indicators including income, education, race and ethnicity, geography, and whether a child is in the home.[17] Historically, households with broadband Internet tend to be white or Asian, higher income, and higher educated.

The devices that we use to access the Internet are just as important as whether we access the Internet. During the period of our fieldwork, African Americans were less likely than whites to access the Internet on a desktop or laptop computer, but they were 70 percent more likely than whites to access the Internet on a handheld device.[18] The data from this period strongly suggest that two different pathways to the Internet were emerging for black and white Americans. The Pew Research Center adds that "to an extent notably greater than that for whites, wireless access for African Americans serves as a substitute for a missing onramp to the Internet—the home broadband connection."[19] Pew also concluded that English-speaking Latinos were the heaviest users of wireless on-ramps to the Internet.[20] What are the social implications of these trends?

Not surprisingly, analysts have viewed the adoption of the mobile web by African Americans and Latinos in two competing ways: as a sign of progress or as a sign of continuing deficits. However, the story is a bit more complex. It turns out that what was really happening was the emergence of adaptive, even innovative behaviors—namely early adoption of the mobile Internet. As early as the mid-2000s, futurists were predicting that mobile was the future of the connected and computing worlds. When Steve Jobs introduced the iPad in 2009 to an eager Apple audience, he repeatedly noted that "it was like holding the Internet in your hands." It turns out that in the United States, a population of unlikely early adopters, blacks and Latinos, were already holding the Internet in their hands. The key question, of course, is, what kind of Internet were they holding? Going online via a mobile platform emerged as the norm among populations that historically have not been associated with the class of early technology adopters.

These different pathways to the online world also structure different opportunities to participate in the online world. Predictably, homes with access to broadband Internet accrue several advantages compared with homes without broadband. Households with broadband, for instance, are much more likely than those without to use the Internet for a wider array of activities—social, educational, political, and recreational. Youth with home access to broadband have more opportunities than youth without to build rich interest-driven learning ecologies that promote digital exploration, experimentation, and content creation. It is not that youth without home broadband access are unable to build interest-driven learning ecologies, but rather that they must be especially resourceful to do so. Throughout this book we explore how Freeway students designed a number of creative and flexible solutions to ensure greater access to and participation in digital media culture.

The mobile lives of black and Latino youth raise a number of interesting questions regarding the ever-shifting currents of the digital divide and represent, more generally, what we call a *mobile paradox*. On the one hand, the adoption of mobile phones and the mobile Internet among African Americans and Latinos suggests that they are early adopters and mobile trendsetters in the United States. On the other hand, the conditions that shape black and Latino teens' mobile practices suggest that they continue to grapple with the social and economic challenges associated with life in the digital edge.

Even as black and Latino youth are early adopters of mobile, they are less likely than white or Asian youth to grow up in households with access to broadband Internet and the associated benefits. Home broadband expands the opportunities for young people to develop the social networks and technical competence that are associated with more robust forms of digital media practice, production, and participatory cultures. Put another way, the opportunities to cultivate more dynamic forms of digital literacy and social capital are severely limited when young people must rely on broadband Internet access through school, a public library, or someone else's house.[21]

The mobile path to the online world for Latino and black youth also raises some concerns. Smartphones can be a tool for youth creativity, learning, and civic engagement (i.e., Black Lives Matter, The March for Our Lives). However, there are credible concerns that teens who are restricted to mobile phones for home Internet use may also be restricted to social worlds, media literacies, and cultural practices that rarely, if ever, afford access to the social and technical currencies that power whole new kinds of learning pathways and opportunities in the networked world. From a more technical perspective, mobile Internet connections lag in comparison with the high-capacity Internet connections associated with broadband or fiber optic cables in terms of data, speed, and network capacity.[22] This explains, for example, what is call the "homework gap," or the recognition that students who only have mobile phone access to the Internet at home are severely limited in their ability to execute school assignments. In short, homes with mobile-only Internet are at a social, technical, and educational disadvantaged compared with their broadband counterparts.

Historically, early adoption of consumer technologies has been viewed as an indicator of a privileged status. However, the early adoption of the mobile Internet by blacks and Latinos tells a more complex story. More specifically, their early adoption of the mobile Internet reflects the degree to which social and economic inequalities persist even when they appear to have diminished.

Anytime/Anywhere: The Transformation of Teen Media Consumption

Predictably, the increase in mobile media ownership contributes to the increasing amount of media young people consume in a typical day. In its 1999 study, The Kaiser Family Foundation reports that American youth spent about seven hours a day consuming media.[23] By 2015, a Common Sense study that included similar methods to and one of the authors from the Kaiser report found that teens averaged about nine hours a day of media use.[24] A decade after its first study of young people's media use Kaiser summed up its key takeaway this way: "The story of media in young people's lives today is primarily a story of technology facilitating increased consumption."[25] Several studies also report significant racial and ethnic differences in young people's media consumption. The Common Sense study finds that African American youth spend about eleven hours a day with media compared to nine and eight hours, respectively, among their Latino and white counterparts.[26]

A 2010 Kaiser study found that Latino and black youth were significantly more active on their mobile devices than white youth, suggesting that mobile adoption in the digital edge has been in the making for some time.[27] For instance, Latino and black youth spent more time texting and talking with their mobile phones than their white counterparts.[28] The racial gap in mobile media consumption was even wider. Compared with white children and teens, black and Latino youth were heavy consumers of media content via mobile devices. Both black and Latino youth spend more time than white youth using mobile to consume music, games, and video.[29] Mobile is the ultimate media consumption platform and easily provides teens with what Nielsen Media Research calls "entertainment Nirvana."[30] The consumption of entertainment media was a major impetus in the coveting of mobile devices among many of the students in our study.

The twin brothers Miguel and Marcus wanted mobile devices to access Facebook and play games. Selena wanted mobile so that she could listen to her favorite bands and post pictures on social media. Sergio believed that a mobile device would keep him connected to his favorite bands. The role of mobile as a platform for media consumption was clearly evident from the initial focus group that we conducted with students. Many of them echoed a similar sentiment: "I use my mobile for everything." Translation: "I consume much of my media entertainment via my mobile device." For many young people, their participation in pop culture is increasingly facilitated by their adoption and use of mobile content including, among other things, music, video games, apps, video, memes, social media, and photos. But the significance of mobile in the lives of teens extends well beyond the media that they consume.

Mobile, for example, is a source for peer community and social identity. In their adoption of mobile, teens align themselves with certain peer groups, tastes, cultures, and what sociologist Pierre Bourdieu refers to as "distinctions" in their acquisition of peer-inflected forms of cultural capital.[31] Among young people, mobile technologies are clear markers of social status.[32] Students at Freeway noticed when their peers acquired a new mobile device. When Diego received an iPhone as a gift from his mother, his standing in his peer group immediately rose. Students without handheld devices, like Miguel and Marcus, experienced varying degrees of frustration and social isolation from their peers. Whereas technology is often decried for making young people less social, a new reality has emerged: not owning a connected device may actually lead to greater social isolation from peers.

Several factors—social, structural, and financial—provide greater perspective on the rising rates of mobile media consumption among black and Latino teens. Over the course of our fieldwork we noticed that many of the students at Freeway lacked access to enrichment opportunities outside of what the school provided. As we discuss in chapter six, many families at Freeway did not have the resources—money or the time—to invest in costly or time-consuming after-school learning and enrichment activities for their children. This partially explains the higher amounts of leisure time among youth in lower-income households and lower amounts among youth in higher-income households.[33] Consequently, youth from lower-income households find themselves with substantial amounts of free or unstructured time on their hands. Equipped with a rising number of screens, including handhelds, some children and teens may be filling some of that free time consuming mobile games, videos, music, and social media.

A conversation between one of our researchers and Gabriella, a young sophomore student in our sample, highlights how unstructured time, boredom, and access to a mobile screen can lead to increased media consumption. Discussing her use of social media, Gabriella says, "I would say that I am addicted to Twitter during the summer because I have nothing to do so I keep checking it every five minutes. Even when I log out and go to eat or something and then five minutes later I need to go back." She also explained that she is trying to "break myself from Twitter," a platform she called entertaining.

"Why do you want to break from Twitter?" a member of our research team asked.

"Because it's annoying after a while. It stops me from doing other things," Gabriella responded.

We are not convinced that Gabriella's constant engagement with Twitter is attributable to a social-psychological disorder—Internet addiction. Rather, the likely unstructured leisure time induces her to use mobile media to occupy time and ease the annoyance of boredom.

The racial, ethnic, and class trends in media consumption noted above are not new. Historically, social and economic factors have influenced differences in youth media consumption. High levels of entertainment media consumption tend to correspond with lower economic status.[34] Although mobile devices did not create the media consumption gaps reported above, the rising rates of mobile media ownership in black and Latino households might certainly be accelerating these trends.

The broad diffusion of handheld devices among young children and teens is certainly changing their media consumption behaviors, and the implications—health, educational, social—for youth in disadvantaged households are worth noting. Compared with older forms of screen-based media, such as television, video, console-based games, and computers, mobile devices introduce new dimensions to teen media consumption. First, mobile privatizes young people's media consumption more than ever before, making it increasingly difficult for parents, teachers, and other adults to monitor. Second, and perhaps more important, is the ability to consume media on the go and across different settings. For a number of youth in our study, the consumption of media takes place early in the morning and late in the evening, in school and out of school—in other words, anytime and anywhere.[35]

However, the focus on screen time obscures other substantive issues. Rather than ask, how much media do young people consume?, the more relevant question is, what kinds of media are young people consuming? The latter question shifts the focus to quality, not quantity, and considers the different repertoires of media use. In today's environment, media can be a diverse experience, one marked by production rather than consumption, participation rather than isolation, and skill building rather than time wasting. Even as studies document the rising rates of media consumption and screen time, it is important to acknowledge that not all screen time is equal.

The data and adoption trends discussed above confirm that mobile figures prominently in the lives of many black and Latino youth. Still, we know very little about how mobile media matter in their everyday lives. In the end, the more substantive issues related to mobile are less about devices and more about practices. That is, what are Latino and black youth doing with the mobile devices that they are adopting, and how, if at all, are mobile technologies transforming life, learning, and opportunity in the digital edge? The next three sections offer more texture and context to our mapping and understanding of the mobile lives of the students that we met at Freeway.

Mobile + Learning: The In-School Perils and Possibilities

Throughout the interviews, students consistently mentioned the use of mobile devices in the classroom despite the fact that school district policy prohibited such use. In most cases students described the use of mobile technologies for texting with friends, playing games, listening to music, or browsing social media like Instagram. In some cases, students received permission to listen to music as they completed homework assignments in the classroom.

Amina, for example, used her iPod in class to listen to music when, according to her, "I have nothing else to do." In her government class, Amina worked "pretty fast" and usually spent the remainder of the period listening to her music because she has no friends in the class. "If I'm absolutely not doing anything, and if there's no one that is important in that class." In instances like these, permission to use mobile devices may be a reward for completing assigned classroom tasks and maintaining an orderly classroom.

Jada confirms this perspective, noting that if "teachers see you multi-tasking, you're texting and you're doing your work, then they don't care. Some of them don't."

Gabriella indicated that her math teacher allows them to listen to music "when we are taking a quiz or if we're just working independently, like just finishing our own papers."

The decision by individual teachers to permit the use of mobile phones in the classroom is an indication of how, district policy notwithstanding, teachers and students devise their own policies and norms to negotiate the presence of personal tech in schools.

The integration of mobile devices into the academic learning experience was not a common occurrence in the observations that we conducted. In fact, we rarely noticed students using their mobile devices for explicitly academic-related purposes. This can be attributed to both institutional and attitudinal factors. From an institutional perspective, mobile was largely constructed as a distraction, a tool that negates rather than supports learning. Consequently, the school's framing of phones and other devices as antithetical to learning effectively extinguished the prospects for utilizing mobile in the formal academic setting at Freeway. By dismissing mobile, schools miss the opportunity to expand how students think about the utility of mobile devices, leverage the anytime/anywhere affordances of mobile and the opportunity to link in-school and out-of-school learning, and engage students in ways that are not only technologically relevant but also culturally relevant. Students have woven mobile into the fabric of their daily lives and see the devices as a complement to nearly everything they do.

Like most resource-constrained schools, Freeway struggled to provide students with basic resources and standard curricula. Consequently, Freeway's vision for mobile learning was essentially nonexistent. Some students managed to adopt mobile for academic purposes, but most of these practices were limited to accessing information or textbooks more efficiently. Jack was the only student in our sample who owned a tablet, which he occasionally used for schoolwork. "I lost my book for U.S. History, so I end up needing it [iPad] for a lot of assignments. I read books on it sometimes. I've downloaded a couple of my English books on there," he said during an interview.

Some students preferred downloading and reading their textbooks on their mobile devices. Unfortunately for these students, district-wide prohibition of personal devices in the classroom nullified any serious or sustained engagement with mobile for academic purposes while in the classroom. Occasionally we noticed some students pulling out their mobile devices in class to conduct a quick Wikipedia or Google search for facts or information related to a school assignment or project. A primary barrier to in-school mobile learning was that engagement with personal devices was discouraged by school district officials.

Tied to a regime of curriculum design and instruction that reduces learning to seat time, memorization, and test-taking skills, most schools continue to ignore the potential of mobile as a learning platform. Learning is largely constructed as an experience that is bound to the four walls of a classroom and composed of worksheets and the consumption of facts. The transformational potential of mobile—real-time data collection, locative storytelling, place-based learning, augmented reality, multimedia production, citizen journalism, and, of course, anytime and anywhere engagement—will revolutionize how and where students learn. Indeed, as the New Media Consortium writes, "Tablets, smartphones, and mobile apps have become too capable, too ubiquitous, and too useful to ignore . . . in schools."[36]

The Austin MASD's approach to mobile is not unique. It reflects a national ethos that is remarkably shortsighted when it comes to comprehending the power and potential of mobile in learning environments. Ultimately, schools like Freeway must generate a philosophical rather than technological solution to the learning challenges they face. What should learning look like in the connected world? How can we leverage technology to design better learning futures? Technologies are tools to help build better learning futures; they are not, in and of themselves, indicators of better learning futures.

Far beyond the walls at Freeway, mobile learning is a rapidly evolving enterprise that encompasses a diversity of strategies and pedagogies. While only a small percentage of young people today are using mobile devices as a powerful learning or civic tool in schools, the percentage is growing. The question is not whether rich and meaningful mobile learning ecologies will develop. As the New Media Consortium's *Horizon Report: 2011 K–12 Edition* shows, they already exist.[37] Rather, the real question is, will these mobile learning ecologies be distributed in ways that address America's learning and skills divide? In other words, will schools and students in the digital edge have access to these kinds of learning and civic opportunities?

Finally, this underscores another dimension of the mobile paradox: even as Latino and African American youth are early adopters of the mobile Internet and spend just as much time using mobile devices as their white and more affluent counterparts, they still find themselves among the least likely to have access to school, curricula, and learning opportunities that support mobile learning in any meaningful way.

Reimagining Mobile: The Out-of-School Creative Practices of Teens

That Freeway did not endorse the use of mobile devices in support of academic endeavors did not deter some students from integrating mobile into their informal and creative learning endeavors. This was especially evident in some of the interests that students pursued, including, for example, writing, photography, and video production. The examples of Jasmine and Antonio illustrate how mobile was a constant presence in the out-of-school creative identities and practices that some students carefully cultivated.

Mini Case Study One: Jasmine

Jasmine rarely, if ever, used her mobile device for academically oriented learning, but she used it frequently for interest-driven learning. Like some of the other students that we followed closely, Jasmine was actively involved in the Cinematic Arts Project (CAP). Her role on the cinema project was assistant camera operator, but because the primary camera operator was not excited about the assignment, Jasmine took on a lead role.

Jasmine tolerated her teachers and academic life at Freeway. Her effort in school was inconsistent, and she struggled to feign interest in many of her classes. This was in sharp contrast to the extended effort that characterized her involvement in the after-school activities at Freeway, especially her engagement with interests related to digital media production. The most dedicated students in the CAP worked long hours on the project, often to the dismay of their parents or guardians, who occasionally complained about how much time an informal and voluntary after-school activity occupied. For these hardworking students there was very little time for homework, and the CAP took on, at least for some, features of a part-time job. In addition to long hours after school, some students devoted substantial portions of their weekend to work on the CAP and their own creative projects.

As we got to know Jasmine, we also learned that her literacy practices outside of academically oriented instruction were quite inventive. She frequently kept notes and wrote short stories about her friends and the various encounters with them on her mobile device. "I have a short memory so I write stories that I want to remember—I'll change the name and turn it into a children's story or something or a real-life story," she said during an interview after school.

Jasmine added, "Later, if I want to change it to a script it'll be on my mobile."

When asked why she adopted her mobile as her primary writing platform, Jasmine responded the way many of the students respond when the question is about mobile: "Because I always have it with me." She used the Notes application on the mobile to record her initial version of a story. "If I want to turn it into a script there's an app called Scripts." Jasmine did most of her informal (i.e., out of school) writing on her mobile. She says that it is easier than using pen and paper or even her computer.

"I write so much that my hands will cramp up—my fingers could cramp up but they usually don't do that." She adds, "It's faster when I'm typing rather than just writing. I can read it and if I want someone else to read it they can read it too. I write too small."

We found Jasmine's preference for writing with her mobile device interesting in light of growing concerns that students are spending less time engaged in more traditional literacy practices such as reading and writing.[38] During the course of our fieldwork we met many students like Jasmine, that is, students who cultivated their creative interests and out-of-school learning in ways that reflected engagement with more traditional forms of literacy. A few students maintained elaborate sketchbooks to engage and capture their creative ideas. The students who developed a passionate interest in film were constantly jotting down ideas for scripts, stories, and specific scenes. The students who developed an interest in games frequently maintained notebooks with character art and game play scenarios. In the case of both film and games, students drew storyboards, a common technique for visualizing ideas.

Students like Jasmine did not draw sharp distinctions between traditional and new literacy practices. She sought out ways to leverage mobile and digital technologies to enhance traditional literacy practices. The students who pursued interest-driven learning pathways also tended to be involved in interest-driven reading that combined a mix of genres such as books, comics, anime, and graphic novels and interest-specific websites, blogs, and social media. During our fieldwork we noticed a wide range of interests, including, for example, automotive design, fashion, fantasy sports, games, art, photography, film, writing, music, and the culinary arts.

What was especially interesting was the degree to which Jasmine linked her traditional literacy practices—writing—to learning that took place informally, after school, and in a more creative context. The informal learning practices of students like Jasmine encouraged interest-driven learning, creative expression, content production, and the adoption of various technologies including mobile. In instances like these, mobile emerged as a crucial node in the out-of-school learning ecologies that students designed. Mobile served less as a device for consuming and more as a device for doing.

Mini Case Study Two: Antonio

Mobile was also an important node in Antonio's informal learning ecology. This was clearly evident as he developed an interest in digital photography during the year. Antonio shared his burgeoning interest in digital photography with Javier, Sergio, and Nelson. In chapter six we describe how the creative aspirations of this particular network of peers propelled the formation of a distinct informal learning ecology in an after-school digital media project. Javier spent his early formative years growing up in Mexico. Sergio's family moved to Texas from California when he was in middle school. Nelson, who is African American, was a recent Freeway graduate and mentor in the CAP. Despite their varied backgrounds they were drawn to each other through their common desire to be filmmakers.

The learning ecology that they created was a crucial source of social and cultural capital. None of them thrived in the traditional school setting. They viewed school as a space that was both constraining and alienating. And yet, they each crafted dynamic creative identities and opportunities in Freeway's informal learning setting. If school was often laborious, the after-school space could be liberating. If they struggled to find their voice and paths to opportunity in school, they derived great satisfaction from the voices and paths they crafted in the after-school space.

Antonio and his peers in the informal learning ecology relied on each other for inspiration and technical information. In the case of digital photography, for example, they routinely shared tips about camera models, shooting angles, lenses, filters, and editing software. They were constantly capturing digital images for the others to not only view but also offer critical feedback on aesthetic matters such as editing and lighting. The feedback was a source of both social support and creative engagement. Accordingly, they took on many different roles in this interest-powered activity, including photographer, editor, artist, learner, and teacher. Most importantly, their efforts catalyzed something that most of the classes at Freeway failed to generate—the opportunity to connect their interests, creative work, and learning across many different settings. Their media production practices linked school, after school, home, and peers in creative activities that were social, experiential, and the very embodiment of connected learning.

Antonio and his peers made an informal pact with each other. While they each wrote their own scripts, they agreed to cobble together the few resources that they had to help shoot each project. The planning and design work that they did was far more intense and creatively stimulating than anything they were required to do in school. But they seldom looked at this as "work." Instead, the projects that they developed ignited their imaginations, provided an outlet to pursue their aspirations, and established a vehicle to express their artistic visions through creative storytelling.

Filmmaking and photography were more than an interest for Antonio; these creative activities shaped his identity, enlivened his ambitions as a visual and digital media artist, and were a source of reputation and recognition among his peers. Antonio was generally ambivalent about school but remarkably animated when it came to his out-of-school and creative pursuits. Like the others in his interest-driven learning ecology, Antonio devoted substantial time and energy to his creative endeavors. They often spent several hours after school and on the weekends in the digital media lab working on their projects, messing around, and simply enjoying the chance to share and grow their interests in the digital media arts with each other. Though Antonio did not have a high-end digital camera, he did have a camera on his mobile phone. Consequently, his personal mobile device emerged as a valuable resource in the cultural identity he crafted, the creative projects that he pursued, and the informal learning ecology that he inhabited.

Antonio regularly looked for ways to continually hone what he described as his "cinematic style" or way of seeing the world, primarily through the lens of his mobile camera. "Well, even just walking, I would think of how I would shoot something, just to make it more interesting," he told a member of our team. Antonio used his mobile phone to hone his visual point of view.

"I go on bike rides with just my phone, and I always take pictures of random things, just so I can keep a cinematography style in my head."

He added, "I'm always looking to make things I shoot more interesting through a lens, in a camera, just so I can keep that in my head, and not lose it."

Antonio was determined not to let his passion for digital photography fade despite not having access to equipment that was commensurate with his aspirations. Though he lacked what he regarded as the proper camera, Antonio was determined to cultivate his technical and cinematic vision. His mobile phone became a tool for cultivating his visual style and art-making voice. In this context, his mobile phone was a source of media making, creative inspiration, and identity formation.

For young people like Jasmine and Antonio, mobile devices are a dynamic source of personal expression, exploration, media creation, and reputation. Despite the misgivings that district officials have about mobile in the school learning environment, some of the students that we met recognized the affordances of mobile to craft their creative selves and spark their creative interests. These competing attitudes about mobile devices offer insights into the dispositional divide that exists between educators and students. Whereas most educators continue to view mobile as an impediment to learning, many students view mobile as a pathway to cultivating new learning worlds.

The Making of a Mobile Media Sharing Economy

Immersion in the day-to-day world of Freeway students also provided an opportunity to discover some of the more subtle aspects of life in the digital edge. One notable example is our discovery of an informal mobile media sharing economy that some students participated in. More specifically, this is a reference to the improvisational practices that students devised to gain access to mobile devices and, more important, the media content and social connections that are so highly desirable among most teens. The inventive methods deployed by students to access mobile devices invite consideration of a long history of informal economies and social networks that the poor have designed as a means of survival, mobility, and opportunity in the face of limited social, material, and financial resources.[39]

During the course of our fieldwork we frequently noticed students swapping, exchanging, and bartering to gain access to highly coveted mobile devices such as iPods and phones. Unable to afford new devices or the customary two-year plans that accompany most new mobile phone purchases, some of the students in our study turned to each other and their inventive swapping practices to access mobile technologies.

The formation of this informal sharing economy underscores the fact that access to mobile devices and mobile networks does not come easily for lower-income youth. Despite the mobile adoption patterns noted above, youth living in lower-income households face constant challenges to access the kinds of mobile devices and media experiences that teens covet. Students without handheld devices often had to wait until family finances improved or the accumulation of personal savings from after-school employment to acquire a mobile device. Waiting for a change of financial fortune was no certainty. Faced with potential prolonged periods without a mobile device, some students resorted to peers, informal economies, and sharing practices to gain access to a mobile device.

Life in the Mobile Sharing Economy

Good examples of the mobile sharing economy are the schemes that Cassandra and Amina devised to upgrade their phones and find a replacement for a phone that was no longer functioning properly. Both Cassandra and Amina coveted their phones, but like many teens they were also hard on the devices and needed to replace them frequently. But phone replacement can be a problem when families that are already stretched financially are unable to take on a seemingly innocuous expense like a new mobile device.

When her phone broke, Cassandra found herself frustrated because it meant, among other things, that she could no longer communicate easily and frequently with her friends via text or social media. After a couple of weeks without a phone she experienced a great sense of alienation from her peer group. "I was missing out on everything that my friends were doing and talking about," she explained. Cassandra's parents could not afford another phone, but this did not end her quest to obtain a working device. When she discovered that her friend Devon was looking to sell his phone, she saw an opportunity to acquire a mobile device.

Convinced that the $80 asking price was affordable, she asked her parents for the money. After some familial deliberation, her parents decided that $80 was both a good deal and the only way they could purchase a phone for her, considering the family's financial situation. Her mother was struggling to find work, and her father, a construction worker, had seen his income fall precipitously during the Great Recession housing bust.

Amina was constantly in the market for a new phone, usually because she had lost or damaged her device. Once she went swimming and forgot that her phone was in her back pocket. On another occasion the device slipped out of her back pocket and fell into the toilet. In one of our conversations with her, Amina mentioned that she was preparing to purchase a phone from a peer. "I kept telling myself I was going to buy a phone but I was trying to save money, but I was like, 'Why should

I buy a brand new phone if I'm gonna lose it,' so I just bought this off my friend for $40—a Blackberry Curve."

She was not sure whether the purchase was a good deal, but because she could not commit financially to a new phone or a customary data plan, it was her best option to get a device or else run the risk of a rather prolonged period without one. The Blackberry that Amina purchased was limited in many respects—she could not access the web or use applications. Moreover, the back cover was falling off what was essentially a backup device for the previous owner. She preferred her iPod Touch to the worn-out Blackberry device she purchased. The former, in her view, "is pretty much everything but calling."

Amina was not only a buyer in Freeway's informal sharing economy; she was also a seller. She was in the market for a new phone but was short on finances. Her mother, who was working and going to school, had limited funds for discretionary spending. Amina worked but realized that she would need to supplement her income in order to upgrade to an iPhone. Her solution? Amina decided to sell her iPod to help defray the cost of switching from her old phone to an iPhone. She used the iPod but preferred the iPhone because it combined the features of the former with several phone-specific functions. She paid about $240 for the iPod but was prepared to sell it for $80.

Freeway's informal mobile media and sharing economy served two main purposes. First, it provided an opportunity for students facing limited financial means to acquire a mobile device through alternative channels (no family credit checks) and cheaply. Second, this informal economy also provided an opportunity for students in need of money to acquire funds. In some cases the money collected from the sale of a device was used to upgrade to a better device. In other instances the money was used to address a personal or familial financial hardship. Devon, the young man who sold his phone to Cassandra, needed the money to purchase gas so that he could drive to work.

The devices and funds circulated freely and without any discernible improprieties or conflicts in the informal economy that Freeway students created. On the one hand, this sharing economy reflected the ingenuity of Freeway students. Faced with uncertain familial finances and the exorbitant service and interest fees common in lower-income communities, routine participation in the mobile consumer marketplace was simply not an option for many Freeway students. Additionally, the informal economy that they created established an alternative social and economic milieu for participating in a youth consumer culture increasingly predicated on access to smartphones and mobile networks. On the other hand, this sharing economy illuminates the fragile circumstances, stifled aspirations, and limits to fuller participation in teen mobile media practices that many Freeway students faced.

The swapping and borrowing of mobile devices was another common practice at Freeway. Students shared devices and passwords that helped to form a sharing economy that was predicated on trust and reciprocity, that is, forms of social capital. We rarely, if ever, heard of instances in which students abused the sharing of devices, peripherals (earbuds), and passwords. According to Amina, Freeway students frequently borrow personal devices in school. Jada often loaned out her iPod to friends so that they could listen to music or play games during the school day. Jasmine rarely used her iPod in class, which prompted her friends to borrow it during the school day. Most Freeway students preferred a smartphone. For those who could not afford one, the iPod Touch was an alternative on-ramp to the mobile media world.

Why the Mobile Sharing Economy Is Important

We view the making of this informal sharing economy as an extension of a practice that has been documented in previous studies that examine the tactics and techniques of the poor to navigate their lack of financial and material resources. The manner in which students bartered and borrowed for mobile handhelds illuminates, once again, the extent to which the poor leverage available social networks and resources to sustain themselves and address their needs by making provisions for services and material goods that are difficult to attain. This was one of the many findings generated by Carol Stack in her classic study of how the poor leverage kinship networks as a source of sustenance, survival, and social capital.[40]

Specifically, Stack considers what she calls networks of exchange, the improvisational ways in which those who lack resources develop "swapping" practices that provide access to goods that would otherwise be difficult to obtain. In Stack's ethnography, the poor swapped furniture, food, clothes, and a host of other items to help them get through the pain and strain of poverty. According to Stack, this form of improvisation "is an adaptive style of behavior" and illuminates the creative strategies by the poor to navigate circumstances marked by depleted resources. "This powerful obligation to exchange," Stack writes, "is a profoundly creative adaptation to poverty."[41]

Stack argues that rather than viewing poor families as dysfunctional or disorganized, analysts would do better if they began to understand the "interpersonal links between those individuals mobilized to solve daily domestic problems."[42] In Stack's analysis the poor emerge as creative, resourceful, and capable of maneuvering through tough circumstances. This is the lens through which we make sense of the swapping practices and exchange networks that formed at Freeway.

In the world of teens, no product is more coveted than the smartphone. It is, quite simply, the principal gateway to virtually all of the things that shape teen interests, social relations, and aspirations. Mobile is central to the identities that teens craft and perform. Mobile is the primary node in the social connections and peer networks that teens belong to. And mobile is a gateway to media and pop culture, a sphere that has long held special resonance in the subcultural milieus, practices, and identities fashioned by young people. But not all teens have access to smartphones and the array of practices, media, and connections associated with their use.

Immersed in a consumer culture that has rendered mobile devices an indispensable aspect of teen social life, some of the youth in our study displayed "adaptive style behaviors" to hack through the barriers that limited their access to and use of mobile technologies. Teens purchased heavily discounted and pre-owned handhelds from peers, shared their devices and passwords with each other, and, along the way, built a distinct mobile media sharing economy in the face of social, familial, and economic circumstances that made mobile adoption a real challenge.

The making of this informal sharing economy illuminates the extent to which life in the digital edge situates particular forms of participation in the media worlds that teens are creating. The students in our study were not shut out of this world, but their participation was structured by social and economic circumstances not of their making. Many of the teens at Freeway exercised creativity to realize their mobile media aspirations. The making of this informal sharing economy is yet another example of how black and Latino students at Freeway were actively remaking but not necessarily eliminating the disparities that persist in the digital world.

Is Mobile Bridging the Digital Divide?

The widespread adoption of mobile devices among Latinos and African Americans provokes an inevitable question: Is mobile bridging the digital divide? If you define the digital divide largely as a matter of access to technology and the Internet, then smartphones, to the degree that poor and working-class families can afford them, may be bridging the access gap. It is clear that network-powered handheld devices provide a clearer path to the online world for black and Latino youth, especially in cases where home broadband is not available. In the United States, Latinos and African Americans are just as likely as whites to own smartphones.[43] Moreover, studies consistently show that Latinos and blacks are more active mobile media consumers. However, if you define the divide along more subtle dimensions, such as repertoires of participation and the acquisition of capital-enhancing resources (i.e., rich social ties, digital literacy), the relationship between mobile phones and equity becomes more complex.

A case can be made that the rise of households with mobile-only Internet may be perpetuating rather than eradicating digital disparities. To date, such households are much more likely to be consumers of digital entertainment—music, games, video—than producers of digital content. Participation in the digital world is growing more complex. And while mobile broadens access to the Internet, the technology does not necessarily broaden access to the resources—vibrant social ties, knowledge, expertise, and dynamic creative ecosystems—that support and sustain more robust participation in the digital world.

The mobile media trends discussed in this chapter—the hyper-privatization of children and teens' media use, increased media consumption, and constant connection to peers—typify teen practices more generally. What may be unique among teens in resource-constrained schools and homes, however, is the overwhelming reliance on mobile connectivity for their participation in digital media culture. Educators, policy makers, and researchers are just beginning to understand the implications of "underconnectivity" for youth and their participation in the digital world. For example, growing up in mobile Internet only households often means that young people are restricted to social and technical milieus that limit their access to social, informational, and creative networks that are capable of expanding their literacies, social ties, and participation in a networked media culture that is, paradoxically, becoming more pervasive and elusive at the same time.

3

Technology on the Edge of Formal Education

Jacqueline Ryan Vickery and Vivian Shaw

Digital media technologies are an integral part of daily life at Freeway. Simply walk through the halls during passing period and you cannot help but notice the presence of media and mobile devices. However, connect to the school's Wi-Fi or one of the many wired computers and attempt to access your Facebook, YouTube, or Twitter account and you will immediately discover the limitations imposed on students' digital media engagement. Like many high schools, Freeway is a highly regimented space that attempts to strictly regulate students' use of technology, especially social media and personal mobile devices. The official school policy states that personal electronic devices "cannot be seen nor heard" during school hours. Additionally, Freeway blocks students' access to material deemed inappropriate or uneducational and blocks access to social media and videos. Students are often denied access to what they consider the most desirable and even educational spaces (e.g., games, social networking, and videos). And owing to financial limitations within many families at Freeway, they experience the "edges" of the Internet both at home and at school.

At Freeway, students' and teachers' use of media and technology is shaped by daily tensions and struggles over who can use what devices, for what purposes, when, where, and how. On the one hand, Freeway embraces the potential of digital media by offering courses that afford students opportunities to develop skills and digital literacies. For students facing precarious social and economic situations, digital media can provide alternative opportunities and experiences not typically afforded them in traditional educational institutions. On the other hand, the school attempts to restrict and heavily regulate students' digital media practices. These contrasting and seemingly contradictory perspectives highlight a unique historical moment of tension in which schools (and society) are struggling to incorporate digital media into traditionally formal and controlled spaces, such as the classroom.

The question at Freeway is not should technology and digital media be a part of formal education, but rather *how* should digital media be incorporated into formal learning environments? While such questions are certainly not unique to low-performing schools like Freeway, they take on a distinct resonance due to the high stakes and limited opportunities that such schools and their students face. To highlight the challenges Freeway faces in regard to incorporating digital media into the formal learning environment, this chapter considers tensions between institutional perspectives and students' perspectives within the localized social and economic context of Freeway. We illuminate some of the contradictory ways in which discourses about the future of twenty-first-century learning—such as critical thinking, problem solving, and collaboration—influence the educational practices and opportunities at Freeway. The key aim is to elaborate on the contradictions, tensions, and opportunities associated with the integration of technology into the social and educational life of Freeway.

Valuing Technology in Formal Education

Part of the dialectical struggle over how technology is shaped within schools harkens back to questions regarding how technology itself is constructed. Are smartphones considered tools for learning or are they a means of distraction? Are chat rooms considered harmful spaces lurking with creepy predators or do they connect students to diverse perspectives and ideas? Are social network sites breeding grounds for bullying and drama or do they provide spaces for students to share ideas and receive valuable feedback? The ways in which technology and digital media are discursively constructed impact how they are regulated, incorporated, and adopted by schools. Federal, district, and local school polices overtly attempt to regulate technology at Freeway. Although students and teachers struggle with and at times outright resist rules, it is important to understand how the district policy perspective values technology use. Despite continuous research demonstrating the positive, constructive, and educational uses of digital media in the classroom, many protectionist federal and state policies reflect misinformed conceptions of risk, and thus detrimentally impede schools' use of digital media.[1]

We do not deny schools have a responsibility to protect young people from risks and harms that they may encounter online. Nor do we want to overlook the fact that digital media present challenges to classroom control, student attention, and optimal learning environments. Technologies challenge the traditional order of classrooms. However, risks are often overstated and deemed unacceptable, which leads to overly restrictive policies that exacerbate problems rather than resolve them.[2] Van't Hooft points out that policies regulating students' and teachers' use of technologies often blame technologies for much bigger societal problems and distract us from solving other issues.[3] As a result, many policies intended to protect students are actually misguided and are problematically techno-phobic and/or moralistic.

Rules and Policies

Federal policies in the United States have mobilized fears and anxieties around young people's use of the Internet. There have been many policy attempts to restrict young people's access and engagement online, such as the 1996 Communications Decency Act, the 1998 Children's Online Protection Act, the 2000 Children's Internet Protection Act, the 2006 Deleting Online Predators Act, and the 2007 Protecting Children in the 21st Century Act. While a full history of all these acts is unnecessary here, it is important to note that risks associated with young people and the Internet get mobilized through restrictive policies.[4] Undeniably the Internet presents potential harms, but media panics tend to construct all youth activity as risky and ignore the benefits of teens' online practices.[5]

Because Freeway is a low-income school, it is financially dependent on federal E-rate discounts for telecommunication services; therefore it must also comply with the Child Internet Protection Act. The act stipulates that any school receiving federal funding must use filters to prohibit students from accessing information deemed inappropriate, such as nudity or pornography. In practice, the filter also blocks educational materials such as sexual health information, art, and news sites depicting violence. At the time of our study there was not a system in place for students to challenge the administration if a website they tried to access was blocked. For example, teachers were not equipped with codes that could override the filters. Teachers could, however, put in a request to the Informational Technology (IT) department to have the site unblocked, a process that ranged from a few days to several weeks.

Additionally, the Austin MASD, of which Freeway is a part and by whom Freeway is governed, chose to block students' and teachers' access to all social network sites (Facebook, Tumblr, Instagram, etc.). Furthermore, the school district blocked students' access to all video sites, including YouTube, Vimeo, and even embedded videos on news sites such as CNN.com. For a while, teachers were also denied access to videos. However, the policy was later revised so that teachers were allowed to access YouTube from one computer at a time (verified by teachers' account log-in information), yet they were still completely banned from social network sites.

It is problematic that students receive mixed messages about the value of technology: on the one hand, courses such as the Tech App class teach students that mastering technology and online tools could provide a valuable pathway to future success; on the other hand, they are told that technologies pose threats that they are not responsible enough to handle or learn to negotiate.

Undoubtedly technologies present both risks and opportunities, yet the school largely focuses on restricting use and minimizing risky encounters rather than enabling students to responsibly identify and navigate risks. As the video game production teacher Mr. Warren noted, "We are the classrooms that help define the twenty-first-century classroom and it's unfortunate that we're sending out a mixed message; and the people that really are frustrated are the students." The ambiguity reveals the tensions and challenges schools face as they attempt to integrate technology into the classroom that supports student academic achievement and future opportunities.

Students' Perspectives of Technology and Rules

It is no surprise that students resisted, and at times even resented, school policies that limited their online engagement. In part, this was because there were ambiguities and disconnects between official rules and on-the-ground enforcement in classrooms and hallways. Students constantly and persistently bent or outright ignored the rules, and teachers did not consistently enforce the rules. On a deeper level the ambiguity reflected a more general uncertainty about the school's overall value of incorporating technology into the school's values.

For example, Sergio noted that the school "is really anti-technology, but then it supports the technology program that it has, so it's just anti-technology toward the students using it in the hallways and in class, unless the classroom involves that." His statement acknowledges the abstruseness of Freeway's relationship with technology and the growing disconnect between how students prefer to learn and how schools perceive learning. Sergio went on to say, "I would change the electronic rule at school because it just limits the students to be free." By and large, all participants stated that they were frustrated by the restrictive rules and generally felt the school should allow students more freedom with technology because it would help maintain their interest and aid in schoolwork. These attitudes also reflect research demonstrating the ways mobile media, for example, can enhance learning.[6] Anna, a senior, told us the rules were there to

> keep people on task. Try and keep them working on schoolwork so everyone can pass, the district looks good, they get paychecks, everyone gets paid. Because if you're sitting there on YouTube all day you might not be learning anything at all. . . . Then at the same time it sounds like they're going too far with it in general. I don't know. It's one of those situations where you're not really sure why the rule's there, but at the same time if it wasn't there it might be worse. At least it stops some people who don't know what the proxy is or something from getting on [to blocked sites]. Then again, who's to stop them from just sitting there not doing anything in general?

Anna's statement echoes other participants who also expressed ambivalence toward the technology rules. With the exception of explicit technology-focused classes, participants largely felt teachers did not encourage them to use personal devices to seek out information or enhance their learning opportunities. For example, in several interviews

Jasmine complained about the school's technology policies regarding personal devices. She thought students should be allowed to use their iPad or iPod in the classroom: "I have books on my mobile, and I want to read those, but [teachers] were like, 'Just go get a different book.' But I don't want that book because I'm already on a different book. I left the physical book at home, but I have the other book on my mobile. I should be able to use that."

Jasmine's experience is an example of the ways in which blocking personal technology limited opportunities for academic engagement. Rather than allowing Jasmine to finish a book on her mobile, her teachers would rather she begin another book that is physically available in the classroom or library. It is not hard to imagine a not-so-distant future where all reading in all classrooms will be performed on personal mobile devices, yet as Watkins discusses in chapter two many Freeway teachers did not embrace these opportunities.

We repeatedly observed that students at Freeway developed ways to covertly use mobile and social media during school to exert agency over their learning environment. For example, they would text under their desks, hide earbuds under their hoodies, bypass technical filters via proxies, and negotiate leniency with particular teachers. Taylor describes these acts as "locally assembled resistance against an established set of social structures or 'rules.' "[7] It is within this vein that we consider the resistive (as well as the compliant) tactics participants exercised to cope with constraints.

Drawing from de Certeau's concept of resistive tactics, Morgan O'Brien argues that disciplined subjects subvert power with whatever possibilities at hand, but is careful to point out that tactics only allow subjects to "escape without leaving the dominant order."[8] In other words, students work within institutional discipline without completely overruling it. Participants' resistant maneuvers are agentive tactics to cope with the everyday institutional restrictions and power to which teens are subjected. Teens' resistant tactics may seem inconsequential, but O'Brien writes these practices "are a part of the way through which everyday life is rendered livable for young people."[9]

Some of the participants' tactics were intended to deliberately subvert or disrupt institutional power and discipline; other practices demonstrated how some teens did not summon the energy, will, or desire to challenge restrictions. The back and forth between the school rules and student practices reflected the ongoing tensions shaping whose values were privileged at school.

Working around School Blocks

Several participants were experts at finding proxy servers that allowed them to bypass the school's Internet filter and access restricted sites. Others who did not know how to find a proxy relied on friends to show them how to bypass filters. For example, students such as Antonio and Sergio were adept at finding proxies and discussed their success with an air of pride; they knew they were skirting the system and enjoyed being able to deliberately bypass filters. They used proxies to gain access to online tutorials, videos, and other content that was blocked. Their practices actually reinforced and reflected educational goals, but were not officially sanctioned at school. Some students even belonged to a Google Group called Free Proxy a Day as a way to stay one step ahead of the institutional restrictions blocking access to websites. Despite their best efforts, though, students also expressed frustrations because the school typically discovered proxies and blocked them; thus they were pushed to find a new one to use until it too was eventually discovered.

However, other students such as Javier found proxies more trouble than he thought they were worth. When asked if he used them, he responded, "No, it's too much work. You go to one and then the next week it's blocked so you try another, and then you ask someone, and that one is blocked too. It's too much, I just quit trying." Interestingly, like Antonio, Javier mentioned the sites he was trying to access were usually tutorials or images and music for his films—sites that enhanced rather than detracted from educational goals. Many students actively chose to bypass filters and regulations, but we must be careful not to assume all students necessarily want to bypass constraints. Some students reluctantly complied with school rules, even if they did not agree with the values behind them.

Another tactic participants used to resist institutional restrictions was to download a different browser onto mobile devices, which enabled them to bypass the school's technical filters. The majority of participants demonstrated they could access Facebook and YouTube from school using Opera and other browsers on their mobile devices (the school's Wi-Fi filters were set to block sites in only certain browsers). Students also used alternative apps to access videos and social networking sites. Jasmine showed us an app on her mobile that looked like Facebook but it was not blocked at school. Interestingly, she was not the one who installed the alternative app on her mobile; it was one of her friends.

Jasmine did not check Facebook on a regular basis throughout the day, so it did not bother her that she could not access it from school. However, her friend Bianca, who had a limited text message plan, borrowed her iPod Touch all the time. Bianca was the one who downloaded the app as a way to access Facebook at school. Peers often relied on each other to learn how to bypass filters using browsers, proxies, or apps. Peers developed networked economies of sharing as a way to resist institutional limitations and enhance their educational or social lives.[10] Students did not necessarily have to possess the technical prowess to bypass restrictions; instead, they drew from resources available within their respective peer networks. These examples demonstrate the ways social and peer norms actively competed with institutional regulations shaping the value of digital practices.

Finding Balance between Risk and Benefits

Freeway was understandably concerned about the risk of distractibility that arises with the incorporation of social and mobile media in the classroom. Undoubtedly we witnessed plenty of moments in which students were distracted by their mobile devices during class. However, to justify completely banning mobile devices on the premise that it reduces distractions is problematic on at least three accounts.

First, arguing that technologies ought to be banned because they present a distraction in the classroom presumes there was ever a time that students were not distracted. Mobile devices can be disruptive; however, students have always been (and likely will always be) distracted. Prior to mobile devices, students would doodle, pass notes, sneak a magazine into their book, daydream, make to-do lists, and so forth. Technology possibly exacerbates the potential to be distracted, but mobile devices certainly did not create the problem. As we reported in chapter two, several students told us they preferred to use their phones when they were bored in class. But as noted earlier in this book, we contend that the biggest distraction in the classroom is not media, but rather a dumbed-down curriculum that generates consistently low expectations and rote tasks for many Freeway students.

Second, the always-on presence of technology and the potential for distraction is a real-world adult experience that students will have to learn to manage at some point. Banning mobile devices to create "distraction-free" learning at school constructs a superficial environment that ignores the reality that young people, just like adults, must learn to negotiate the distractions posed by mobile media. Sheltering students from these distractions does nothing to prepare them to manage these situations when they are no longer "protected" in the contrived environment of the classroom. Arguably, the consequences of distractions in the classroom differ from distractions in the workplace, namely, that it is (at least in part) the school's responsibility to enhance learning environments in which students can focus. This differs from the adult workplace, wherein employees are held responsible for their decisions and practices (and thus also held responsible for the consequences of distractions).

Rather than attempting to outright ban mobile media distractions, schools could institute a scaffolding approach that would allow students to earn the privilege and responsibility of incorporating mobile media in the classroom. Such an approach would integrate students' preferred modes of learning and help them learn how to manage distractibility in school and beyond. There needs to be a balance between completely restricting mobile media and forgoing any level of control.

Third, students miss out on the benefits of mobile learning in the restricted environment like the one Freeway created. Student's understand, to a certain extent, that the rules are designed to keep them "on task"; however, virtually all participants felt the rules went too far. Some students believed the rules limited creativity. Some students believed that they were more productive when they could listen to music, look up online tutorials, search for information online, or take notes on their mobile devices. For example, Cassandra got frustrated when teachers did not allow her to use her phone for class. "I like using the notepad on my phone [to take notes], but I can't because of my teachers. And sometimes we have to turn in our notes or [we're allowed to] use our notes on tests but I can't have my phone out during a test looking at my notes." Other participants also commented that they preferred to take notes on their mobile devices because it was faster and more convenient, and they always had their device with them.

Rather than harnessing the educational potential of mobile media and validating the diverse ways teens are already using mobile media, banning it sends the message that mobile media are not valuable in the formal learning environment. But in fact, research has demonstrated the ways mobile media can enhance learning, particularly for disengaged teens.[11] By incorporating media into the classroom, teachers could capitalize on the educational ways teens are already integrating mobile media into their learning ecologies outside of school. Instead, banning media altogether invalidates teens' practices and preferences.

Not all teachers tried to control technology and mobile media. Mr. Lopez believed the educational values of digital media outweighed the risks, including the risk of distractibility. While he incorporated some personal devices into the classroom, he thought schools should be doing more. He argues that schools should take advantage of the fact that most students own a mobile device. He told us: "Students should be able to bring whatever devices they have. You should have activities in class where you're like, 'Okay, go ahead and take out your cell phones or your mp3 players or whatever. You're going to sit down in a group. Go ahead and record what you discuss and we're going to upload that recording and we're going to do this with it'; things like that. Teach them how to use it." Just as adults must manage distractions presented by technology, so must students. Outside of school, students' use of technology is not strictly managed; they must learn to use it responsibly, and that includes resisting temptations of distractibility.

The Role of Social Norms in Shaping Practices

Current policy regulations have neglected to account for the role of social norms in regulating teens' media use. Prior to mobile phones, earlier technology studies have shown that users develop norms for how, when, and what purposes to use new information and communication technology.[12] Feldman describes norms as "the informal rules that groups adopt to regulate and regularize group members' behavior."[13]

Norms develop differently among different groups and within different contexts. Beyond an educational context, participants discussed how social norms regulated mobile media use within peer networks. For example, in several interviews students mentioned the social accept-ability of checking one's phone while hanging out, but also noted that at times it was considered rude. Jada said friends usually teased each other in a playful manner when someone was being rude by checking his or her phone too much. She said it was not a big deal, but it usu-ally got the point across. In other words, in social situations outside the classroom, peers regulated when and how often they were distracted by mobile devices, along with the circumstances dictating the appropriate-ness of such distractions.

It is not hard to imagine how social norms within the classroom, alongside acceptable-use policies, could also serve as a mode of regula-tion that would be less restrictive than outright prohibition of mobile devices.[14] When discussing the school's no-technology policy, Anna commented, "When a teacher's lecturing, that's incredibly rude, you can't have your headphones in. You can't be texting your friends when someone is up there trying to get your attention and teach you some-thing. But in your free time [in the classroom] it really shouldn't be a big deal as long as you're doing whatever you're supposed to be doing."

As another example, Amina, a confident and high-spirited east African senior, talked about listening to music in class: "I'll listen to music if we're not doing anything, we're just silently doing our homework [in class]. . . . If you do it while [teachers] are talking it's just rude, you can't do that. I think we've grown up to be like, we know what's rude and we won't do it, and it's not even just not to be rude, it's cause we want to get our education and we're not freshmen anymore, we're not acting like kids."

Amina's comments demonstrate how social norms can serve as a mode of regulation that distinguishes between inappropriate and ap-propriate uses of personal technology in the classroom. We believe that schools would benefit from incorporating mobile media into edu-cational settings, recognizing the central role mobile plays in the way teens communicate and navigate the world around them, and playing an active role in teaching students how to manage distractions and risks. Valuing media in the classroom validates students' perspectives and practices, and acceptable-use policies move beyond merely banning technology but recognize teens' agency to use media in responsible ways.

Critical Digital Literacy in the Age of "Look It Up" Culture

The Internet provides young people (and adults) access to an unprecedented amount of information and resources. We live in a culture that allows us to easily look up the answers to all sorts of queries from the educational to the hyperpersonal. Greater access to information certainly benefits educational opportunities and encourages autonomous learning. Yet, as the recent "fake news" crisis demonstrates, discerning the accuracy, motivation, and context of the information we encounter online requires fine-tuned critical and digital literacy.[15] Fabos connects critical media literacy with digital literacy when she writes that students need to understand "how political, economic, and social context shapes all texts, how all texts can be adapted for different social purposes, and how no text is neutral or necessarily of 'higher quality' than another."[16] Although not entirely unprecedented—amateur and citizen media, of course, predate the Internet—the Internet nonetheless provides students greater access to amateur voices, including their peers, which provide complex literacy challenges.

Digital media texts require a more nuanced approach to determining the value of information that moves beyond an understanding of reliable or unreliable, but require us to understand the value of different voices, texts, contexts, and platforms. Students could proficiently look up information, but they needed to develop the critical skills necessary to become digitally literate. This section addresses the ways restrictive federal policies and Freeway rules inhibited students' ability to more fully develop critical digital literacies within their formal learning environments.

Search Engines

Participants said teachers encouraged them to use the library databases to look up information rather than use online resources. In and of itself this is not problematic—the more resources to which students have access, the better. However, from talking to students it seemed many teachers encouraged library resources in lieu of online resources such as Google, Wikipedia, or YouTube, sites students consistently told us they preferred to "look up information online on their own." This highlights tensions between the school's intended incorporation of technology and students' own practices and values. Schofield and Davidson suggest that student learning is enhanced when students are allowed to experiment with their own procedures for solving problems of seeking out information and to pursue their personal interests.[17]

Teachers' policies and practices, which aim to control students' use of search engines, are antithetical to the ways research tells us students prefer to learn. Students noted that teachers do not necessarily discourage the use of Google, but few recall teachers actively encouraging Google searches. The exception to this was Mr. Lopez, whose students noted he often encouraged them to look up information online using resources such as Google.

School databases are certainly valuable resources; however, as quickly as information changes and evolves, it is a disservice not to encourage and teach students to use other online resources. Unlike static resources, such as books and databases, the Internet can stimulate learners to find the most up-to-date information in a short amount of time. While search engines have become increasingly easy to use, search results require nuance and critical engagement. Discerning reliable information is not an innate skill; it must be honed through experience and teaching. "Fake news"—an umbrella term used to describe disinformation, propaganda, satire/parody, journalistic inaccuracies, partisanship, and hoaxes—is often intentionally disguised to appear as credible and factual news that both students and adults may not be able to easily decipher.[18] It is vital that formal education help students fine-tune what Rheingold refers to as their "crap detector"—that is, the ability to critically asses the validity, accuracy, and motivation of information they encounter online.[19] The need to help students develop the competence to discern "fake news," real-time information, and a data-driven world is especially urgent in the aftermath of the 2016 U.S. presidential election and rising concerns about data privacy and data literacy related to big tech companies like Facebook, Google, and Twitter.

When asked how they determined whether a search answer was accurate, some students said they compared answers between sites. In other words, if the same answer appeared elsewhere they assumed it was accurate and reliable. This was not necessarily a bad strategy; however, few participants said they paid much or any attention to the source, URL, author, date, or publication type (e.g., they did not distinguish between user forums and actual published articles), nor did they utilize advanced search features such as placing phrases in quotation marks or using a dash to filter out results they did not want.

Jasmine, a junior very involved with the CAP, said, "You can just tell if a site looks right or not." Javier agreed, "You have to use common sense [when determining whether a source is accurate]." Although these were not misinformed strategies, clearly there were missed opportunities for critical digital media literacy. Such skills should not be taught in artificial simulations, but rather could be incorporated into real-time classroom situations, which arise as students seek out information in classroom learning environments. This reflects how digital media is compartmentalized into special courses, when in fact it should be more seamlessly and fully integrated into all aspects of students' learning environments.

By not encouraging students to use everyday search engines in class, teachers missed opportunities to fully engage students with critical digital literacies, which would take into consideration the media content, media grammar, and medium literacy of information. In virtually any class, teachers could incorporate aspects of critical digital literacy by having students look up information and then discuss not only the reliability of the information but also elements of design, ownership, and the values or connotations therein. For example, if a student finds an article that appears credible but is determined to be politically biased misinformation, teachers could help students think about why the article was written, who benefits from its circulation, how algorithms shape the popularity of search results, and how to find and verify information that is accurate. If there was ever a time to teach young people about the implications of algorithmic literacy, it is now.

Although Freeway's filters purported to block objectionable and harmful material, they did not block advertisements, which aim to capitalize on teens' insecurities (ads for beauty products, diet pills, etc.).

Frechette poignantly argues that "educators, librarians, and parents need to ensure that [filters] serve the *public* interests, rather than private commercial interest."[20] Schools have a responsibility and opportunity to help students think critically about information and challenge a consumer culture that profits from their online practices.

Wikipedia

Wikipedia provides not only an opportunity for information literacy to move beyond mere critical consumption, but also collaborative participation. As in many schools, students at Freeway were not explicitly encouraged to use Wikipedia, because it is often considered an unreliable source.[21] However, information literacy scholars note that the site has a lot of value in the classroom. For example, Sormunen, Lehtio, and Heinstrom write:

> Wikipedia has explicit guidelines of the accepted practice in writing, using sources and citing them. In school assignments, these guidelines form the framework which students have to consider and reflect on. Open publication of articles furthermore makes the requirements authentic (real world vs. school based norms) which may be an important motivational factor in the learning process (Every, Garcia & Young, 2010, Forte & Bruckman, 2010). Writing for Wikipedia also has potential in helping students to understand Wikipedia as an information source, how its contents are created and how to critically evaluate the information it offers.[22]

Unlike more static online resources, Wikipedia provides the opportunity for students to simultaneously learn to critically evaluate information while also contributing their own knowledge. However, students were unlikely to actually contribute to Wikipedia; they knew "anyone" could contribute, but they had never considered contributing. Concerns have been expressed that the community of contributors often devalues the contributions of others, especially women and people of color, creating a relatively unfriendly environment for participation.[23] This may be one explanation as to why students at Freeway are unlikely to contribute to Wikipedia.

In addition to lack of institutional support from the school, this references how social capital (e.g., connections to individuals who are likely to be makers and not merely consumers of web-based content) and cultural capital (e.g., knowledge and understanding of the subtleties associated with participation in online communities) shape degrees of engagement in online participatory cultures. Schools could help students view themselves as knowledge contributors and facilitate the acquisition of information literacy through the evaluation of Wikipedia. New technologies create learning opportunities that challenge traditional learning models and allow students to play a more agentive roll in constructing personal learning ecologies and networks.

Activist projects such as "feminist edit-a-thons" have emerged as a powerful way to mobilize marginalized communities to contribute to databases of knowledge such as Wikipedia. The events bring underrepresented communities together with the goal of intentionally editing Wikipedia entries (or creating new ones) to include more information about women and issues of interest to women that are overlooked or missing from the site.[24] Likewise, teachers could encourage students to identify interests or perspectives that are not represented on Wikipedia, and as a class they could contribute to the growing body of knowledge about that topic. As a lesson in critical digital literacy, this requires students to think critically about the consumption and production of information and to view themselves as active participants in their digital media ecologies.

Many participants noted that teachers outright discouraged the use of Wikipedia. While some students still used it, only a few participants engaged with Wikipedia in ways such as clicking on embedded links, checking cited sources, or viewing the editing history. Yet, there were some students, such as Sergio, who viewed Wikipedia as a resource rather than an authoritative text. He told us: "Sometimes people say don't use Wikipedia because it's not always accurate, but I'm not using it for accuracy. I'm using it more as a guide to compare one thing to another to see if they're the same—similar—and that way I'll understand. Wikipedia's more like enlightenment, a little part of the subject, but then I'll do more research." Through his own practices, Sergio has constructed a learning ecology, which tapped into the benefits of Wikipedia and simultaneously acknowledged the limitations of it.

Still, other students avoided Wikipedia altogether (at least for traditional educational purposes) because they were concerned it might not be accurate information. Fabos draws attention to the ways digital media literacy often privileges "authoritative" and "accurate" information from professional sources and, thus, tends to marginalize amateur texts.[25] She argues that rather than seeking an objective "truth," all texts ought to be considered within different contexts and recognized as serving different purposes. Sergio's use of Wikipedia as a starting point for further research demonstrated his ability to critically engage with Wikipedia in a productive way.

Rather than using Wikipedia as a site for critical digital media lessons, teachers seemed to write it off as a less than valuable resource and dismissed students' values and cultures of learning. To an extent, students echoed these views as well. Schools are doing students a disservice when they fail to embrace easily accessible and free resources available to students. Although the Freeway policy stated teachers should be equipped with up-to-date technology and online skills, which they were expected to incorporate into student curriculum, in practice participants were largely navigating the Internet without much classroom guidance or teacher support. Policies missed opportunities to validate students' learning practices and develop critical digital literacy. Wikipedia is an educational resource that can facilitate deeper understanding of power, representation, and the construction of knowledge.

YouTube

There is a sense of irony in the fact that students are learning how to write, produce, and edit their own videos in the classroom, yet they are denied access to videos at school. This explicitly reveals the tensions facing Freeway with regard to digital media. Students repeatedly and consistently reported using YouTube as a source for online tutorials and help. Videos have a long history of being used in the classroom to help visual learners understand difficult concepts.[26] Jones and Cuthrell demonstrate how YouTube has been successfully incorporated into the class to aid in teaching virtually any subject, including math, literature, and social studies.[27] Mohamed Ally writes, "Just-in-time learning encourages high level learning since learners access and apply the information right away rather than learn the information and then apply the information at a later time."[28]

Blocked videos and online tutorials that would support just-in-time learning were a source of constant frustration for students. For example, active CAP participant Sergio complained that the school blocked so many useful sites including videos.

> Sergio: That's another thing I didn't like about the [school's] computers. Like, a lot of the tutorials seemed really cool when I got the visual [preview] of it, but when I tried to open it, it would be blocked, because apparently it had some unknown content that the school didn't want. And sometimes I would try to download images from file-sharing sites, and they wouldn't let me, and I really needed those images to compose an art piece.
>
> Interviewer: Yeah, that's kind of a bummer, right?
>
> Sergio: Yeah. Like, YouTube is blocked, here, and at home, YouTube is one of my main sources for tutorials, because then I get a spoken kind of tutorial rather than just going back and reading it, . . . someone would just be speaking on what I need to do, and that way it would be more efficient.

Blocking social media in this way reflects one of the long-standing fears that the selective prohibition of resources will disproportionately impact low-income students. For students without broadband at home or Internet-enabled phones, the school should be a place that provides a more equitable learning experience for students and should embrace new tools for learning. The restrictive policies exacerbated digital inequalities when they limited students' access to valuable online resources such as YouTube tutorials. Further, in chapter five we explore how blocking online videos seriously impacted both the quality and opportunity for students to learn in the school's game design class.

Blocking YouTube also impeded an opportunity for students to learn to responsibly share their work in a networked public and connect with other amateur filmmakers. Henry Jenkins writes, "In a world in which knowledge production is collective and communication occurs across an array of different media, the capacity to network emerges as a core social skill and cultural competency."[29] Mr. Warren, the video game production teacher, recognized the importance of networking and the fact that the game industry expects young people to be using social networking sites as tools for reputation management and self-promotion.

During an interview, Mr. Warren discussed how the current policy inhibited students' opportunities to network and demonstrated how YouTube and social network sites could enhance his classroom. He was working on a classroom project between his Freeway students and students in Cambodia. As he explained it:

> Right now I'm working with a number of students in Cambodia. These students are going to be uploading, downloading, and sharing stories, pictures of their families, their environments. Today we had some [Freeway] students bring some of their favorite foods from their cultures. And we're going to share those pictures and those stories with the Cambodian students. These students are designing games that will be teaching about the history and art of Cambodia. . . . A group of my students wants to design a game that every time you win a game, rice is being sent to Cambodia. So now we've got games that can help a culture, help a community evolve, survive. That's brilliant, and it's not my idea. It's theirs and when it's their idea, they own it. And when you own it, they're more passionate about it.

The project was severely limited because the videos the Cambodian students were sharing were available only on YouTube, which Freeway students did not have access to at school. Research demonstrates YouTube fosters communication, collaboration, interaction, and learning.[30] In this instance, the decision to block YouTube not only restricted the scope and complexity of school-related work that Freeway students could produce; it also restricted their ability to connect with students, ideas, and projects in a global economy and reified their position in the digital edge. We noticed these kinds of challenges and contradictions throughout our fieldwork at Freeway. On the one hand, teachers like Mr. Warren and Mr. Lopez were open to new kinds of learning models and experiences. On the other hand, their efforts to pursue these pathways were often constrained by forces—including filters and the lack of professional development—that they simply could not control.

Access, Friendship, and Disengagement

In examining how Freeway's digital policy tends to constrain a number of opportunities for digital learning and development of critical literacies, we argue further that the costs of these limitations are particularly intensified for students in the digital edge. We agree that educational institutions such as Freeway have reasons to be concerned about the use and "abuse" of digital technology at school. Our interviews with students suggest that the boundaries around appropriate and inappropriate applications of digital technology within and outside school time are blurred based on differing levels of access to and practices of meaning-making around digital technology.

In considering how these ambiguous practices of digital media shape learning at Freeway, we argue that access to technology at home and in their broader social lives shapes how students are able to participate in digital technology as a learning medium. The restrictive structuring of student access to digital media at school and separation of certain types of usage as "educational" vs. "recreational," therefore, is particularly problematic due to students in our sample often lacking access to technology at home. We explore this point specifically through the case of Amina and Cassandra's sharing of personal digital technology.

Moreover, as we demonstrate with our discussion of Selena, such digital policy might have significant impacts on students who are both interested in digital media and creative practices more broadly and disengaged from traditional academic curricula. Ultimately, the realities of how socioeconomically marginalized students navigate digital use should be considered by schools as they develop digital use policies.

Case Study One: Amina and Cassandra

Amina and Cassandra referred to each other as best friends, and in our study often participated as a pair—in focus groups, interviews, and in-home visits. They were both graduating seniors at the time of our study. However, whereas Cassandra gushed enthusiastically on a range of topics from her cell phone to her love for alternative music, Amina was less prone to such cheeriness, instead more likely to narrate her long nights working at her part-time job after school and to offer up sarcastic, if not at times cynical, observations about life inside and outside Freeway.

The two girls were, despite differences in their attitudes, uniquely bonded through their living circumstances. For several months of our study, Amina was living with Cassandra's family, though she continued to return home to her mother's apartment for visits. They rarely talked about the reasons behind their living arrangements, but their sharing of space clearly shaped many details of their daily lives, down to their iPod Touch. The device was actually Amina's, but she regularly shared it with Cassandra while she was at work, allowing her friend access to music and to social media websites such as Instagram. In Amina's narrative, through the development of their friendship the device had taken on a status as shared property. Amina explained how this practice of lending initially emerged from a fix to a temporary problem—that of Cassandra's mother punishing her by taking away her phone—into a more enduring practice, and one with important social meanings:

> So basically I was like, "Look, you can borrow my iTouch until you get your phone back." And that's just how comfortable it got with her. She was just like, "Oh, that's really nice of you." Yes, I let her do that. Now we live together, we basically share everything. Basically. Her phone is still her phone, my phone is still my phone, my iTouch is still my iTouch, but if she'll be like, "Hey, you're going to work. Do you mind if I borrow your iTouch?" I'm cool with that. I'm going to go to work, I'm not going to use it anyway. She won't steal it I'm pretty sure. When I go home it will be there in my room charging. But yes, basically I'm comfortable sharing stuff with her.

Unlike some of the other students in the room that day in our study more broadly, neither Cassandra nor Amina was a member of Freeway's digital media club. Instead, they tended to use digital technology strictly for personal and social reasons—to listen to music, to socialize on Facebook and Twitter, and to text with friends and parents. It was clear from their practice of sharing the iPod Touch that such technology played an important role in their social experiences.

Through their collective ownership, the two girls were able to mutually compensate for compromised access to digital technology. Beyond the scope of her cell phone punishment, Cassandra continued to borrow this device because it appeared more user-friendly and conducive to social media applications such as Facebook and Instagram than her own phone. Although they were able to house Amina, Cassandra's family had its shares of financial concerns, which limited their ability to keep fully updated with technology. Cassandra alternated between referring to her parents as "unemployed" and "self-employed," with her father and mother both depending on independent contracting work for their income.

Outside of school and Cassandra's house, Amina reported limited access to the Wi-Fi necessary to use her iPod Touch. In fact, when we asked her more generally about her access to digital technology, Amina's answer was often shifting and dependent on her living arrangements, a status that frequently changed. At her mother's house, she had some access to a shared family laptop, but was less able to use some of her personal devices. Similar to the sharing practices that we observed among other students in the study (and discussed in greater detail in chapter two), Amina and Cassandra's sharing of a mobile device illustrates the importance of social life in creating access to media and meaning-making with technology.

The way that the two friends engaged with digital media, furthermore, disrupts a strict binary of home versus school in the landscape of the digital edge. Here, we argue that the school's policies are predicated on the assumption that students' use of technologies might be better served within a home environment. However, in the context of digital edge communities, this idealized separation between recreational (and occasionally risky) and academic use is complicated by the fact that students do not always have quality access to technology in both home and school environments. Wi-Fi is one example of this, but as the case of Amina and Cassandra demonstrates, compromised access is also visible in terms of lack of access to hardware—old and shared computers, and malfunctioning phones. Considering the social meanings of access not only in relation to students but also in the context of their families is important considering how technology takes on important meanings in "hybrid" families as in the case of Cassandra and Amina.

Case Study Two: Selena

Selena was also a graduating senior at Freeway. Meeting for the first time in the school's digital media lab along with other student participants in a focus group, we noticed her dark wardrobe and eyeliner and generally quiet demeanor. In one-on-one interviews, Selena was more forthcoming about her opinions, of which there were many. For instance, she commented that stores like Hot Top are inauthentic, not truly "gothic"—unlike the realness of her own personal goth style. Just as easily, she critiqued peers at her school for acting "hard" but believed her background growing up in a small town in west Texas had granted her a deeper knowledge of the meanings of this adjective.

Selena is an example of a student who is typically labeled "at risk" according to a number of variables; she had a high school record flagged with academic missteps. Selena spent a year at a nearby alternative high school program where she was sent after getting into multiple fights and failing the tenth grade. As a senior she was struggling with transferring her credits from that year and was making up schoolwork in hopes of graduating.

Selena was forthcoming with her frustrations and feelings of disengagement from the classes at Freeway. In fact, compounding academic troubles from her past, Selena occasionally raised concerns about her ability to graduate from high school, which was also complicated by the fact that no one in her family had a high school diploma. Alienation from her school environment contributed to these worries. When describing her feelings about school, she said: "It just gets on my nerves and I can't pay attention. So, lots of times I usually skip a few days." Despite skipping class, she would come back to school to meet us for interviews or use the school's computer labs.

When we asked about her group of primarily Latino friends, Selena was able to offer a litany of derogatory names: "potheads," "skaters," and "stoners." These names were ones that Selena had heard others use in reference to her peers, but she admitted that these stereotypes were not without some truth. However, despite this image, she credited her friends as offering some support for her academic success, with several of her friends encouraging her to stay on the path to graduation. Of her group, she was one of the few to avoid both dropping out of high school and using drugs "harder" than marijuana. When talking about her family life, Selena also describes a complex situation involving both emotional support and instability. During the course of our study her mother was unemployed and struggling to find work. Disruptions in Selena's academic record were shaped by a history of moving back and forth between west and central Texas. Her relationship with her single mother was tenuous, but they respected each other. Her mother even maintained contact with a trusted teacher via text message, asking him to check up on Selena's progress at school.

Despite appearing to be at the border of several risk factors, Selena was motivated by her passion in the creative arts, which encompassed a range of activities including writing, painting, and music. Moreover, she was interested in digital technology and cites her tech classes as some of her favored experiences at Freeway. She enjoyed her freedom in her art class, using software such as Photoshop for projects in her digital media class, and making music. As she puts it, "Yeah. I like making different stuff. I like making music in there sometimes." Selena also acknowledged YouTube as an important source of inspiration and critiqued the school's policy of restricting the website:

Selena: Mmhmm. YouTube they block, but what they don't realize is YouTube is very helpful.
Interviewer: How is it helpful? What do you use it for?
Selena: YouTube, God dang. I learned so much stuff from YouTube.
Interviewer: Like what? Can you think of examples?
Selena: I've learned how to make a tattoo gun out of YouTube. YouTube's what taught me how to play the piano.[31]

Given these interests, Selena's involvement in the after-school digital media club and film project was fitting. However, despite starting the school year as an active member, by the middle of the term Selena reported losing interest and rarely attended meetings. She struggled with finishing and submitting a script for the group's international film project and felt the sting of rejection when her work was not accepted, in part contributing to her decision not to participate in the film project.

The contradictions present in Selena's status as an at-risk student suggest that Freeway's restrictive digital policies might unintentionally exclude students at the margins or who are interested in forms of learning that have historically been devalued or overlooked within traditional curricula. Moreover, as with other students in our study, Selena's abilities to access technology of a sufficient quality outside of school was compromised by financial limitations—she and her family shared a computer that was reportedly from 1997; they did not have cable or Internet access at home. As Alex Cho, Vivian Shaw, and S. Craig Watkins discuss in chapter seven, the sidelining of creative interests to extracurricular activities and alternative tracks can be particularly problematic for socioeconomically and racially marginalized students.

While such "alternative" approaches to education do not always explicitly address "at-risk" students, conceptualizations of risk are certainly embedded in both the school's administrative policies around technology and its academic curricula. Thus, cases such as Selena's raise serious questions about the need for a more thorough integration of digital technology and creative themes in academic learning.

Arguably, the ways in which both learning and risk are framed within the context of contemporary schooling often resort to a disciplinary model for dealing with those who fit outside the "academic" mode of students. In other words, in understanding the shape of school policies around digital risks—as well as the ways in which the school values students' technological practice—it is also necessary to interrogate how marginalized students who attempt their own paths of creative and intellectual exploration often encounter significant structural limitations and, unfortunately, get frequently constructed as "risky" and prone to misbehavior.

Conclusion

This chapter demonstrates the challenges Freeway faces when incorporating digital and mobile media. Students, teachers, and policies are often at odds with regard to the appropriate use of technology at school. Daily life at Freeway is fraught with struggles and tensions regarding the value and appropriate use of digital media. Students understandably desire to incorporate digital and mobile media into their educational lives. They have demonstrated the value that online search engines, social network sites, peer communication, and online video tutorials have in their lives away from school. Teachers understandably want to ensure optimal learning environments with minimal distractions. And of course school districts have a responsibility to minimize students' exposure to inappropriate or harmful content. The different goals, values, and practices that are developing around and through media are competing to shape policies, curricula, and opportunities at Freeway.

The incorporation of technology should not be isolated to formal technology courses, but should be embraced as part of an overall digital culture that values digital literacies and practices in all aspects of students' learning ecologies—creative, recreational, and educational. Technology is an integrated aspect of students' lives, thus they require adult guidance and support as they learn to navigate new terrains. Until schools more fully recognize and embrace the cultures and values of today's generation of learners, they will continue to miss a multitude of opportunities to help students become responsible and engaged digital citizens. Schools have a responsibility to prepare students for their future, and this goes beyond merely teaching them how to use digital media and mobile technologies; it also includes fostering critical thinking, responsible use, and a sense of efficacy. This is particularly true for students in the digital edge, whose access to material resources and digital literacy is already marginalized.

4

The STEM Crisis in Education

S. Craig Watkins

Something interesting happened during the course of our fieldwork: games emerged as a viable component in the effort to make academic learning more relevant for students. A host of games-based platforms, most notably *Minecraft*, were adopted as technologies for accelerating the design of new learning futures. The rise of games as a catalyst for rethinking schooling and learning was driven primarily by the urgent call to raise the science, technology, engineering, and math (STEM) literacy rates in U.S. schools. Its limited resources notwithstanding, Freeway launched a new game development track just as we were about to begin our ethnographic inquiry with the school. Freeway adopted games as a way to draw students into classes and learning environments that provided a more deliberate path to developing STEM skills. The decision to offer a game development course also reflected the school district's inconsistent policy and pedagogy toward technology (discussed in chapter three).

One of the classes that we spent the most time in during our fieldwork was Freeway's advanced game design class, which was held in what was informally called the Game Lab. The room was impressive. It was outfitted with about twenty-five iMac computers with large monitors. All of the Apple computers were loaded, for example, with powerful graphics applications, digital video editing software, and game authoring tools. Students also had access to a couple of Samsung Galaxy Tablets, a Wacom graphics tablet, a digital music keyboard, and two small digital cameras. The computers were Internet enabled, which meant, *in theory*, that students could connect to the proliferation of data, information, and distributed expertise available online. A large projection screen in the classroom enabled live video conferencing.

In contrast to the view held by outsiders and even some Freeway students that this was a "ghetto school," the Game Lab was a technology-rich space. It was also the space in which the school district, Mr. Garcia (the school's principal), and Mr. Warren (the advanced games class instructor) had made a significant bet on the future of learning at Freeway.

The decision by Freeway to leverage games to expose students to STEM education was consistent with broader national trends in education. The widening effort to incorporate design, systems thinking, and coding into the K–12 curriculum is an indicator of a broader push to strengthen STEM literacy among U.S. youth. Schools around the nation are involved in what is tantamount to a rebranding campaign in an effort to align their curriculum with STEM-based skills. Among other things, there are serious political and economic incentives for schools to offer more robust STEM learning opportunities.

School administrators run the risk, politically, of being out of step with a widening ethos that has made STEM learning the main measure of success in public education. Moreover, powerful institutions from the White House (under Barack Obama) to the National Science Foundation have issued compelling economic incentives for schools to invest in STEM readiness and education. The nationwide emphasis on STEM is a response to several factors: a steadily evolving knowledge economy, skill bias technical changes in the labor market, and concerns about America losing ground in the global race for supremacy in education, technology, and innovation.

But Freeway's embrace of new learning futures faced some serious challenges. The school, it turns out, did a relatively good job of securing tech for students. However, it struggled to offer a curriculum and instructional environment that was commensurate with the technological resources that it provided. For example, the school's strict vision on workforce development—learning specific tech skills to get a job—demonstrated little awareness of the more nuanced STEM-based competencies. STEM education is important not only as a means to a good-paying job but also as a catalyst for sparking curiosity, creativity, and a questioning disposition among students.[1] An effective STEM education encourages students to ask probing questions, analyze the world and data around them, develop critical thinking skills, and cultivate the disposition to test new ideas. These skills, we believe, are useful across a wide spectrum of life's activities, including social, educational, economic, and civic life.

This chapter and the one that follows offer a close-up view of the challenges and opportunities resource-constrained schools face when they embrace the call to ramp up STEM learning. More precisely, we focus on Freeway's adoption of games and the quest to prepare students for a rapidly evolving STEM economy. In this chapter we address how the institutional limitations in resource-constrained schools severely challenge the efforts to integrate STEM-based instruction and learning. Also, we consider the broader social context and inequities that conspire to limit the development of a more diverse pool of STEM talent in the United States. If STEM is the future, then the failure to provide the nation's fastest-growing segment of students—Latino, immigrant, and lower-income—with the academic skills required to succeed in that future is unethical. The challenges facing Freeway in its efforts to catalyze STEM learning are symptomatic of a broader national crisis.

The next chapter identifies some of the creative strategies that a group of Freeway students, many of them only modest academic achievers at best, employed to turn the game development class into a unique learning experience. Their resilience in the face of compelling institutional barriers such as inadequate curriculum design and instructional expertise suggests that these students were capable of far more than what their teacher or school expected from them in the formal academic setting.

The Opportunity to Learn STEM

To frame our analysis of how the games class structured STEM-based learning, we turn to the work of education scholar Jeannie Oakes.[2] She contends that some of the most common institutional practices in schools structure different kinds of learning opportunities, which can often lead to disparate academic outcomes. In her analysis of educational inequalities, Oakes considers what she calls the "opportunity to learn." She writes: "What happens if different kinds of classrooms systematically provide students with different kinds of learning experiences?"[3] Further, she asks: "Do these differences mean that some kinds of students have greater opportunities to learn than others?"[4]

Even as digital media, games, and STEM education make their way into a wider mix of classrooms, not all twenty-first-century learning is equal. That is, the degree to which students gain mastery in STEM skills varies significantly by school and the resources—social, technical, and instructional—available to them.

Our yearlong immersion in the advanced game classes allowed us to assess to what degree the class provided regular and substantive opportunities to cultivate STEM-based skills. This was especially true in terms of the opportunity to engage more cognitively complex activities in relation to game design. We organize our analysis of the opportunity to learn STEM via the game design class around three primary themes. First, we consider what students were expected to learn in the game design class based on state education standards. Second, we address another key aspect of academic-oriented learning—the quality of the learning environment, including, for example, the amount of time-on-task that students were able to devote to game design and, by association, STEM literacy. Third, we explore how the teacher's perceptions of student ability shaped students' opportunities to cultivate greater competency in STEM education.

STEM Learning Standards

To better understand the kinds of things that students were *supposed* to learn in the game development class, we reviewed the Technology Applications standards prepared by the State Board of Education Texas Essential Knowledge and Skills Committees.[5] The Technology Applications curriculum has six strands:

- creativity and innovation
- communication and collaboration
- research and information fluency
- critical thinking, problem solving, and decision making
- digital citizenship
- technology operations and concepts

The standards that our research team reviewed online were presented in open and iterative form and candidly recognized that courses like game design are under constant revision as a result of the technological innovations and shifting practices and platforms that are continually reshaping the games industry. The primary purpose of the six strands is to provide some general learning guidelines, goals, and outcomes related to the development of the social, technical, and educational skills necessary to demonstrate mastery in digital-, media-, and technology-oriented classes.

According to the Technology Applications standards developed for high school, it would be reasonable, for instance, to expect Freeway students to create a prototype game that includes, among other things, multiple game levels with increasing difficulty. This reflects the ability to design not only different levels but also different problem-solving strategies. The standards also imply that students' games should reflect examples of physics, which may include lighting, shading, perspective, motion blur, and reflections. Game design is also part art, which means that students might demonstrate some degree of aptitude regarding color theory, texture, balance, skinning, and drawing. Moreover, a carefully designed game might layer the game play experience with different points of view and camera angles. Games are dynamic systems that reflect varying degrees of artificial intelligence, mathematical functions, and creative and artistic expressions. It is, after all, the combination of these features that makes game design such a promising domain for academic-oriented learning.

How did the learning goals established in Freeway's game design class compare with the Technology Applications standards? In the advanced game design class at Freeway, students were expected to create a game using a platform called Gamestar Mechanic. The decision to use Gamestar Mechanic reflected the core dilemma that shaped this "advanced" game design class. Mr. Warren, the course instructor, envisioned the class as a catalyst for igniting student engagement with STEM-based literacies, but in reality the lack of a sharp curriculum vision undermined any opportunity to foster a rich formal learning experience. Gamestar Mechanic was designed primarily as a game-authoring tool to teach elementary and middle school students some of the rudimentary aspects of game design. The adoption of the platform in a high school advanced class was peculiar and illuminates how curriculum-poor conditions established relatively low standards and limited opportunities for students to engage more robust forms of STEM learning.

Coding

Some of the standards, not surprisingly, involved developing greater fluency in programming languages. In a multiplatform world, the art and science of programming is a steadily evolving skill. For example, the differences across platforms, such as coding for a personal computer or mobile device, require nuance. Despite the growing calls to expose all students to basic coding literacies, virtually all of the Freeway students that we met had never been introduced to even the most rudimentary aspects of programming.

During our fieldwork, a number of enrichment programs (in Austin and beyond) devoted to introducing a greater diversity of students— girls, African Americans, Latinos—to the basic aspects of coding began to grow and attract attention from media and philanthropists. Tech companies, led by Google and Facebook, have launched educational programs and national campaigns encouraging students to learn to code. Two students from the game design class had played around informally with coding languages but had no real proficiency. Their efforts to learn coding involved going online to find tutorials. Freeway did not offer any courses in coding.

The absence of computer science courses at Freeway was actually typical as the overwhelming majority of U.S. schools in which black and Latino students are the majority generally lack even basic instruction in computer science.[6] Computer science courses are a principal gateway to STEM-oriented career tracks. Many of the most highly compensated and high-status occupations in STEM are computer related. Learning to code has become so central in the digital economy that some states have even considered education legislation that would allow learning a coding language to be a substitute for learning a foreign language.[7] Critics, however, charge that learning a foreign language is substantially different from learning programming language. Learning to code is as much about learning to problem-solve—dealing with complexity—as it is learning the technical aspects of programming. One indicator of the low number of black and Latino students having access to high-quality computer science education is the extraordinarily low number of Latino and black students who take the college AP exam in computer science every year.[8] The data strongly suggest that significant proportions of black and Latino students are locked into schools and learning environments that do not prepare them for future opportunities in STEM.

Quality of the Learning Environment

From the very beginning of the class it was clear that there was no curriculum or plan for the kinds of games that students were expected to create. For instance, there were no clear-cut instructions, guidelines, or rubrics for students to consider. Moreover, there were no discernible pathways to level up, that is, produce subsequent games that demonstrated more complex ideas or game play mechanics over the course of the semester. For example, students could have been asked to produce board games, paper prototypes, or simple digital games as a way to make their ideas actionable through rapid ideation and prototyping techniques. In addition to providing a foundation for building their design and game creation skills, these kinds of early assignments could help students foster creative confidence and academic efficacy.

One of the few students who consistently worked hard on his Gamestar Mechanic project complained that the version of the platform available in the class lacked many of the assets that were required to produce richer games. He wanted to enter his class project in a Gamestar Mechanic student competition. His expectations for the class—producing a game high enough in quality to receive outside recognition—were considerably higher than Mr. Warren's expectations.

Throughout our time in the class (the entire year) there were no lectures or any teacher-led discussions about the features of the game creation software available in the class specifically or game design principles more generally. Further, Mr. Warren did not provide textbooks, handouts, or online learning materials related to game design for students to consult. How was this possible? First, we learned that Freeway, already facing severe budget constraints, could not afford instructional materials for the course. Second, Mr. Warren's lack of teaching experience limited his capacity to design a classroom environment that supported students' opportunity to learn some of the basic principles of game design.

Learning materials like books and electronic resources not only support instruction and provide guidance; they also help establish certain expectations for the learning climate. When no materials exist for students to consult, the possibilities for learning are seriously undermined. Students were expected to learn mainly through individual or collaborative exploration, experimentation, and discovery. While a few of the students tinkered with Gamestar Mechanic, many used it only on the rare occasions when Mr. Warren insisted. Consequently, their time spent on game creation tasks was limited.

Time to Learn STEM

Oakes contends that one way to assess the opportunity to learn is to consider the amount of time students are able to devote to learning. She found that when it comes to the time to learn, students in higher-track classes benefit in an assortment of ways—quality instruction, more time on task, academic rigor, regular attendance—that enhance the amount of time they are able to devote to learning compared with students in lower-track classes. Admittedly, observing learning is a challenge due to the subtle and often invisible aspects of learning. Even when students appear to be listening, working, or following instructions, it does not necessarily mean that they are learning. Thus, we focused on *engagement*—that is, the extent to which time was allocated for interacting with some of the more cognitively demanding elements of game design referred to in the state standards, such as critical thinking, prototyping, and technical operations.

The significant relationship between time and learning, however, is not simply about the amount of time set aside for learning (quantity of time); it is also about how the available time to learn or engage subject matter content is spent (quality of time). What made our analysis of learning more challenging than usual was that there was very little instruction from Mr. Warren. There were also virtually no assignments. Teachers are generally expected to introduce students to specific texts, concepts, ideas, and techniques and then require them to demonstrate their understanding through an essay, test, homework, experiment, or creative product.

In the games class, for example, students might be expected to read documents and textbooks that offer insights into the mechanics of game design. Typical assignments might require students to spend some of their time writing, sketching, and building prototypes. These kinds of

classroom activities—engaging course learning materials and participating in the demonstration of proficiency—support engagement with
STEM-based literacies such as hypothesis testing, design, coding, or research and information fluency.

And yet, students spent very little time formally engaged in these
kinds of learning tasks. Instead, several students played games in class
but generally not for the purpose of informing their own approach to
the design of games. In other instances, students used the classroom
Internet connection to watch videos, listen to music, or consume content that did not appear to have any relevance to the main goals of the
class—learning how to design and build games. Students were rarely
required or expected to engage in game design learning tasks during
class time.

Many education researchers believe that *time-on-task* is a critical factor to consider when assessing the opportunities that students have to
learn.[9] If students do not have sufficient time to devote to tasks that
encourage engagement with core class concepts and ideas, then the likelihood of meaningful learning outcomes is substantially reduced. From
the outside looking in, the students in Mr. Warren's class had substantial time (each class was an hour and a half) to learn the basic components of game design. However, if the attainment of STEM skills in
game-based learning settings is at least partially contingent on students
devoting time to tasks like systems thinking, computer science, iterative
design, multimodal storytelling, media production, or building playable
prototypes, then the opportunities for cultivating STEM literacies at
Freeway were, in fact, limited.

Perception of Student Abilities

The learning opportunities that schools provide their students are insti-
tutionally created and perpetuated, in part, by perceptions of student
ability. When teachers think that their students are capable of stretch-
ing cognitively, they are much more likely to assign rigorous tasks.
Conversely, when teachers think that their students are incapable of
handling challenging academic work, they are much less likely to assign
rigorous tasks. Oakes writes, "We know that the learning opportunities
teachers are able or willing to create in classrooms are affected in some

ways by their perceptions of the characteristics of the groups of students they encounter."[10]

Although he had a great rapport with many of his students, Mr. Warren's lack of attention to curricula-related details, coupled with the near absence of any projects from students to assess, strongly suggests that he did not have high expectations for what his students might be able to accomplish. During our fieldwork, students were never required to produce some of the basic artifacts that reflect substantive engagement with the creative or rigorous cognitive activities associated with game design. For example, students were not asked to produce design documents, research, artwork, storyboards, or prototyped games for feedback and assessment.

Moreover, even if Mr. Warren wanted to design a rich curriculum and require his students to produce game-based artifacts for teacher feedback and assessment, his lack of classroom experience combined with no expertise in game design severely handicapped his ability to do so. The decision to appoint Mr. Warren as the instructor for the game development class despite his lack of expertise was not an aberration. Researchers call this "out-of-field teaching," and it is much more likely to occur in high-minority and lower-income schools than in predominantly white and higher-income schools.[11] The higher percentage of out-of-field teaching in lower-income schools means that even when students have access to STEM courses, the instruction that they receive may not be on par with the instruction that more affluent students receive.

This is less a critique of Mr. Warren than it is of an educational system that routinely places teachers in classes that they are not prepared to teach. His appointment in the class was one of many indicators that when it came to implementing Freeway's vision for a game design track, the school's curricula planning and learning resources were incommensurate with its ambitions. Mr. Warren cared about his students, and they often spoke very highly of him. However, like so many others, Mr. Warren succumbed to the view that simply providing lower-income students access to technology—computers, game-authoring software, graphics applications—was an indicator of achievement. By emphasizing the acquisition of tech over the acquisition of high-quality instruction, the class was simply not built to deliver a robust STEM learning experience.

Our research team pondered whether the relatively low standards set in the class would have been permitted in a school with more affluent families. Our conclusion: likely not.

The Costs of Curriculum-Poor Conditions

Curriculum-poor conditions like the ones we learned about at Freeway are consequential. More specifically, students pay a steep price and one that has long-term effects on their future readiness and life chances. Classrooms that lack a clear curricula vision do not just limit the opportunity for students to learn in that class; the cumulative effect is often much greater. Curriculum-poor classrooms severely restrict the ability of students to develop the full range of skills that adequately prepare them for postsecondary education and an economy that values higher-educated and higher-skilled persons. Next we offer two examples that illuminate how curriculum-poor conditions cost students.

In the first example we consider how the curriculum-poor conditions failed to ignite interest in media and technology of two students who enrolled in the game development class with high hopes for learning and their future. The second example considers how the curriculum-poor conditions failed to develop a repertoire of skills that enhance the ability of students to make important industry and real-world connections. The first example illustrates how curriculum-poor conditions limit the capacity of students to grow their *human capital,* while the second example illustrates how these conditions can also limit the capacity of students to grow their *social capital.*

Looking for a Spark: The Consequences of Curriculum-Poor Classrooms

A number of students enrolled in the game design class optimistic that they would be able to ignite specific interests and, in some cases, forge open future-oriented pathways in areas such as game design, art, graphics, and engineering. The limitation of the class notwithstanding, Mr. Warren was a caring teacher for the students who displayed an interest in games and digital media production. He sincerely valued the interests that students were developing out of school and encouraged them to bring those interests, skills, and projects into his class. Further, he invited students to take a greater ownership stake in their own learning. For some students this was an invitation to dive deeper into interests that they were developing, work on outside projects in school, or tinker with emergent interests.

As a result, Mr. Warren created an opportunity for a learning experience that softened the boundaries between formal and informal learning spheres, academics and pop culture, school work and play, and adult-driven and peer-driven modes of learning. However, as we discovered during our fieldwork, allowing students to bring outside interests into the classroom does not guarantee that they will encounter rich learning opportunities or develop depth expertise or a stronger sense of academic efficacy in school.

The stories of Caroline and Emmanuel illustrate how the curriculum-poor aspects of the game design class undermined the ability of students to meet some of the learning outcomes established in the Technology Application standards or realize their own interest-driven aspirations.

Caroline and Emmanuel

Caroline was one of the few female students enrolled in the advanced games class offered at Freeway. Mr. Warren championed her as one of his prize pupils. Like a proud parent, he boasted about her art skills. Caroline, a junior when we met her, enjoyed drawing and was especially fond of anime—the Japanese art/animation style that is popular in comics, children's cartoons, and games. When we saw her sketchbook, it was full of drawings that appeared in a classic two-dimensional anime style. There was a mixture of black and white as well as colored-pencil drawings that reflected a bold style. The eyes of some of her characters seemed to possess life. Caroline was self-taught and started drawing when she was in sixth grade. Her inspiration was a cartoon that she watched as a kid, Naruto.[12] She liked to practice, and, as she told us, "every drawing just gets better and better the more I do it."

During the school year we had the chance to learn more about Caroline. For example, we discovered that she did not like attending Freeway. "The students here are too rowdy," she told one of our interviewers. And like many of her peers, Caroline thought that homework was a waste of time. Even more disheartening was her claim that "most of the teachers here don't really care how well you do." Her ambivalent attitude about school made the sketchbook that she maintained even more intriguing. If school failed to motivate Caroline, her interests in anime had the opposite effect.

Her reasons for enrolling in the games class were partly aspirational and demonstrated the degree to which Caroline was engaged in some sophisticated translation work. Unlike some of her peers, she did not view Mr. Warren's class as a career path to games but rather as an opportunity to explore a different career track. "I want to make animation and manga art for books and television shows," she told a member of our research team. Caroline said that she took the class "to see if it would help me in designing an anime show that I want to make when I get older."

Emmanuel also viewed the games class as an opportunity to connect an interest he pursued outside of school to the game design class. This was Emmanuel's first year at Freeway, which may explain his occasional shyness and tendency to recede into the background whenever he collaborated with students in the game design class. He intentionally chose engineering, art, and game design classes to engage his true passion—drawing cars. Emmanuel, also a junior, made repeated references to his love of cars.

Similar to Caroline, Emmanuel maintained a sketchbook full of pencil drawings. Most of Emmanuel's pictures were side-profile views of cars, often tweaks and modifications to real cars on the street. The pencil sketches displayed clean lines, careful shading, and interesting interpretations of well-known car brands. In one series of drawings he had a Lincoln Continental merged with a Cadillac DeVille, several cars based on Bentleys, and two drawings sourced from BMWs. In addition to the technical illustrations, his collection of drawings included a couple of two-dimensional drawings of female friends and a rough sketch of his dog. He even tried a self-portrait.

Emmanuel carried his sketchbook around like a badge of honor, a physical manifestation of something that he had committed time and creative energy to make. He occasionally sold some of his drawings to classmates. Through many conversations with him, we learned that Emmanuel enrolled in the game design class because he was excited by the prospects of seeing his drawings in three-dimensional aspects on the computer. Emmanuel, in short, was hopeful that the class would spark his creative aspirations.

Failure to Spark

Caroline and Emmanuel came to the game design class with specific goals in mind related to art, design, and animation. Their stories are additional examples of how student aspirations and academic dispositions at Freeway belied the "at risk," "low achievement" narrative that drove the largely negative perceptions of the school. This is a crucial point insofar as it suggests that even students labeled as "average" or "low performing" may have interests that if acknowledged and supported can lead to important educational breakthroughs.

Caroline and Emmanuel were not exceptional students by traditional standards. Their grades and academic ambitions were modest, at best. Neither articulated postsecondary aspirations. Moreover, both Caroline and Emmanuel were uncertain about how to translate their interests in art, design, and animation into postsecondary or career opportunities. And yet, they each had imaginative ideas regarding how the game design class could help them cultivate their artistic and technical skills and connect them to creative and career-oriented trajectories that were personally meaningful.

Each student was looking for an opportunity to spark a distinct interest. Caroline envisioned an interest-to-career trajectory. "I'd like to draw for an animated television show one day," she confessed. Emmanuel had aspirations that the class would help take his artwork to the next level, 3D animation. They were ready for a novel academic experience, but the class, unfortunately, was not designed to deliver one.

The level of a person's interest is believed to have a powerful influence on learning. Hidi and Renninger write that "interest as a motivational variable refers to the psychological state of engaging with particular classes of objects, events, or ideas over time."[13] When students bring an outside interest into a class we might expect that they will be motivated to engage, perform, and achieve. However, the direction and development of that interest is influenced by external conditions.

In the two examples that we sketch above, Caroline and Emmanuel came to the class with an *emerging individual interest*. That is, both exhibited "the beginning phases of a relatively enduring predisposition to seek repeated reengagement with particular classes of content over time."[14] And while this emerging individual interest is generally self-generated it requires external support to be sustained. The educational environment is a context presumably equipped to help students develop and sustain their interests by supporting their ability to go deeper, acquire knowledge, and attain greater proficiency.

Caroline and Emmanuel embodied aspects of emergent individual interest. The effort that they exerted in the maintenance of their sketchbooks suggests that they valued this interest and reengaged it over time. They enrolled in the game design class because they believed it was an opportunity to continue engaging their interests in art and also cultivate new interests in digital media production, animation, and design. In theory they were right. School, and the game design class in particular, should have been an opportunity to explore and further cultivate their interests in digital media content creation.

Studies show that educators can help students nourish and develop their interests through modeling and innovative task organization, and by offering feedback that encourages students to maintain attention and grow more curious and competent about an interest.[15] Educators can also establish the learning environment and conditions that not only create the opportunity for students to reengage an emergent individual interest but also deepen that interest.[16]

As high school students, Caroline and Emmanuel were at a crucial point in their emergent individual interests: their interests as digital media artists were poised for further development. This is a period when an interest's relationship to postsecondary education and career-oriented trajectories becomes more salient for some students. Educators—both in and out of the classroom—are in the unique position to build the conditions that help students link their interests to future opportunities. The failure to design an educational environment that offers learning opportunities that deepen engagement with an interest, for example, can lead to reversal or an interest becoming dormant or disappearing altogether.[17]

Throughout their time in the game design class, Caroline and Emmanuel struggled to find learning opportunities that enriched their interests in the digital media arts, design, and animation. Caroline hoped to connect her interests in anime to the games class and articulate a career-oriented trajectory. She needed a curriculum, instruction, and learning climate that fostered the ability to explore the areas of art, story, and character development in greater depth. Emmanuel had no substantive experience with graphics software prior to the class, so what he really needed was hands-on instruction, guidance, and feedback to enhance his design, art, and technology skills. Unfortunately, in an environment that offered no instructional expertise, instructional materials, or innovative tasks, Caroline and Emmanuel had to develop their design and technical competencies on their own. As a result, the class was of very little value to them, and midway through the semester their interest began to wane.

We highlight the stories of Caroline and Emmanuel to note that interest-driven learning does not happen simply because a student can pursue an outside passion in school. Rather, interest development has to be organized through rich curriculum design, supported by instructional expertise, and deepened by cognitively demanding tasks. Our observations and subsequent analysis compel us to conclude that linking interests to the formal learning environment is an important aspect of more relevant learning but is insufficient alone to produce learning that is deep, robust, and connected to future opportunities.

Designing the Networked Classroom

If Mr. Warren struggled with developing a curriculum-driven vision for the game design class, his persistent efforts to connect his students to the various stakeholders in Austin's burgeoning innovation economy were considerably more robust. Austin is a mini-hub for game development companies including Electronic Arts, Disney, Sony, and Blizzard Entertainment. Equally noteworthy are the small independent game, interactive, and mobile media start-ups dotting the city's creative economy landscape. Throughout the school year Mr. Warren maintained an open-door policy, inviting journalists, educators, school board members, state elected officials, and members from local game studios to his class.

Mr. Warren strongly believed that for his game design class to reach its potential it was imperative to expose Freeway students to the industry and cultivate meaningful social ties. As we discuss in the book's conclusion, one of the more urgent challenges that Freeway students confront is their isolation from the social networks and information channels that are the real links to opportunity and economic mobility in a knowledge-driven economy. In this section we explain how curriculum-poor conditions undermined Mr. Warren's ability to fully catalyze the social ties he labored to turn into an asset for his students.

A visit by Catherine and Jillian, two twenty-somethings from a local game studio, was a clear example of a great idea—exposing students to industry professionals—falling short because of curriculum-poor conditions and naïveté about employment in the creative sector. These arranged encounters with industry and other local VIPs were often a missed opportunity for Freeway students to learn valuable lessons about the world of creative work and the significance of cultivating meaningful professional connections.

At the start of their visit Catherine and Jillian stood in front of the class to answer questions. Many of the questions that the students asked were understandably inexperienced. "What's the best way to get a job in the video game industry?" "What kinds of positions are available at your studio?" Many of the students were half-interested at best in the two visitors. Some of the members from the UT Crew (a group of students you will meet in the next chapter) showed slightly more interest. Working to try to keep students attentive, Mr. Warren announced, "Ok guys listen up. . . . If you want a job in the industry here's your chance."

The two visitors talked about their own paths to careers in game design. Catherine noted that she studied art and design at the University of Texas and made her own way to games via that track. "There was no one in my department who worked with games," she said. Jillian traveled a more unconventional path. "I got my degree in a field that is far from the industry, Asian studies," she said. But she picked up a skill in college—writing—that she believes serves her well in the games industry. Her strong writing skills led to her first job in quality assurance, where she was able to point out flaws in games and write powerful descriptions.

"You have to be able to write in the industry; it's actually quite important," Jillian explained.

Both Catherine and Jillian emphasized the importance of going to college and developing your skills as a writer and a thinker. To make her point about college even more pronounced, Jillian pointed to Watkins, a university professor, and stated, "That's the guy that you need to know."

The suggestion that the ability to write and think was a key element of finding opportunity in the game industry illustrates an important point about literacy in the era of smart technologies and knowledge-driven economies. Digital literacy is routinely championed as a key feature in the new world of learning and preparation for the economy of tomorrow. But as Jenkins et al. argue, a key aspect of education in the twenty-first century is the twin mastery of the long-standing literacies associated with print culture and the newer forms of literacy associated with digital media culture.[18] Jenkins et al. also note that before students can thrive in the digital realm, "they must be able to read and write."[19] Importantly, they note that "youth must expand their required competencies, not push aside old skills to make room for the new."[20]

In his book *The Art of Game Design: A Book of Lenses*, Jesse Schell lists writing among the various skills a good game designer needs.[21] He identifies two distinct forms of writing, creative and technical. Whereas the former includes creating the fictional world, characters, and events that will shape the game world and gameplay experience, the latter includes, for instance, the creation of design documents that clearly map all of the game details. The perspectives from Jenkins et al. and Schell reiterate the idea that the ability to write and communicate effectively remains critical in an economy driven by knowledge, technology, ideas, and innovation. When we reviewed our field notes we were stunned to find virtually no reference to students submitting any type of written work. The curriculum-poor conditions neither required nor expected students to demonstrate proficiency in any form of writing, creative or technical.

Further, Catherine explained that oftentimes employers want to see your work and suggested that students maintain a portfolio of the creative content they generate. This could include anything from drawings to artwork to blogs and even games. She offered her website as a sample of a digital portfolio that included, among other things, information about her work experience, samples of her work, and a repertoire of art, design, and social skills. In addition to her technical proficiency with software such as Unreal 3, Maya, Photoshop, and Illustrator, Catherine performed management and supervisory roles. She also touted her writing, editorial, and communication skills as assets that could support the achievement of team-wide objectives.

After Catherine and Jillian left, our research team reflected on what the visit suggested, more generally, about the class. Ideally, the students would have conducted some research on the studio and prepared a set of questions related to, for example, the studio's mission, previous and current titles, and adaptations to an industry that is undergoing wide transformation as a result of social gaming and mobile platforms. This kind of preparation—conducting research on a company and industry-specific related data and trends—is quite common among those seeking jobs in today's hypercompetitive economy. Additionally, the encounters with local talent—game designers, tech companies, and media professionals—presented opportunities to help students not only connect to industry talent but also gain experience cultivating the social skills that are a prerequisite for entry into the knowledge economy.

For example, during the visit by Catherine and Jillian, Freeway students could have handed out business cards and shared their games, sketchbooks, music compositions, and other content for creative and professional feedback. The outside visit presented a great opportunity to learn about internships and other potential opportunities to make connections with the studio. These kinds of interactions and the rich lessons they might provide require a curricula vision that is responsive to the needs of students and cognizant of industry trends. Additionally, a well-designed curriculum could help students use the informal knowledge gained through these exchanges to inform their academic pursuits and creative aspirations.

* * *

The curriculum-poor conditions failed to spark the emergent interest development that some students articulated when they initially enrolled in the game design class. In many instances the inadequate curriculum design severely limited the opportunities for students to grow their human capital in STEM-related areas. As we noted above, the formal aspects of the class fell far short of the state standards in digital media and technology.

In addition to the educational costs, the curriculum-poor conditions led to important social costs. Entry into creative work is as much about social capital (who you know) as it is about human capital (what you know). The many encounters, for example, with game industry studios and personnel provided unique opportunities for Freeway students to learn more about the creative industries in Austin. Equally important, they provided an opportunity to practice some of the networking skills that are essential in creative economies.[22] The curriculum-poor conditions resulted in a missed opportunity to help students gain some experience building the social capital skills—networking and cultivating social ties—that are part and parcel of the knowledge economy. Students like Caroline and Emmanuel paid real costs for a game design class that articulated lofty goals but failed to produce the curricula conditions and learning climate to realize those goals.

The $TEM Economy

Among the many reasons why schools like Freeway have intensified their focus on STEM education, none may be more significant than the widely held view that the best-paying occupations in the United States require STEM skills. Most STEM occupations offer wages that are significantly above the U.S. average.[23] The hegemony of the STEM economy—the rising premium on technology skills, high educational attainment, complex problem-solving skills—will continue to influence education policy discourse, curriculum planning, and future visions of learning.

According to the U.S. Bureau of Labor Statistics, STEM employment will far outpace non-STEM employment in the expected rate of job growth.[24] Whereas the projected growth rate for all occupations between 2014 and 2024 is 6.5 percent, the growth projections for STEM occupations are notably higher.[25] For example, mathematical science occupations are projected to grow 28 percent and computer occupations by 12 percent during the same period.[26] STEM workers, on average, earn 26 percent more than their non-STEM counterparts.[27] Furthermore, STEM professionals are less vulnerable than their non-STEM counterparts to periods of joblessness or unemployability.[28] In an economy increasingly defined by technological transformation and a bias toward more nuanced cognitive skills, the value of STEM-oriented competencies—complex problem solving, data analysis, computational thinking, experimentation, and mathematical and statistical analysis—will only increase.[29]

These shifts more broadly are connected to what Frank Levy and Charles Murnane call "the new division of labor."[30] The pervasiveness of computers in the workplace has profoundly transformed the occupational structure of postindustrial economies. As we discuss in greater detail in the chapter's conclusion, some economists argue that the computerization of work drives a sharp demand for more cognitively complex skills such as expert thinking, solving uncharted problems, and complex communication.[31] These trends assert greater pressure on educational institutions to cultivate the skills that align with the new division of labor. This is precisely what the emphasis on STEM education intends to do, that is, accelerate the capacity for schools to build a more highly skilled workforce.

Even as the STEM economy is projected to be a significant feature of the larger U.S. economy, only a small number of Latino and African American students are adequately prepared to enter the STEM education and career pipelines. The underdevelopment of STEM talent in lower-income schools is one of the essential challenges driving the education crisis in the United States.

The School-to-STEM Transition: Alternate Paths

The lack of information about and exposure to STEM careers is a significant barrier facing many lower-income youth like the ones we met at Freeway. Most of the students in our study were simply unfamiliar with the many different career options in STEM. The misinformation regarding what types of education and training establish different pathways to STEM employment is also an impediment to opportunity. For instance, there is widespread belief that the attainment of a bachelor's degree is the route to a career in STEM, but alternative educational pathways exist. The STEM labor market is heterogeneous and comprises many sectors, including government, academia, and private.[32]

The U.S. Department of Commerce, for example, found that nearly one-quarter (23 percent) of STEM professionals completed an associate degree or at least some college.[33] In a report titled *The Hidden STEM Economy*, the Brookings Institution presents what it calls a "new portrait of the STEM economy."[34] The report maintains that half of all STEM jobs are available to workers without a four-year college degree. Jobs that require some degree of STEM knowledge but only sub-bachelor's level training, the Brookings report notes, can be found across various sectors such as the health care, construction, and installation and repair industries.

Whereas STEM jobs that require at least a bachelor's degree tend to be clustered in certain regions and major metropolitan areas, STEM jobs requiring only a sub-bachelor's degree are more widely distributed across the U.S. metropolitan map.[35] And while these STEM occupations may not offer wages comparable to those with more education and in higher-skilled STEM sectors, such as software and computer systems design, the wages certainly exceed low-skill service-sector employment.

Findings like these suggest that the STEM economy is much more diverse in the education and training required than is generally recognized. Consequently, the emphasis on the attainment of a four-year college degree obscures the other paths to meaningful employment opportunities in STEM. Information about these other educational and training tracks to STEM would be especially encouraging for many of the students at Freeway who had not been adequately prepared for post-secondary education in STEM or any other discipline. This points to another challenge that severely undermined Freeway's efforts to prepare its students for life beyond high school—the many choke points along the K–12 pipeline to develop students capable of entering the pathways to STEM education.

Diversifying the STEM Talent Pipeline

The persisting difficulties in building a more diverse talent pipeline in STEM—one that includes women, Latinos, and African Americans—shed a critical light on the unique pressures that resource-constrained schools face in preparing their students for an economy that is certain to maintain a bias for STEM-related skills into the foreseeable future.

Freeway's desire to develop more STEM-ready students was weakened by a combination of factors including, for example, the enduring effects of low-quality education in the early schooling years. There are persistent choke points along the kindergarten through high school pipeline that steadily diminish the pool of black and Latino candidates eligible for college degrees or careers in STEM. Curious about the education pipeline directing the students in our study, we examined the STEM readiness of students from Central Texas Middle School, the primary feeder school for Freeway.[36]

Among the nearly one thousand students attending Central Texas Middle School, 72 percent were designated as low income. The school was racially diverse, but Latino (49 percent) and black (22 percent) students made up nearly three-quarters of the school's population. In addition, 16 percent were categorized as English language learners. The combination of low social-economic status, race and ethnicity, and English language learners makes Central Texas Middle School an especially challenging environment for academic development. Specifically, we looked at the college- and career-readiness data compiled by ACT Inc. in two STEM-related areas of coursework, math and science.[37]

ACT defines college and career readiness as "the acquisition of the knowledge and skills a student needs to enroll and succeed in credit-bearing first-year courses at a postsecondary institution (such as a 2- or 4-year college, trade school, or technical school) without the need for remediation." How did Central Texas Middle School fare?

Whereas 90 percent of eighth-grade students were designated as passing mathematics, less than half, or 42 percent, were designated by ACT as career and college ready in mathematics. The outcomes in science were worse. Whereas 81 percent of students received passing scores in science, only 28 percent were identified by ACT as college and career ready in science. This suggests that even when students receive passing grades in their math and science courses, their grade-appropriate readiness for postsecondary schooling in these two areas was notably weak. By the time a majority of these students enter Freeway for ninth grade, the chances of them successfully pursuing academic tracks that prepare them for STEM studies in a postsecondary institution are extremely low. Even if Freeway had developed a robust STEM curriculum, the likelihood that the majority of students could operate at a high level was undermined by inadequate academic preparation during their earlier years of schooling.

The STEM career- and college-readiness status of Central Texas Middle School students is even more striking when you compare it with the status of students from West Hills Middle School, an affluent middle school located across town.[38] West Hills is located in what the *Washing-*

ton Post classifies as a "Super Zip Code."[39] These are zip codes containing families that are in the ninety-fifth percentile for median incomes and college degrees. Austin had eight Super Zip Codes, and one of them was home to West Hills. In the zip code that was home to Central Texas Middle School, 33 percent of the adults had college degrees compared with 79 percent in the zip code that West Hills calls home.

Among the 915 students attending West Hills, only 3 percent were designated as low income. The median household income in the zip code, $129,188, was more than double the U.S. average. The school was predominantly white, 77 percent. Latinos made up 2 percent of the student population. English language learners and African Americans made up 2 and 1 percent, respectively. A combination of factors such as an overwhelmingly upper-income, white, and English-speaking population made West Hills an especially advantageous environment for academic development. While 99 percent of West Hills eighth graders passed math, a respectable 78 percent were identified by ACT as college and career ready in the subject. The outcomes in science were comparable. Ninety-five percent of students received passing scores in science, and 67 percent were designated as career and college ready in science. The educational disparities in STEM readiness between Central Texas Middle School and West Hills are substantial and consequential.[40]

Sadly, the choke points that diminish the pool of Latino and black students able to pursue postsecondary STEM degrees begin long before students reach the middle and high school grades. Kids from lower-income households are more likely than their counterparts from higher-income households to enter kindergarten behind in terms of cognitive and non-cognitive development.[41] In a study of three age cohorts of children, researchers found that gaps in early cognitive skills are highly predictive of gaps at later ages, establishing what they call "a trajectory of cumulative disadvantage for black children over time."[42] In other words, skills acquired in early education beget more skills in primary, secondary, and postsecondary education.

Much of the educational evidence suggests that from early childhood through high school, children from lower-income families face enormous hurdles in sustaining access to high-quality educational opportunities. As a result of these early childhood disadvantages, many of the students that we met at Freeway faced significant hurdles in what

Claudia Golding and Lawrence Katz call "the race between education and technology."[43] It is a painful reality to accept, but by the time many Freeway students enter ninth grade their educational and economic futures have largely been determined.

The college-readiness disparities at Freeway parallel national disparities. Consider the data on high school STEM coursetaking in the United States. In 2009, Latino and black students were less likely than their Asian and white counterparts to have completed higher-level math and science courses. Whereas 42 percent of Asian/Pacific Islander and 18 percent of white graduates had taken calculus only 9 and 6 percent, respectively, of Latino and black high school graduates had.[44] Similar coursetaking patterns emerge in science courses. Fifty-four percent of Asian/Pacific Islander and 31 percent of white graduates completed the combination of biology, chemistry, and physics courses in 2009. By contrast, 23 percent of Latino and 22 percent of black graduates completed this combination of science courses in 2009.[45]

The disparities throughout the K–12 pipeline are certainly linked to the low number of STEM college degrees that black and Latino students receive. A 2016 study by the National Student Clearinghouse confirms the escalating concerns about the STEM degree attainment gap in the United States between black, Latino, and white students, for example.[46] Whereas 15 percent of students from higher-income schools earned a STEM degree within six years of high school graduation, only 7 percent of students from lower-income schools did. Even though the growth in the number of black and Latino high school graduates and college enrollees has been outpacing that of whites, the former are still less likely to earn STEM degrees.[47]

The low number of STEM degrees is even more remarkable when you consider the growing number of underrepresented youth who report that they want to earn a STEM degree. Since the 1980s blacks and Latinos have been just as likely as their white counterparts, for example, to express aspirations for attaining a STEM degree.[48] However, compared with their Asian and white counterparts, they are significantly less likely to leave college with a STEM degree in hand. There is no STEM aspiration gap between Latino and black students and their white counterparts. Rather, Latino and black students tend to lack access to the educational preparation necessary to realize their desire to earn degrees in STEM.

It's Hard to Be What You Cannot See

In addition to the education choke points noted above, several other factors help explain the low numbers of black and Latino students in the STEM education pipeline. Among them, for example, is the fact that many lower-income students are simply unaware of the opportunities in STEM and what is required to credibly pursue related career tracks. This is further compounded by the fact that lack of exposure to science- and technology-oriented professions makes these career choices less visible, tangible, or even imaginable. We commonly met students at Freeway who could articulate aspirations for high-status careers. Students, for example, expressed interests in filmmaking, software engineering, and the digital media arts. But in many of these instances it was clear that students had insufficient access to role models or information about how best to realize their aspirations.

Critics often bemoan the fact that so few Latino, black, and female youth pursue STEM careers, and yet how we message who is most likely to occupy these careers is seldom interrogated. To what extent do narratives about STEM literacy, competency, and opportunity routinely imply white, college-educated men?[49] Latino and black students are less likely to see other Latinos or blacks in STEM careers compared with their white and Asian American counterparts. This suggests a need to actively rebrand computer science, information technology, and STEM-related professions.[50] A different set of images, messages, and narratives about STEM might appeal to a more diverse group of young people, prompting even greater interest in the field. This all suggests that it will take a comprehensive approach to substantively diversify the STEM pipeline, even rethinking the kinds of cultural representations that inform who we think of as designers, engineers, computer scientists, and tech gurus.

Marvel Inc.'s blockbuster Black Panther (2018) was widely recognized for its box office success that debunked the many industry claims that black-themed films could not succeed in a global marketplace. But many championed another feature of the movie—the portrayal of Shuri, a young black woman, as the design and tech savant in the fictional world Wankada. Her STEM skills were a critical part of the narrative. Historically blacks in general and black women specifically have seldom been portrayed as designing, thinking, and problem-solving with technology. These cultural representations and the racial, gender, and behavioral scripts they construct not only entertain us; they also reproduce common sense notions about who has the agency to adopt and leverage tech to build better futures. [51]

These issues are especially significant in light of the workforce trends at technology companies like Google, Facebook, and Apple. In 2014 many of the big tech companies began releasing their workforce data after initially refusing to do so. The data have consistently revealed two decisive trends in tech: the employees in technical and leadership positions are overwhelmingly white and male. At companies like Google and Facebook, black and Latino workers make up about 2 percent of the workforce. The lingering question, of course, is why are these huge disparities in tech employment the norm?[52] Thus far we have highlighted the disparities in education—that is, inadequate preparation in the knowledge and skills (human capital) necessary to gain access to STEM occupations. But the gross underrepresentation of blacks and Latinos in STEM occupations is attributable to insufficient social capital, too.

The Significance of Social Capital in STEM

The STEM employment hurdle that black and Latino students face is not simply a matter of inadequate education; it is also attributable to shortcomings in the diversity and reach of their social networks. For example, as we explained in the introduction, Freeway students live literally on the outer edges of Austin's vibrant tech and knowledge economy, leading to spatial isolation. Importantly, spatial isolation contributes to social isolation.[53] Whereas spatial isolation can limit access to certain physical resources (resource-rich neighborhoods and schools), social isolation generally limits access to important social resources (diverse informal social networks and rich channels of information).

Informal social networks are the primary channels through which ideas, knowledge spillover, tips, and rumors about employment and other opportunities circulate.[54] This is social capital. Access to social capital among students comes largely in the form of the social capital acquired by the adults in their lives, including, for example, parents, other adult relatives, teachers, coaches, mentors, and faith leaders. Thus, any solution to the STEM employment crisis must not only bolster the education and training that black and Latino students receive; the solution must also bolster the social networks, information channels, and STEM role models that black and Latino students have access to.

Redesigning the quality of education available to lower-income students in the K–12 pipeline is a significant challenge. Redesigning ways to fortify their social networks and the informal exchange of knowledge and information is even more formidable. Whereas the former requires enhancing the quality of schools and instruction that students have access to, the latter requires expanding the informal social networks, people, and information channels that students have access to.

Conclusion

The adoption of games at Freeway was a sincere effort to embrace the future of learning. In our view there was one fatal flaw above all other shortcomings in the game design class at Freeway. Although students had access to technology, they did not have access to a clear curriculum vision and learning climate that cultivated human capital (STEM-oriented academic skills) and social capital (STEM-oriented social ties). The primary goal of the course was to encourage high school students to tinker and make games with a piece of game-authoring software that was designed for middle school students developing a novice interest in game creation. Making digital "stuff," it turns out, is actually quite common throughout the K–12 embrace of games specifically and the adoption of technology more generally. The singular focus on making digital content, in our view, is a mistake.

We urge educators to broaden their vision for what STEM classes can accomplish. It sounds strange, but learning how to use a specific piece of software or even building a game should not be viewed as the most important aspect of a game design class. The primary focus should be on outcomes that are neither technology nor product dependent. While the accomplishment that comes with making a game is certainly noteworthy, the real test of progress is whether technology classes can spark greater academic efficacy among students—that is, the confidence that they can thrive and chart their own destiny to opportunity in formal educational settings.

At Freeway the mere access to technology—high-powered computers, an impressive mix of software, and the Internet—was considered a sign of achievement. Access to technology is certainly important, but having access to curriculum-rich classrooms and cognitively challenging tasks that promote level-appropriate expert thinking, problem solving, and complex communication skills is even more important.[55]

Games are viewed by a surging number of educators and tech entrepreneurs as an opportunity to ignite more robust learning experiences and academic outcomes. Media and technology in the classroom—film, television, video, computers—have long been viewed as a remedy for the ills plaguing education.[56] Games have been positioned as a viable pathway to the STEM literacies and careers that are generally associated with the future of work, opportunity, and social mobility. While this may be true, our fieldwork also suggests that the mere provision of tech-rich and game-based learning classrooms does not, by itself, establish the opportunity to cultivate STEM skills.

New learning futures should not be measured in terms of how much technology schools acquire but rather how technology is used as a platform for growing the academic competency and efficacy of students. Freeway is a powerful reminder that even as the spread of technology and technology courses accelerates in U.S. schools, not all tech-rich classrooms and the opportunities for STEM learning are created equal.

5

Gaming School

How Students Strive to Learn in Technology-Rich, Curriculum-Poor Classrooms

S. Craig Watkins

In the previous chapter we examined the curriculum-poor conditions of the game design course and the struggles to engage the emergent interest of students and the educational standards established for technology classes. And while the academic conditions certainly limited the opportunities for students to learn STEM, they did not completely prohibit them from gaining something of value from the game design class. This was precisely the case with a group of students who entered the class with a set of expectations that exceeded those developed by the teacher or the school.

One of the notable advantages of ethnography—in our case, spending considerable hours in the classroom, after-school settings, and homes—is the opportunity to discover practices that greatly enrich our understanding of individual and institutional processes. During our fieldwork we observed a small group of students turn the curriculum-poor conditions into an opportunity to remake the class into a rich learning and creative experience. Although Mr. Warren did not require any substantive deliverables, the students created their own set of deliverables that made them accountable to each other. Some of the students exhibited a creative resilience that was fiercely determined to learn STEM skills even when the class conditions appeared to limit the opportunity to do so. For these students, games were more than just a source of recreation; they were also a source of experimentation, academic innovation, and identity exploration.

The creative resilience of the students even managed to engage some of the education standards for technology courses in ways that the formal course did not. Students made a space to spark conversation, share ideas, and participate in active forms of learning and engagement in the face of classroom conditions that were not built to cultivate STEM learning. This aspect of life and learning at Freeway suggests that the students were capable of much more than what was expected of them. In fact, students were not only open to learning; they were determined to learn even when the school struggled to provide the necessary resources. Working with each other and our research team, the students codesigned a learning environment that supported their interest in making games, cultivated leadership skills, and further developed their talents for digital content creation.

In this chapter we explain how students employed inventive techniques for gaming school or, more precisely, mobilizing their resources, interests, and expertise to transform a curriculum-poor classroom into a space for creative exploration and learning.

Embracing the Future

After a series of meetings before the school year began with Mr. Warren, the course instructor, and Mr. Garcia, the school principal, it was decided that our research team would focus on the two advanced game development classes. But rather than assume the role of the proverbial fly on the wall, our research team proposed something different. We asked and received permission to get involved with the class by coordinating a game design project and working side by side with students. As a result, we were not just onlookers in the classroom; we were participants. Our immersion in the games design classes afforded unique access to students, the classroom climate, and day-to-day life at Freeway. What did students really think about school, education, and their own life chances? What interests, if any, did students have in technology courses in general and games-based courses specifically? How do students perform academically in a class that has no curriculum vision and few expectations?

Resource-constrained schools face unique and complex challenges when they integrate digital media technologies into the classroom. Building a technology-rich space, it turns out, is only part of the challenge. Over the course of the year we gained a fuller understanding of the challenges that students and teachers face in today's schooling environment and why the effort to build twenty-first-century classrooms is about much more than building technology-rich classrooms. Designing a carefully coordinated curriculum that promotes engagement with complex cognitive tasks and problem-solving skills is, without question, the more substantial challenge in building better learning futures.

The introduction of the game design course was a novel experiment that injected elements of the debate about education, technology, and innovation into the academic climate at Freeway. None of the stakeholders at Freeway—administrators, teachers, school board members, parents, students—knew exactly what it meant to integrate games into the menu of course offerings at Freeway. Still, the decision to move forward with the initiative committed some of the school's limited resources to the theory that games could stimulate students, accelerate STEM learning, and lead Freeway into the future of learning.

Games + Learning

There are many descriptions of game-based learning, but this definition by the Institute of Play is clear-eyed and consistent with the approach our research team adopted with Freeway students: "A learning approach that emphasizes engagement, learning by doing, collaboration, reflection, iteration, frequent feedback and sharing. The approach structures learning activities around real-world or fictional challenges that compel learners to take on a variety of roles as they actively identify and seek out the tools and multi-disciplinary information they need to generate solutions."[1]

This definition suggests that game-based learning is not simply about mastering a specific technical skill (e.g., coding) or making a playable game (e.g., prototyping). Instead, robust game-based learning settings situate opportunities for the development of a combination of competencies including the ability to seek out the appropriate information, tools, expertise, and skills necessary to address challenges in more innovative ways.

Educators have traditionally dismissed games as play, leisure, and a detriment rather than a complement to academic engagement. Over the years games have been criticized for promoting antisocial behaviors such as violence, sexism, and racism.[2] These and other factors explain why schools and the adults who lead them have been reluctant to embrace games in the formal school setting. But alternative perspectives about the social, emotional, educational, and health benefits of games are gaining momentum.[3]

The big shift in the games and learning movement is the emphasis on developing more complex cognitive skills. Deep engagement with games includes a mix of competencies that extend far beyond producing a playable game with a specific set of rules and core mechanics. For example, it also involves the ability to think critically and creatively about a specific problem space. What makes game creation a potentially rich academic activity is the degree to which it engages art *and* science, language arts *and* math, risk taking *and* rule making, and individual tenacity *and* collective agency.

Games scholars have identified a number of learning principles in the architecture of games. These include the ability of games to foster experiential learning, creativity, persistence, cooperation, support, and helping behaviors.[4] Games have also been acknowledged as capable of promoting civic-mindedness.[5] Even the concept of play is undergoing a revision as researchers develop a more nuanced appreciation for skills related to inquiry, exploration, and experimentation.[6] Games, more generally, are championed as engines for the development of commonly referenced twenty-first-century skills such as problem solving, critical thinking, and innovation.[7] Importantly, these skills differ from the skills that traditional schooling typically emphasizes, such as following directions, mastering predefined concepts, test taking, and obedience.[8]

Further, good games are "sandboxes" that encourage risk taking, hypothesis testing, exploration, and iteration. James Paul Gee describes this aspect of games as "pleasantly frustrating . . . in the sense of being felt by learners to be at the outer edge of, but within, their 'regime of competence.'"[9] Schools, as many observers note, rarely offer the space and the encouragement to take risks, explore, or fail. Whereas failure in games is an invitation to employ a new strategy or simply try again, failure in school typically leads to harsh evaluation (i.e., low grades), feelings of inadequacy, and marginalization.

The adoption of games as a platform for academic learning reflects the degree to which games are now viewed as a multifaceted medium capable of engaging a variety of social and human experiences. Game designer and scholar Ian Bogost urges us to begin thinking about the many different uses of video games and, in his words, "how together they make the medium broader, richer, and more relevant."[10] Games, Bogost claims, "have seeped out of our computers and become enmeshed in our lives."[11] Bogost offers this intriguing probe: how to do things with video games. Accordingly, as games become more enmeshed in our schools, educators must carefully consider how to do education with the medium. In some cases the adoption of games in schools can reflect superficial engagement and trend following. In other cases, the adoption of games can reflect academic rigor and trendsetting.

It is, of course, one thing to theorize about games and learning and another to design real classroom settings that expertly leverage games for the purpose of cultivating more complex thinking and making skills. This was the challenge that Freeway faced and one that this chapter explores in greater detail.

The UT Crew: A Class within a Class

Once it was decided that our research team would be working side by side with students, we had to assemble a team of learners to work with. Students were given the option to work with our project or pursue their own individual game design projects in the class. Among the twenty-one students, roughly half (ten) chose to work with the two members of our team from the University of Texas. This created an interesting dynamic—a class within a class. One class would be working with our research team on a project that was semistructured and committed to a shared purpose—designing the components for a health-based game. The other class involved students who would be working largely in autonomous fashion on projects driven by their individual interests and motivations. Both sets of students represented distinct social and learning ecologies and typified the varied academic dispositions and practices at Freeway. One day Mr. Warren randomly referred to the students who joined our project as the "UT Crew." The students embraced that identity and it became their informal moniker.

Though they were in the same classroom, the academic engagement of the UT Crew and that of the autonomous students were miles apart. The students who chose to work on their own sat along the periphery of the class, often facing a computer screen and the wall. Spatially, their engagement with the class was isolated, insular, and individualized. Some of the students in this group worked on projects related to game design, but others used the relative physical isolation of their location in the classroom to play games and watch videos that had little to do with the presumed learning goals of the class—making games. By contrast, members of the UT Crew often convened at a long table that was placed near the center of the room. The computers that they claimed resided squarely in the middle of the room, which made it easier to see and talk to their classmates. Spatially, their engagement with the class was open and collaborative. The in-class differences between the two groups were not merely spatial; they were also social and experiential.

While the students on the periphery of the class usually worked alone, the students in the UT Crew worked together and toward the common goal of designing a health-themed game. At the beginning of each class, Michael, the elected team leader, would call out, "Ok, can I get my UT Crew together." Occasionally students were slow to make their way to the lengthy table where they met, but, generally speaking, they gathered as a collective most days. These meetings provided an opportunity for students to participate in design-based exercises, conversation, and the exchange of ideas. They used these daily kickoff sessions to sharpen the vision, story, and other elements of their game. These meetings also presented a chance to provide a status report on the work that they had been tasked to perform. With only a little bit of prompting from the UT researchers, the team cultivated a project that embodied the principles of shared purpose. That is, game making and learning was collaborative and committed to delivering a class project that was more communal than individual. As Ito et al. explain, "When learning is part of purposeful activity and inquiry, embedded in meaningful social relationships and practices, it is engaging and resilient."[12]

Working together gave students frequent opportunities to share knowledge, learn from each other, and engage in collective inquiry.[13] Importantly, the *shared purpose* aspects of the project also gave students *individual purpose*. For some students, work on the project encouraged them to dive deeper into distinct areas of interests like level design, graphic arts, sound production, and management and leadership skills.

In short, the shared and collective aspects of the project generated note-worthy individual benefits too.

The Social Aspects of STEM Learning

The social and communal methods created a distinct learning-by-doing experience for the UT Crew. In fact, learning for the UT Crew took on some of the key properties of twenty-first-century learning identified by Jenkins et al.[14] In their report on learning in the digital age, Jenkins et al. identify several skills and literacies that are keyed to the currents of the networked world and emergent forms of knowledge creation. According to Jenkins et al., the skills required for the mastery of twenty-first-century literacy are not simply technical; they are also social. More precisely, the researchers explain that these social skills should be seen "as ways of interacting within a larger community, and not simply an individualized skill to be used for personal expression."[15]

The distinction between technical skills (i.e., proficient navigation of technology) and social skills (i.e., proficient navigation of people) is critical. The latter point to more nuanced levels of participation and performance in knowledge cultures. A social and connected learner is conscientious and engaged with the world of information and data around him or her and amenable to meaningful forms of social exchange, cross-disciplinary expertise, and collaboration.

Next, we briefly consider two of the new literacies identified by Jenkins et al.—*collective intelligence* and *negotiation*—to illustrate the sociable features of the learning environment the UT Crew codesigned.

Smarter Together: Collective Intelligence

While some members of the UT Crew knew more about games and game making than others, no one person knew everything. From the start it was clear that students brought different bodies of game-based knowledge, skills, and experience to the project. Whereas Broderick was heavily invested in designing graphics for games, Taylor was more interested in audio and sound design. Whereas Jason considered himself a good writer, Kevin was an aspiring programmer. Diego focused on building the game levels, while Michael concentrated on building the team. Nicolás had worked on a summer project that gave him some experience with collaboration, the agile method, and an appreciation for maintaining a production schedule.

This mix of interests, expertise, and experience encouraged members of the UT Crew to tap the varied forms of knowledge within the group to make the whole team and their approach to game design smarter. Pierre Levy refers to this process as "collective intelligence."[16] When practiced effectively, collective intelligence can be a powerful source for communities for learning, problem solving, and innovation. This process is a sharp contrast to how schools typically structure and facilitate learning—largely as an individualized and highly competitive enterprise. Instead of working together to solve problems students are expected to work against each other in competition for individual evaluation and grades.

The autonomous students' learning experience was more traditional. Rather than share their interests, projects, and knowledge with others in the class, they journeyed alone and without much input from or engagement with their peers. While it was common to see members of the UT Crew moving around the class, sharing their knowledge, exchanging ideas, and working side by side, the autonomous learners were often stationary, seldom shared expertise or exchanged ideas, and worked in a more isolated fashion.

The kind of learning and game-making culture that the UT Crew experienced—collaborative and social—parallels the rapidly evolving twenty-first-century workplace. A growing number of organizations are adopting elements of the collective intelligence model to promote knowledge sharing and spillover, grow their insights, cut costs, and kindle a culture of creative problem solving.[17] As the world of work retreats from the top-down, bureaucratic models of knowledge production and problem solving, it is adopting practices that encourage cross-disciplinary expertise and open innovation.

Negotiation

Because the students brought distinct personal, educational, and cultural experiences into the classroom, the ability to manage multiple perspectives and competing opinions regarding the build of their game was crucial. What was the story? What was the aesthetic? And what about the core gameplay mechanics? These were just some of the decisions that the UT Crew had to settle. Jenkins et al. contend that the ability to "understand multiple perspectives, respecting and even embracing diversity of views . . . and negotiating between conflicting opinions" is, increasingly, a valuable skill in the design of twenty-first-century learning environments. Specifically, the researchers refer to this skill as *negotiation*. Skills like these, as Jenkins et al. note, are social. We would add that negotiation skills are a key element in facilitating more critical thinking skills among students or the ability to not only listen to diverse views but also translate those views into actionable forms of knowledge.

As we discuss below, the UT Crew certainly had to navigate competing perspectives and diverse opinions, especially during the initial phases of building their game. One of the first collaborative and knowledge-producing exercises that we created for the students prompted them to identify some of the factors in their school, homes, and communities that contribute to food insecurity and childhood obesity in lower-income neighborhoods. The students generated several factors ranging from the behavioral to the social and environmental. After sorting these factors into recognizable clusters, students had to pivot and figure out the core or defining elements of their game. Consequently, students had to present credible data, stories, and examples to support the causal factors that they endorsed. Moreover, they had to listen to each other, offer feedback, and contemplate divergent perspectives. By sharing and embracing diverse ideas and perspectives, the students were able to generate richer insights that ultimately provided a spark for building compelling concepts, stories, and scenarios for their game.

Affinity and Diversity

Members of the UT Crew played a wide mix of games, including Big Box titles like *Halo*, specialty games like *Minecraft*, and casual mobile games like *Angry Birds*. Many members of the UT Crew were especially curious about how games were made, thus they also had an affinity for some of the specific competencies—design, story development, character art, game play mechanics—that contribute to the production of games. Their affinity for games opened paths for deepening their interests, finding a community, and fashioning a repertoire of activities that extended far beyond the mere recreational consumption of games.

The Game Lab was an important space for the students who gravitated toward a deeper engagement with games. It was one of the few spaces where "geeking out" about games outside the privacy of their homes was not only possible but also vigorously supported by their peers and adults. In the Game Lab, students could talk incessantly about even the most esoteric aspects of games. Further, the Game Lab was one of the few spaces where knowledge about the history of games or the contemporary gaming landscape was a source of cultural capital, conferring status and prestige within peer groups. Sports, most notably football, were the primary after-school platform for status and prestige at Freeway. With the exception of Michael, who played football, most of the UT Crew expressed very little interest in sports, thus validating a claim that Diego once proudly made to a member of our research team, "We are the nerds in the school." In the Game Lab, students could explore their cultural identity as gamers and digital media makers without fear of being labeled or treated as outcasts.

Despite their affinity for games, the UT Crew was far from a monolithic group. For example, members of the group represented a broad range of academic interests and dispositions. Michael was on the college-bound track. Russell and Ben were on the general academic track and had expressed a slight interest in community college. Other members of the UT Crew had no plans to pursue postsecondary education and were uncertain about what awaited them upon graduation. Miguel and Diego had experienced the "English language learner" track earlier in their academic career.

Members of the UT Crew brought distinct motivations and aspirations to the class. Enrollment was influenced by several factors. Some members of the UT Crew were interested in pursuing a career in the game industry. Diego, for example, viewed the class as an extension of his investment in games, computers, and technology. Michael planned to study engineering in college and saw the class as an opportunity to explore his curiosity in design and software. Students like Caroline and

Emmanuel (see chapter four) viewed the class as an opportunity to cultivate their interests in digital media and the creative arts. Others enrolled in the class because a friend was in the class and it was an opportunity to enjoy each other's company.

There was, however, one aspect of the class that clearly lacked diversity: the low number of females. There were only three female students among the forty-two students that were enrolled in the two advanced game design classes that we worked with. Our research team noticed the gender imbalance immediately and eventually attributed it to three factors.

First, we discovered that the game design classes and the Game Lab had been constructed primarily as a "sandbox" for boys. The sandbox metaphor in this instance refers to the extent to which games and the game design class function as an open space for play, exploration, and discovery. From our perspective, the male dominance of the space could be credited to the social norms and milieu that the boys created. This was a space that privileged certain forms of knowledge and expertise about games—especially the masculine and action titles that boys preferred. Even though girls play action titles, the opportunities to discuss them, share gameplay tactics and techniques, or build alliances may be severely limited in social spaces dominated by boys.

Second, the dominance of teen boys could be attributed to the presence of Mr. Warren. Some observers note that girls are much more likely to be interested in technology-related initiatives when they have access to female role models in technology- and STEM-related fields.[18] Even though girls and women make up a significant portion of the game-playing marketplace, they are typically underrepresented in the education (e.g., game design instructors, coding instructors) and industry professions (e.g., programmers, character artists) most associated with the creative aspects of game design.

Finally, Freeway's emphasis on game making as a vocational pathway likely asserted particular kinds of narratives about career opportunities and trajectories in games that were more welcoming to male than female students.

The three young women in the class were never treated in a hostile manner. Still, the sheer number and presence of their male counterparts made it difficult for them to establish a meaningful voice or presence in the formal and informal learning activities that took place in the Game Lab.

Design Thinking

As part of our work with the UT Crew we decided to introduce them to some of the techniques associated with design thinking, a set of principles that intend to spark inquiry, problem solving, experimentation, and innovation. There has been a growing amount of attention devoted to the movement to expand the presence of coding in primary and secondary schooling. Across the United States and around the world, design consultancies, educators, and business leaders have been quietly making a case for bringing design thinking into the K–12 environment.[19] Chris Pacione, director of the LUMA Institute in Pittsburgh, believes that design should be as pervasive as reading, writing, and arithmetic. Pacione lays out the case for how design literacy or "pervasive competency in the collaborative and iterative skills of 'looking' and 'making' to understand and advance our world" could represent a breakthrough in the history of common literacy.[20]

Moreover, many of the ideas associated with design thinking align with the view that learning is meaningful when it is inquiry based rather than rote, experiential rather than abstract, production oriented rather than test and memorization heavy, and situated in a broader universe of experience and expertise rather than the four walls of a classroom. Throughout our work with the UT Crew we insisted that they leverage their world, their experiences, and their expertise to inform and enrich the story they wanted to tell about food insecurity and childhood obesity in their community. We wanted to foster a learning environment in which students could link the game design process to settings, interests, and conditions beyond school. Also, we subscribed to the view that connecting game creation to their everyday lives would make the project more relevant and the learning experience more meaningful.

Specifically, our design challenge required students to build a game prototype that addressed the issue of childhood obesity. We chose this topic for three reasons. First, Freeway was located among a sequence of zip codes populated by youth from lower-income Latino, African

American, and immigrant households. Children and teens from these areas were disproportionately more likely than teens from white, Asian, and affluent zip codes to be obese for a variety of reasons including geography, income inequality, and food desert conditions.[21] Second, because childhood obesity intersects with a mix of academic subject areas including science (i.e., biology), health (i.e., nutrition), and social studies (i.e., social inequality), we concluded that the project could support the development of academic skills such as inquiry, writing, and analysis. A series of prior discussions with the teacher and the district officials led us to select a project that could model how digital content creation could intersect with already established academic courses.

Finally, we wanted to select a topic that facilitated an opportunity for students to experience real-world engagement with their community in the design of their game. The very neighborhood that students lived in could serve as an effective setting for catalyzing youth civic engagement, media making, and voice. As Hart and Kirshner explain, "Clear, present, and compelling issues are more likely to engage adolescents in civic and political activity than are complex concerns."[22] Thus, we hypothesized that students could see how issues of food insecurity and childhood obesity converged with social justice issues to affect their community.

Our project anticipated students taking on multiple roles including, for instance, artists, researchers, writers, and project managers. Importantly, we wanted them to also take on a design disposition. Designers strive to change existing situations into preferred situations.[23] We wanted our students to see themselves and their actions in the classroom in a similar fashion. At Freeway, like most schools, this was a radical idea, one that opposed virtually every definition of schooling and learning familiar to students and teachers alike. Rather than simply consume information students were encouraged to be producers of ideas that they could translate into tangible and creative action. Rather than ask what they needed to know (for a test) students were encouraged to generate the questions they needed to seek out for problem solving and game creation. In addition to building their technical and game creation skills, it was important for students to build their critical thinking and questioning skills.

This approach to schooling has the potential to not only enhance learning but also empower students to be change agents in their schools and communities. Further, this approach asserts that the mission of our learning institutions is to create engaged, critical, and future-building citizens. Schools must do more than train students to be good workers, especially in a world in which the very notion of work is evolving. Schools should be community resources that help students develop the competence and the confidence to intervene in the making of a future that is more equitable, desirable, and sustainable.[24]

Schools are quite effective at shaping how the various stakeholders—administrators, teachers, students, and parents—understand learning. Design thinking differs from more traditional forms of instruction, academic engagement, and learning in several ways. In the traditional classroom, learning is vertical or top down and teacher driven. In the design thinking–based classroom, learning is horizontal and inquiry driven. In the traditional classroom, students are expected to answer questions typically generated by teachers. By contrast, the design thinking classroom expects students to ask questions. It is customary in the traditional classroom for students to find answers in the back of a textbook. In the design thinking classroom, students find answers in the world. Whereas the traditional classroom situates learning as a linear path to content-specific mastery, the design thinking classroom situates learning as a nonlinear journey defined by discovery.

Predictably, we found ourselves bumping up against the traditional notions of schooling and learning. As a result, the integration of design thinking techniques was not easy. Schools rarely ask students to take on multiple roles, engage in inquiry-driven tasks, take risks, collaborate in substantive ways, think about problems from multiple perspectives, or demonstrate their knowledge by making their ideas actionable.

Affinity Mapping: Connecting Design Thinking and Everyday Life

One of the first design exercises that we tinkered with was affinity mapping. This is a graphic technique that allows designers to sort seemingly disparate ideas into ordered patterns and categories. We chose affinity mapping because it encouraged students to reflect on their world and identify several factors related to food insecurity and childhood obesity. Further, affinity mapping allowed students to organize a lot of information and ideas quickly and into categories that could facilitate understanding and brainstorming. More importantly, the maps could help team members identify emergent patterns and themes that could inform the design of their game.

We divided the UT Crew into two teams, seated at their own individual tables. We prompted them with this question: What factors contribute to the childhood obesity epidemic? Each student received several sticky notes on which to write or draw their ideas. It took them a few minutes to get started, but once they gained momentum the students produced a stream of ideas. Group One had a fast-food motif. Several team members drew McDonald's arches or identified McDonald's as a major factor in childhood obesity trends. Some of the students referenced how pervasive fast food is in their neighborhood and around the school. "They are everywhere," one student quipped.

The group made a number of thoughtful connections. For instance, one student noted that "video games are a reason for obesity." Another student responded, "But wait, there's a difference between button-mashers and Wii Fit, so that might not be exactly true." During the exercise students became quite vocal as they proceeded to identify a range of factors.

Group Two was also busy generating responses to the prompt. One of our researchers noticed a sticky note with a drawing of pants and could not figure out what it meant. Several students offered an interpretation. "Well, those are big pants, so they don't like being fat," one student explained. "No, they are into fashion and want to be able to fit into these pants," claimed another student. As in Group One, McDonald's was a prominent topic of conversation in Group Two. One person quipped, "Not lovin' it!," which was a play on the hip-hop-inspired jingle widely used in McDonald's global marketing and branding campaigns.

After ten minutes we asked each team to post all of its notes on a large board that was visible to both groups. The students produced a long list of factors, generating enough sticky notes to fill four large poster sheets. Next, we asked them to find patterns and to discuss the relationships among the ideas they captured. Then we asked them to sort the notes into clusters. What patterns emerged and what did these patterns suggest about their own understanding of childhood obesity? After some additional sorting and negotiating with their fellow team members, the two teams generated these clusters:

Group 1	Group 2
Fast food	Family
Society	Media
Family	Lifestyle
Lifestyle	Food
Technology/Video games	Psychological
Bullying	
Conspiracy	

The affinity mapping exercise accomplished three things. First, the clusters provoked conversation about key trends and factors that impact childhood obesity. Moreover, students were encouraged to begin making connections to their own lives, families, and community. The mapping exercise was an effort to make a complex topic—childhood obesity—more easily manageable by identifying themes that could be the focal point of a story and the design of a game with rules, environments, characters, actions, consequences, and rewards. Second, the exercise reaffirmed our adoption of design thinking and its capacity to provoke a questioning disposition among members of the UT Crew. They asked several questions: Should this be a game about fast food? Is this a game about the home environment? Should the story encourage players to think about family, behavioral, and lifestyle issues? In short, students used design thinking techniques to interrogate and engage the possible causes of childhood obesity in their environment.

Finally, the affinity mapping exercise offered powerful insight into the mind-set of the participating students and their thoughts about childhood obesity. We discovered that these were issues that some of them had thought about previously. It was clear that many of the students in the UT Crew brought a critical disposition to their consideration of childhood obesity. Some of them mentioned films such as *Fast Food Nation* and *Food, Inc.* Health researchers who track childhood obesity trends in the United States consistently find relationships to class, education, geography, and race and ethnicity. When prompted to identify factors associated with the health epidemic, our students identified many of the same factors and made direct connections to their environment.

Although several members of the UT Crew were not sorted into the high-track, high academic achievement clusters at Freeway, it was clear from this exercise specifically, and our work with them generally, that they were capable of handling rigorous academic activity. The students did not lack the ability to think critically. Rather, they lacked access to an academic environment that expected and cultivated their capacity for critical thinking. They drew connections between social geography, economic inequality, and health-related disparities in the United States. When students were involved in this kind of work—call it critical inquiry and reflection—they were animated, active, and vocal in ways that opened up opportunities to push their thinking, designing, and game making into deeper and more provocative territory.

Setting the Standards

In the previous chapter we explained how the lack of a curriculum and instructional expertise limited Mr. Warren's ability to create a learning climate that engaged the state's Technology Application standards. After examining the extent to which the formal learning environment in the game design class supported students developing greater competency in areas such as coding, critical thinking, or art design, we concluded that the class was simply not built to support the learning outcomes established by the state standards.

If the formal schooling and instructional environment fell short in engaging the state standards, the informal gaming practices and learning environment that formed in the peer networks and in the after-school and leisure activities of UT Crew members offered a surprise: an opportunity for students to engage some of the skills and competencies identified in the Technology Applications standards. This was possible largely as a result of the creative resilience displayed by students and their determination to build an environment that supported their exploration of games, design, and digital media production.

Take, for example, the state standard for game development classes that says students should be able to "evaluate, analyze, and document game styles and playability."[25] Members of the UT Crew were constantly involved in these kinds of evaluations during school time and out of school. Their discussions could be elaborate and passionate and often involved comparing and contrasting different platforms (e.g., mobile vs. console) and game styles (e.g., casual vs. first-person shooter). Occasionally, these discussions engaged parts of the Technology Applications standards that called for students to "research the dramatic elements in games, including kinds of fun, player types, and nonlinear storytelling."[26] In several instances, student-driven discussions and game related activities engaged the history and evolution of game play mechanics, art, and titles.

Some of the members of the UT Crew also joined a group of students who self-organized what was, in effect, an after-school club inspired by their interests in games. In addition to messing around with new gaming platforms (e.g., *Minecraft* rose to popularity during our fieldwork), this informal group organized social activities such as a Yu-Gi-Oh! tournament. This particular interest-driven activity was complete with player rankings, brackets, and a schedule of matches. It was their version of "March Madness," the popular collegiate basketball tournament made famous for its brackets, spirited play, and intense competition. Informal activities like the tournament established unique opportunities for students to access the social, informational, and technical resources they needed to fortify their interests in game-related forms of play, production, and identity construction. The organization of the Yu-Gi-Oh! tournament is an excellent example of how the informal gaming and learning practices of students engaged state academic standards.

In addition to the technical skills (i.e., coding, animation), the state standards identify a range of social and interpersonal skills that a technology course should cultivate. These skills include, for example, project management, the ability to interpret information and communicate it to multiple audiences; seek and respond to advice from others, including peers or professionals in the design process; and demonstrate personal qualities such as open-mindedness, initiative, listening to others, willingness to learn new things, and pride in quality of work.[27]

The informal learning setting and repertoire of practices that emerged from the Yu-Gi-Oh! tournament align neatly with some of the social and interpersonal skills emphasized in the state education standards. The tournament, for instance, involved project management and communication with peers and teachers. The tournament certainly showcased the initiative that students took to coordinate the entire effort as well as their willingness to try to learn new things. Moreover, the organizers took enormous pride in staging what was a completely student-driven after-school activity.

The coordination of the tournament required time, energy, and creativity. Students, for example, possessed knowledge of the participants and their skill levels. This allowed them to create player rankings and matches that were balanced and promoted genuine competition. The students pitched the idea of the tournament to Mr. Warren and, thus, were able to secure the Game Lab to hold the matches. Tournament game play, however, was just one feature of what was a dynamic mode of out-of-school learning and organization. The tournament also established an opportunity for students to learn more about each other's interests in games, discover new games and gameplay techniques, and cultivate opportunities to collaborate on future projects. Throughout the execution of the tournament, students practiced their communication and networking skills. Furthermore, the level of initiative, leadership, and communication was exemplary and revealed a degree of ownership, planning, and execution that was simply not possible in the formal school setting.

The extent to which these student-driven practices facilitated opportunities for students to engage elements of the state educational standards was completely inadvert. Students did not participate in these activities to comply with state educational standards. Instead, they participated in these activities to enhance their knowledge and interests in games. They used the in-school and out-of-school settings to design creative activities and interest-driven communities to participate in practices that did what the school failed to do: enrich their capacity to engage state educational standards. Members of the UT Crew pursued these activities and potential learning outcomes without a formal curriculum framework or prompting from their instructor. The informal learning settings and creative activities that the students made did more than produce recreational benefits; they produced educational benefits too.

Games and Grit

Another indicator of the UT Crew's willingness to exceed the expectations of the class was their decision to use the game-authoring software GameSalad to build their game. The software that Mr. Warren had introduced to the class, Gamestar Mechanic, was more suitable for an introductory game design class at the middle school level than a high school advanced game design class. Members of the UT Crew expressed a desire to build a game that combined original artwork and audio, multiple levels, and robust gameplay dynamics. They realized that the limited functionalities of Gamestar Mechanic would not support the game they envisioned. A couple of the UT Crew members had participated in a summer game design program that provided access to GameSalad and endorsed the platform's game-making features. The group's discussion of the different affordances of the two systems demonstrated a key competency noted in the state standards, "understanding the role of game engines."[28]

At the time of our fieldwork, GameSalad was a three-year-old Austin-based start-up that was attempting to break into the digital content creation business by offering a free drag-and-drop game development platform.[29] The company's tagline, "Game Creation for Everyone Else," was a reference to GameSalad's mission to democratize game creation. Its value proposition was straightforward: offer a tool to those who are interested in making games but are unable to code. One of the promising features of the software was the option for users to publish their game to Apple's operating system, iOS, prompting GameSalad to promote itself as the YouTube of game design.[30]

GameSalad, more generally, is emblematic of a genre of software that is designed to accelerate content creation for an ever-widening demographic of aspiring digital media producers. While the software does not involve coding it does offer access to a host of drag-and-drop assets that enable the design of commercial-style games in terms of physics, animation, and game play mechanics. The members of the UT Crew were confident that GameSalad would support their desire to create a dynamic game and be a rich learning experience. There was, however, one problem. No one in the class knew how to use the software. Mr. Warren gave his consent to use GameSalad, but he did not have any experience using it or teaching it.

Building a game from scratch is challenging. Building a game from scratch with software that no one knows how to use is especially daunting. In addition to the usual obstacles associated with game design—developing a story and story world, coordinating the gameplay mechanics, creating characters—members of the UT Crew encountered several unusual obstacles. Primary among them was figuring out a way to learn the basic functions of the GameSalad platform when no formal instruction was available. Students spent just as much time trying to secure access to GameSalad learning resources—instructional materials, tutorials, mock-ups—as they did designing and building their game. Undeterred by the fact that neither they nor Mr. Warren had knowledge of GameSalad, the students remained steadfast in their desire to use the platform. Their first solution seemed reasonable: YouTube.

As we explain in chapter three, YouTube has emerged as a powerful node in the learning ecology of students. When students want to learn how to do something they often turn to YouTube as a resource for informal instruction and information gathering. Among teen digital content creators, YouTube functions much like a classroom, a coach, or an instructional resource. This is an example of how distributed knowledge, expertise, and the DIY ethos is transforming learning in the era of digitally mediated social networks. During the school year we witnessed several Freeway students turn to YouTube to learn how to play an instrument, build a gaming computer (see chapter six), and use digital video editing software.

From our perspective as researchers, the reliance on YouTube to support learning at Freeway was both exciting and disappointing. It was exciting to observe how students worked constantly and creatively to learn what they needed to know to pursue their creative interests. But it was also frustrating to see students turn to YouTube as a substitute for rather than a complement to high-quality instruction. Freeway students' engagement with YouTube reflects the many contradictions that mark life in the digital edge. Students in this resource-constrained school had access to technology. They even had occasional access to online tutorials that supported their desire to learn new technical and creative skills. What they consistently struggled to access, however, were instructional and learning environments that supported cognitive enrichment, digital literacy, and academic engagement.

The decision to leverage YouTube for GameSalad tutorials and knowledge building was short-lived because the school blocked access to the popular site. The use of proxy servers—a common student workaround to filters that block access to popular websites—was insufficient for obtaining the numerous videos the group needed to begin learning the basic features of GameSalad. When schools block social media they do more than restrict students' access to videos and other online content they believe distract from learning. They also block a key pathway to how students learn in the digital world through social media and computer-mediated social networks. The decision to block social media can impact all students, but students living in homes that lack access to broadband Internet may be especially disadvantaged. For many Freeway students, school was their primary gateway to the networked world, and in this case their primary gateway to the instructional materials they needed to build their game.

It would have been easy for students to abandon their desire to use a more complex piece of game-authoring software considering the many obstacles they faced. Instead, they contacted the GameSalad office and successfully requested that the company make its tutorials available via compact discs. Once they received the physical discs, members of the UT Crew manually uploaded the tutorials to all of the computers in the class.

Self-Regulated Learning in the Digital Edge

Not every member of the team needed to learn the basic drag-and-drop features of GameSalad. Ben and Russell, the two lead programmers for the UT Crew, spent the most time experimenting with the game-authoring software. They were responsible for inserting into GameSalad the game-based assets that other team members created (e.g., graphics, character art, audio). Additionally, they were responsible for creating the game-play action, including all of the physics, interactions, and transitions in the game. Ben and Russell began viewing the tutorials to learn a few of the basic game creation features of GameSalad. They took the task of building the game as a personal challenge that made an otherwise ineffective classroom experience more interesting.

Russell took the game design class because it was the first time Freeway had offered it. He expressed disappointment that he did not have access to more advanced software, like Maya. He had hoped to gain some of the real-world tech skills that were required to work at one of the game studios in town, especially in terms of 3D modeling or motion capture. Russell was predisposed to be pushed cognitively and creatively by the class. Unfortunately, the limited curriculum vision and few opportunities to learn STEM failed to properly challenge him. Despite the curriculum-poor conditions, however, Russell, like other UT Crew members, was determined to make the class a valuable experience. Even though he received no instruction or guidance from the teacher, Russell worked hard to figure out some of the basic elements of GameSalad. This observation from our field notes by one of our researchers is a good description of Russell's work habits in class:

> I watched Russell program for a while. He has a willingness to improvise and be creative in how he approaches game design. He watched the tutorial then showed me the demo of what he's done so far. No tutorials are doing exactly what he needs GameSalad to do, so he's playing around with different features that control things like the speed ratios and other character actions and gameplay mechanics. By teaching himself how to tinker with the platform Russell was willing to fail; he tries something out, adjusts, and then tries out a different strategy when the results are not satisfactory.

This description of Russell's creative process is revealing in several ways. Here we focus on one in particular: his capacity for self-regulated learning.

In the field note above, we see Russell engaging in what some education scholars refer to as self-regulated learning.[31] This style of learning is important for several reasons. Self-regulated learners set goals in the classroom and then execute strategies to achieve and evaluate those goals. The in-class activities of self-regulated learners distinguish them from their peers. Researchers note that self-regulated learners tend to be more motivated and engaged in learning, elicit higher levels of academic self-efficacy or confidence in the classroom, and perform better on academic tests and other measures of student performance.[32]

According to Zumbrunn, Tadlock, and Roberts, self-regulated learning is reflected in at least three phases.[33] The first phase is *forethought and planning*. During this phase the student analyzes the learning task and sets specific goals toward completing that task. In Russell's case he wanted to build a game scenario that involved a specific series of actions that required precision in speed, movement, and cause and effect.

The second phase is *performance monitoring.* Zumbrunn, Tadlock, and Roberts write that during this phase "students employ strategies to make progress on the learning task and monitor the effectiveness of those strategies as well as their motivation for continuing progress toward the goals of the task."[34] Russell was constantly monitoring his performance with the GameSalad engine. After choosing a feature or action he would immediately check to see how it translated in the game scene he was building. For example, he could see how the speed ratios he selected influenced the game play mechanics. This is one of the many inherent benefits of making learning an action-oriented enterprise rather than one based on memorization of facts. The game design engine provided Russell with instant feedback, which allowed him to easily determine the effectiveness of the strategies he employed.

The third phase is *reflection on performance.* During this phase, students are encouraged to evaluate their performance on the learning task as well as the effectiveness of the strategies that they chose. Russell's ability to remain steady through repeated failure suggests that he managed the reflection work well.

Several other members of the UT Crew displayed a capacity for self-regulated learning even though the environment did not deliberately teach this form of classroom behavior. Some of the other indicators of self-regulated learning that we witnessed among this group of students include a more proactive approach to learning. Students worked with our research team to establish some rather lofty goals for game creation compared with what the teacher required. For example, they selected a more complex game engine to build their game, established studio-like conditions to facilitate the execution of tasks, and created a story and characters to design their health-based game.

Moreover, by electing to sit in the center of the Game Lab, members of the UT Crew enhanced their ability to work in a more collaborative environment.[35] The students also sought out additional resources—tutorials, community forums, and GameSalad mock-ups—to build a more complex game than the class required.[36] Finally, the UT Crew repurposed the learning environment to meet their needs. In doing so they turned an uninspiring learning environment into a dynamic space for creativity, the exchange of ideas, and digital media production.

Russell said that he liked GameSalad. He added that the platform was significantly more challenging than the game-making tool that Mr. Warren had selected for the class. He did not seem to rely on the tutorials as much as was anticipated. Instead, he preferred using GameSalad's community to find ideas that he could incorporate into his game. One of the many benefits of online forums and communities is the sharing of knowledge and experience that distributes expertise. "When I get frustrated with it [GameSalad], I stop for a while," Russell explained. But he always continued and made an effort to reach his goal.

Taylor, the team's other programmer, usually sat on the opposite side of the table from Russell. Taylor had a rough version of level one ready to demo. The level had some background art, which Alonso had designed, as well as a character that Broderick had created. The character's movement was jerky as he evaded oncoming enemy foods such as pizza and french fries. Taylor was working to complete one of the gameplay mechanisms—a feature that included scaling a wall as part of working toward the next level within this mini-game. During class time Taylor worked steadily, quietly, and intensely. When one of our researchers asked him what he thought of GameSalad Taylor said that he liked it.

The researcher followed up: "Do you use the video tutorials to help you learn some of the core elements of GameSalad?"

"Not really," Taylor answered, adding, "I'm the kind of person who just works at something until I figure it out."

His primary mode of operation consisted mainly of tinkering with the numerous drag-and-drop assets in the game creator platform. Because there was no formal instruction in the class, Russell and Taylor spent portions of class time figuring out GameSalad on their own. In a class that offered no instruction or assignments they were focused enough to transfer their tinkering into a productive activity. This, however, was not the case for all of the students in Mr. Warren's class.

Learning how to chart a distinct learning pathway, persist through failure, or practice self-regulated learning was especially daunting for some students. In these instances the strict reliance on video tutorials and online communities as the primary resources for knowledge and instruction posed a steep challenge. The expectation that they would essentially teach themselves how to use GameSalad without any in-class instructional support was a hurdle some students could not overcome. For example, Troy, a student from the other advanced game design class, took on the lead role of programing his team's game. The GameSalad engine offered a seemingly infinite menu of drag-and-drop features for engineering game play mechanics. Thus, while it did not require writing code, it did require at least some recognition of rules related to, for example, game-play physics or cause and effect. These were the kinds of game and design elements that students could have learned in a higher-quality instructional setting and then tested in the GameSalad platform. Unlike Taylor and Russell, Troy did not have the disposition to try, fail, and try again. For Troy the tutorials were largely ineffective and encouraged disengagement rather than engagement with the game design process. As a result, the struggles that this class faced building their game were even more pronounced.

Building a Prototype

A main goal of our work with the UT Crew was to create an environment for students to build a prototype. The likelihood that they would build a fully developed and playable game in a class that produced several learning barriers—poor curriculum development, no instructional expertise, and technological limitations—was not great. As a result, our research team devised realistic goals for the project. Our larger goals for the students included developing a better understanding of childhood obesity, identifying the story elements for the game, and building prototypes of key game elements. These deliverables were reasonable and also demanded that students engage some of the key principles of design thinking.

From the very beginning of the class we wanted students to see the value of looking at the world through an inquisitive lens, generating new solutions, and figuring out ways to bring those solutions to life. This is the strength of prototyping, the process of making your ideas tangible quickly and cheaply. The act of making things reflects what the creators of the Stanford Design School call a "bias toward action." In education, students are rarely asked to act, or in this case turn ideas into something tangible. Instead, learning and achievement are often reduced to the memorization of facts. Throughout the process the UT Crew produced a variety of artifacts that were, in effect, small prototypes of their ideas.

At the outset they identified a cluster of factors that establish the food-insecure conditions that can contribute to higher rates of childhood obesity. After that exercise members of the UT Crew started making content for their game. To start, students wrote brief story descriptions that highlighted the narrative attributes of the game. UT Crew members also produced storyboards to visualize some of the action sequences in their game. Students also developed profiles that mapped out the attributes and motivations of potential characters. Some of the UT Crew generated preliminary character and environment art. Alonso used his interest in audio to begin producing sound effects and music for the game. And Taylor and Russell experimented with building very rudimentary action sequences with the GameSalad engine.

At the end of the semester the UT Crew did not have a full-fledged, playable game, but they did have a number of components that served as the foundation for more refined game creation and iteration. In short, they produced materials that made some of their ideas real and their goal to build a game from scratch a little more possible.

Conclusion

In many ways, the UT Crew's struggle with GameSalad is a perfect illustration of how educational and digital disparities in our nation's schools have evolved and yet persist. In the past, the lack of technology in high-poverty, high-minority schools was considered a roadblock to more robust learning opportunities. But students in this resource-constrained school had access to abundant technology—computers, graphics software, audio tools, game-authoring platforms, and video tutorials. As the pressure to enhance the delivery of STEM education in schools intensifies, it is certain to influence the decisions made by school administrators. An unintended consequence of the push to emphasize STEM learning is the increased pressure to purchase computers and software. School officials have made the acquisition of technology a top priority in their bid to build better learning futures. But our engagement with Freeway strongly suggests that this is a mistake. Rather than investing in hardware and software, schools are likely to fare better—in terms of learning outcomes—by investing in high-quality teachers, professional development, and curricula that support deep learning. If Freeway is any indication, schools continue to view the mere presence of technology as a sign of better learning conditions.

The creative resilience of the UT Crew convinces us that students who are often dismissed as disinterested in learning may, in fact, be determined to learn. In his analysis of the racial academic achievement gap, Angel Harris argues that poor kids do not want to fail in school, despite their poor performance.[37] Instead, he argues, they simply may not know how to succeed in the classroom. Our research suggests that something else is also likely contributing to the low levels of academic achievement among lower-income and lower-opportunity youth. One of the primary challenges that students face in school is not of their own making. As the game design class illustrates, students struggle to access rich instructional and learning environments that support cognitive rigor, deep academic engagement, and the opportunity to cultivate the skills that are increasingly in demand in our rapidly evolving society and economy.

6

After the Bell

Why What Kids Do after School Matters

S. Craig Watkins, Andres Lombana-Bermudez, and Lauren Weinzimmer

During the course of our yearlong fieldwork one thing was positively clear about life at Freeway High School: the after-school hours were a vital feature of student life and learning. When the school day ended, the opportunities for learning continued. Students had access to a wide selection of after-school clubs, programs, and activities that ranged from the conventional (football and debate) to the unconventional (the Gay Student Alliance or a program that involved Freeway students teaching middle school students how to make two-dimensional games).

When we spoke with teachers and students it was clear that the time spent in many of the after-school offerings represented a chance for students to experience learning as a hands-on enterprise that sharply differed from the rigid approach to academics and learning that characterized the regular school day. Whether it was hanging out in Mr. Warren's class exploring *Minecraft* with friends or producing a clever film for a twenty-four-hour student competition, the after-school space was markedly different from school in one notable way: student interests defined the norms and practices that guided the activities. If students were restricted in school by the rigid notions of schoolwork, mandatory exams, and informal tracking processes, the after-school settings at Freeway had no such restrictions, which made it a space for exploration, creativity, and experimentation. In this chapter we consider the significance of after-school activities in relation to what researchers refer to as the enrichment opportunity gap and social capital.

Schools and the Enrichment Opportunity Gap

The academic achievement gap in America has been a focal point of interest and concern among researchers, educators, and policy makers for more than three decades.[1] To date, the bulk of the conversation about America's academic achievement disparities has focused primarily on the learning divides and unequal outcomes that occur in the classroom. Whether it is the learning gaps that begin to take shape in early childhood, the lack of resources or quality of instruction in low-performing schools, or the legacy of tracking in schools, the discrepancies in formal educational settings are typically cited as the driving force in America's unequal learning outcomes.[2] This focus is certainly understandable, but it overlooks the learning and educational disparities that take place outside the formal classroom.

There is considerable evidence that young people from high-income households benefit not only from the advantages that are available to them inside school (e.g., better learning resources, qualified instructors); they also benefit from the advantages that are available to them outside school, primarily in the form of enrichment activities. One of the great disparities between affluent households and less affluent households is the resources parents can expend on their children. In fact, one of the most important forms of social capital that children benefit from is the investment that parents make in their development.

Parents make two primary investments in their children: money and time. Generally speaking, higher family income enables parents to provide resources like books, computers, private schooling, tutoring, music lessons, personal coaches, and travel that provide opportunities for enrichment and development.[3] Between the early 1970s and 2000s the gap in enrichment expenditures between families in the top income quartile and families in the bottom income quartile tripled.[4] Kaushal, Magnuson, and Waldfogel report that the largest gaps in child expenditure happen in activities like music lessons, summer camps, and travel.[5] The increasing gap may be explained, in part, by rising rates of income inequality over the past three decades.[6] As family income increases so do the investments in child-related enrichment activities. The corollary may very well be that as family income shrinks, so does the family financial investment in child-related enrichment activities.

High-income parents are not only investing more money in their kids; they are also investing more time.[7] Ramey and Ramey contend that the increased time investments by parents focus on helping their children cultivate the kinds of experiences, skills, and résumés that increase their odds of gaining admission to a selective college.[8] They call this phenomenon "the rug rat race," a reference to the supercompetitive efforts of college-educated parents to gain and maintain any advantage possible in securing a better future for their children.

Hilary Levey Friedman draws similar conclusions in her analysis of the rising amount of time children spend in activities outside the home and school.[9] More precisely, she argues that middle- and upper-middle-class parents believe that participation in extracurricular activities helps their children gain the credentials they need to earn admission into top-ranking colleges.

Economically hobbled parents have aspirations for their children that are similar to those of their more affluent counterparts—happiness, good health, academic achievement, and economic security. The big difference between the parents, of course, is that lower-income parents struggle to accumulate the financial resources to pursue those aspirations through the consumption of goods and services that are designed to boost the life chances of their children.[10] The majority of the parents in our sample were employed in low-skill service occupations. These jobs offer little, if any, flexibility to control one's work schedule, chauffer kids to activities away from school, or afford the often high costs of out-of-school enrichment activities. Consequently, children from poor-resource households are doubly disadvantaged. Not only do they suffer from poor-quality instruction and learning opportunities in school; they also suffer from poor learning and enrichment opportunities out of school.

A study by Alexander, Entwisle, and Olson found that the academic achievement gaps in school are widened by what happens out of school.[11] In their study of Baltimore students, they argue that one of the key drivers of unequal academic outcomes is the learning gaps that occur over the summer, a period when kids from upper-income households are much more likely than youth from lower-income households to see modest literacy gains. This body of research suggests that out-of-school enrichment opportunities offer a number of academic and nonacademic benefits.[12] In this chapter we focus on the nonacademic benefits, namely, the forms and significance of social capital in the after-school enrichment activities at Freeway.

The after-school programs at Freeway were a crucial resource for students and parents.[13] The diverse menu of after-school options for students at Freeway was a deliberate effort by school officials to bridge the enrichment opportunity gap. School officials and teachers understood that without the after-school programs provided by the school, a substantial percentage of Freeway students would have few, if any, meaningful opportunities for stimulation and activity after the end of the school day. Freeway's decision to make after-school time count in the lives of students resonates with the history of after-school programs in the United States and the effort to create dynamic spaces of engagement, development, and opportunity for poor and working-class youth.[14]

Schools as a Source of Social Capital

Our extensive fieldwork inside the walls of Freeway convinced us that the school was a complex system of social networks and social capital, despite its "at-risk" reputation. We turn to the work of Nan Lin to structure our understanding of how the after-school activities at Freeway, a sphere for enrichment and informal learning, were a pivotal site of social capital or resource mobilization for students.[15] Lin asks two questions that capture our attention. First, how do individuals invest in social relations, and second, how do individuals capture the embedded resources in the relations to generate a return? Lin writes that "the focus is on the use of social capital by individuals—how individuals access and use resources embedded in social networks to gain returns in instrumental action (e.g., finding better jobs)."[16]

Lin defines social capital as those resources available to individuals through social connections. They are resources that someone else may own or control (e.g., reputation, social contacts, money), and your connection to that person gives you access to those resources. Alejandro Portes reminds us of the intangible character of social capital. Portes writes, "Whereas economic capital is in people's bank accounts and human capital is inside their heads, social capital inheres in the structure of their relationships."[17] In this chapter we aim to illustrate how students used the resources embedded in their after-school relationships to gain returns in instrumental action or, to be more precise, gain access to resources that enhanced their lives at school.

The students that we met at Freeway actively cultivated social capital. To be sure, students made different investments that established access to different forms of social capital. Whereas some students made investments in academic-oriented relationships, others invested more concertedly in their peer relations or in extracurricular-related interactions. In the cases below we consider what kinds of returns students received from the social relations available in the after-school enrichment activities that they participated in.

As our understanding of life at Freeway evolved we began to view the school as a pivotal source of social capital for many students. Freeway had a number of intermediaries who were in a position to exercise some degree of influence over the lives and opportunities of students because of the resources that they commanded or had access to. Teachers and their social connections outside school were crucial reservoirs of support for students. Counselors were another source of social capital, as they generally served as the link between students and their school-to-work or school-to-postsecondary transition. Coaches and faculty sponsors of after-school activities were also a source of social capital for students. This was especially true for the students who struggled in the classroom but thrived on the field or court, in the band room, or in the media lab.

Finally, peers were a vital source of social capital for many students. The exchange of knowledge and information through peer-based and informal channels is often regarded as a valuable resource in any social network.[18]

Our analysis is also sensitive to inequalities in social capital. This could be a reference to inequality *across* schools (e.g., lower-income and higher-income schools) or *within* schools, the focus of our study. According to Lin, it is conceivable that social groups have different access to social capital because of their advantaged or disadvantaged structural positions and social networks.[19] So, even though schools are a source of social capital, not all forms of social capital or, more specifically, social resources available through schools are equal.[20]

Capital inequality, Lin explains, may result from two processes, what he calls *capital deficit* and *return deficit*.[21] The former refers to the consequence of a process by which differential investment or opportunities result in relative shortage of capital for one group compared with another. Return deficit is the consequence of a process by which a given quality or quantity of capital generates a differential return or outcome for members of different social groups. Our primary focus is on the latter, with a particular emphasis on the kinds of returns and outcomes students experienced as a result of their investments in after-school social relations and activities.

The students who attended Freeway had varied social positions. Lin writes, "It is conceivable that social groups have different access to social capital because of their advantages or disadvantaged structural positions and social networks."[22] The school-based structural positions and social networks among students are shaped by various formal and informal mechanisms. At Freeway, for example, the students in AP courses maintained a more advantaged structural position within the school compared with the students who were slotted into English language learner tracks. Similarly, the students who were involved in prestigious school-based organizations (e.g., student government) were competitively positioned in the social hierarchy at Freeway.

Importantly, students who are in advantaged social positions typically have access to institutional agents and better resources. Stanton-Salazar and Dornbusch refer to school-based institutional agents as individuals who have the capacity and commitment to transmit directly or to negotiate the transmission of institutional resources and opportunities such as information about school programs, academic tutoring and mentoring, college admissions, and assistance with career decision making.[23]

Consequently, students who are in higher-track courses, prestigious leadership positions, and good standing with institutional agents have a structural advantage relative to students who are in lower-track courses, rarely belong to prestigious organizations, and may not be in good standing with institutional agents. As Lin notes, "Those in better social positions will have the advantage in accessing and mobilizing social ties with better resources."[24] It is within this context that we consider the role of after-school activities and, more precisely, the degree to which they strengthened the ability of students to enhance their social positioning within the school and access to social ties with better resources.

An Introduction to Three Cases

We present three distinct case studies to amplify the possibilities associated with the after-school world that we observed at Freeway. The first case study is an exploration of a creative after-school enterprise we call the Cinematic Arts Project (CAP). The CAP was better situated than much of the in-school learning to foster an environment that offered students opportunities in digital media production, peer-based forms of collaboration, and the cultivation of leadership skills. Next, we turn to two Latina teens, Inara and Michelle, to explore their navigation of the after-school learning opportunities at Freeway. Their experiences are instructive for several reasons. Though the academic trajectories and future orientations of Inara and Michelle moved in decidedly different directions—one was bound for a vocational arts institution, the other an elite four-year college—we believe that the after-school activities they pursued established a framework for thinking about how diverse identities, interests, and pathways can be supported by activities in the after-school sphere. Our final case study is a profile of Diego, a student who crafted a series of after-school activities and relationships that formed a robust social and learning ecology around his interest in games.

Among other things, these case studies illuminate how after-school activities are crucial to enriching the social and educational lives of students. A number of the students in our sample were ambivalent about school, but they were certain about after school. If school offered students shrinking pathways for achievement and affirmation, the after-school setting forged open pathways to opportunity and identity.

Case Study One: The Cinematic Arts Project

The CAP is a collaboration between the directors of a small local film postproduction company, Mr. Lopez (the video technology teacher at Freeway), and high school students. The CAP intended to teach the art of filmmaking and digital storytelling to high school students. To paraphrase, the mission of CAP is to educate, empower, develop, and celebrate the next generation of emerging artists. At its core, the CAP set a goal to empower students to assert greater control over their interests in digital media, storytelling, and the development of their creative skills and professional aspirations.

The CAP fostered passionate engagement, hard work, skill acquisition, peer learning, and the articulation of creative and media-making identities among many of the participants. This was especially true among some of the Freeway students who were also enrolled in Mr. Lopez's video technology class, such as Antonio, Javier, and Sergio, three seniors with Mexican origins who had interests in filmmaking and the digital media arts. These three students found in the CAP an opportunity to build dynamic learning opportunities that cut across the domains of home, school, after school, peer culture, and the local media industry. In short, their participation in the CAP established the opportunity to craft unique out-of-school enrichment experiences, pathways to connected learning, and rich social ties.

Work and Play within the Cinematic Arts Project

The CAP was a unique after-school program. The three main deliverables included a student-produced short film and a web and social media campaign that promoted the film. The primary goal was to submit the short film to a prestigious international student film competition. Although the program was created and managed by adults, had a strong structure and division of labor, and had clear objectives in relation to what students should learn ("the art of filmmaking and storytelling"), it also encouraged creative agency, exploration, and self-direction among student participants. Students completed specific tasks, assumed particular roles, and met production deadlines. The CAP, at once, was a structured endeavor (work) and an interest-driven and creative activity for most students (play).[25]

Students are often drawn to after-school clubs and projects because of the opportunity to pursue interests and activities that are meaningful to them. In the case of the CAP, Antonio, Sergio, and Javier joined the program precisely because they had deep interests in filmmaking, were passionate about the creative arts, and wanted to develop technical skills in digital media production. Furthermore, they wanted to be part of a community of media makers and aspired to create professional-style media content. As Javier explained, "I think projects like this help me to be artistically more mature because you're working with other people that know about what you're doing and you have this big responsibility because now it's not, 'Ah, I'm just doing my short film, whatever.' It's professional, it's good work." Because it offered students many unique challenges that were simply not possible in school, the CAP turned out to be a powerful and highly motivational experience. Antonio worked as an editor and camera operator for the team that produced web-based publicity content for the project. Sergio was assigned the role of camera operator and was responsible for shooting all the scenes for the project's short film. Javier worked as the director of photography and editor for the short film. Students who were fully engaged in the project were able to articulate identities as filmmakers, find a creative voice, connect to a vibrant community of peer media makers and artists, and cultivate social relationships that were richer than the ties that they formed in the formal school setting.

Designing a Space and a Climate for Digital Media Production Practices and Discourses

The activities of the CAP were located in a media lab classroom that was designed and supervised by Mr. Lopez, a third-generation Mexican American. He was also bilingual and maintained a cultural and political sensibility that was influenced by the Chicano activist movement and creative art of an earlier era. Mr. Lopez had assembled a media lab that was rich in computer and video technology tools. The lab was equipped with twenty-four iMac desktop computers organized in three rows next to the walls. The computers ran the latest OS-X operating system, were connected to high-speed Internet, and had several media production software applications, such as Garage Band, Adobe Suite (Photoshop, Illustrator, After Effects), Final Cut Pro, and Celtix (screenplay editor). The layout of the desktop computers left a clear wall for screen projections, as well as an open space in the middle of the room where movable and circular tables could be used for group meetings.[26] Moreover, the lab could be modified according to specific production needs. The media lab was frequently repurposed by CAP participants. On any given day it could be a rehearsal set, an editing station, a casting room, or a place to brainstorm ideas.

Through our observations of his elective video technology class and the CAP after-school program, it was clear that Mr. Lopez was trying to create an environment that supported "learning by making" and what Seymour Papert calls constructionism.[27] His students, in both the formal elective classes and the informal after-school program, had the opportunity to participate in educational and creative activities that were student centered, interest driven, and production oriented. He was a pivotal institutional agent who effectively leveraged the social and technological resources available at Freeway and in the local creative community for the benefit of those students who built close ties with him.

Furthermore, for some of the Latino students who felt alienated from formal schooling and came from resource-constrained working-class immigrant families, having a meaningful relationship with Mr. Lopez enhanced their social positioning in the school and, as a result, their access to valuable school resources.

Mr. Lopez's lab established a space and a climate for students to craft digital media stories and identities. The space was reflected in the digital media tools and technology that were available to the young digital media artists. The climate was reflected in the cultural sensibilities, practices, and discourses around learning and making that fueled their creative aspirations and identities.

Enabling Connected Learning Pathways

Learning to be a digital filmmaker or any other kind of media artists requires hours of practice with the tools of the craft. Editing, camera operation, cinematography, and sound design, for instance, are activities in which access to computers, multimedia authoring software, and recording devices is necessary. Access to expertise, social support, and the opportunity to play and tinker with these tools are crucial too. Because low-income youth face so many obstacles in accessing the media tools and creative and collaborative spaces that support rich media production practices, the CAP was a unique enrichment opportunity.

The CAP became one of the most dynamic and vibrant spaces in the learning ecology of students like Antonio, Javier, and Sergio. Through the CAP they were able to access professional hardware, software, media production gear, and a community of peers and social relationships that supported their passion for digital filmmaking.

Furthermore, as a result of their substantial investments in Mr. Lopez, Antonio, Javier, and Sergio were able to extend their access to technology beyond the school and after-school settings. Mr. Lopez provided them access to technology across five distinct but connected spheres—his elective technology class, the after-school program (CAP), home, industry, and peer group. Mr. Lopez allowed them to borrow cameras, laptops, and audio equipment to take home overnight and over the weekend, trusting that the often-expensive equipment would be returned and undamaged.

The extended access to technology supported an active process of media making and learning that linked different spheres—in school, after school, peer groups, and home—together. Antonio, Javier, and Sergio used the digital media production gear and the time at home and during the weekends to work on passion projects as well as temporary paid jobs they found through Mr. Lopez's active networking with the local creative sector. Sergio, for instance, explained to us that his process of learning how to be a cameraman was enhanced by the opportunity to borrow a professional video camera and being able to practice at home. "When I would learn with the camera I had to take it home, practice filming little things in low lighting, and then messing around with the iris and focus-stop and trying to make it so it would look better, because last year's problem with the film was that it was too dark. So we're trying to fix that this year." Although Sergio, an 18-year-old from a working-class immigrant family, could access video game consoles, an old desktop computer, and Internet connectivity from home, his family did not have a digital camera and the software necessary to level up his media production skills. To prepare for the CAP, he needed to practice with professional tools. By borrowing hardware and software from Mr. Lopez he had the opportunity to tinker and play for extended hours and connect his creative pursuits after school with his digital and literacy practices at home.

In addition to expanding access to technology and to social support, the CAP expanded the opportunities for some students to explore their interests in digital media production in greater depth. Some students, for example, pursued their own passion projects, such as the production of short films, animation, or music videos. In a few instances students parlayed their involvement in the CAP into temporary jobs in the local creative industry. As a result of the networking efforts of Mr. Lopez, Antonio got a temporary job as a camera operator and editor for a television program about Tejano music bands in a local production studio. To complete his tasks for the job, Antonio borrowed a laptop computer and a live video switcher (TriCaster) from Mr. Lopez. Having access to such high-quality media production tools outside of school allowed Antonio to connect his after-school activities and relationships to a professional opportunity with a local media company.

This unique opportunity also enhanced his social status among his peers, reaffirmed his aspirations as a filmmaker, and helped him gain some real-world experience. As he explained in an interview, working on a professional set was one of the most meaningful experiences in his life. Even if television and the theme of the show were not directly related to his filmmaking aspirations, he greatly valued the activities and took advantage of them for advancing his learning trajectory. "I'm very fortunate 'cause I know a lot of high school kids don't get the opportunity to edit a show that goes on TV or get paid for filming. It's not what I want to do 'cause I want to do more filmmaking, like, actual stories and scripts and stuff like that. But, I mean, this is an opportunity that I couldn't resist because it gets me a little bit closer. It gets me more contacts. It gets me more experience. And it just grows."

Peers were another important source of social capital for CAP students. Engaged students like Antonio, Javier, and Sergio were able to pursue side projects such as the making of short films that they could shoot and edit on their own. That was precisely the case when they entered a twenty-four-hour youth media competition. Working together with two additional CAP participants, the three students made a short movie over the course of a day. In addition to borrowing audio recording gear and a laptop computer from Mr. Lopez, they secured access to a video DSLR camera owned by a peer.

Leveraging the different expertise within the team they were able to make a movie that told the story of an immigrant father who struggled to communicate with the sons he left behind in his home country. In this context, peer support and expertise became crucial for experimenting, trying new roles, and developing a creative and authorial voice. Javier, for instance, directed the film and helped Antonio learn about cinematography. Sergio wrote the screenplay from scratch and, after receiving feedback from his peers, was able to create a script and a shot list. Both Javier and Antonio edited the film by alternating use of a laptop computer and reviewing each other's work. The two other partners helped with the sound recoding and music, and also acted in the film. Although they missed the deadline for the twenty-four-hour competition, they continued working on the video and submitted it to an international student film festival, where, much to their surprise, it was accepted.

Conclusion

Like many of the students that we met, Antonio, Javier, and Sergio struggled in the formal learning environment. For a variety of reasons—academic, social, racial and ethnic, linguistic—they experienced a great deal of alienation in school. But if they were ambivalent about school, they were certain about after school and the opportunities that participation in the CAP afforded.

Participating in the CAP was transformational for Javier, Antonio, and Sergio. The after-school program provided them with creative and learning opportunities that they rarely experienced in the formal school setting. Through their engagement with the CAP, they reinvented themselves as creative artists and filmmakers and were able to begin imagining a future career in digital media production. Furthermore, participation in the CAP allowed the three students to cultivate rich social relationships with Mr. Lopez, their peers, and the local industry that significantly improved their access to the technology and knowledge resources they needed to pursue their interests in the digital media arts. Finally, they were able to leverage their social and technological resources to find media production opportunities across multiple settings, including after school, the local media industry, and student film competitions.

Case Study Two: Resisting "At-Risk" Girlhood

The extracurricular activities of two teenage girls in our study, Michelle and Inara, encouraged us to identify some of the varied ways after-school time mattered in the lives of Freeway students. A combination of factors propelled Michelle and Inara toward future opportunity—defined in this section as postsecondary education—including their after-school and interest-driven activities. And though we do not causally link after-school involvement to their eventual enrollment in postsecondary education, Michelle's and Inara's endeavors after the bell certainly helped create the social networks and pathways that connected them to postsecondary opportunities.[28]

While Michelle earned a full scholarship to an elite private university on the East Coast, Inara gained admission to a reputable fashion and design institute located on the West Coast. Their stories are noteworthy in the context of a majority-minority school in which about 60 percent of the students are designated as economically disadvantaged. A substantial portion of Freeway students were also listed as "at risk," a term that we believe stigmatizes the school and its students.[29] When you compare the plight of young Latinas with those of their white female counterparts, for example, Michelle and Inara were significantly more likely to be labeled "at-risk" girls.[30]

Historically, the notion of "at-risk" girlhood has been applied to particular populations of girls. Anita Harris explains: "Young women of quite specific populations have been used symbolically: particular kinds of young women have been constructed as a problem for society."[31] As a result of their racial and ethnic identities (Michelle, a biracial Latina; Inara, Latino), economic situations (both were from working-class homes), sexual orientations (Michelle openly identified as gay), and immigrant statuses (Inara's parents are from Mexico), both girls are emblematic of a community that is understood by outsiders as "a problem for society." The convergence of these social indicators suggests that Michelle and Inara were multiply at risk. But their stories did not stop there.

We view Michelle's and Inara's navigation of school, investments in after-school activities, and their distinct interests and aspirations as a counterpoint to the "at-risk" narrative. The creative ways that both Michelle and Inara "did school," especially after school, cultivated vital social ties and resources that defied their "at-risk" status and forged open, dynamic pathways of opportunity.

Drawing from Julie Bettie's ethnographic work on Latina girls in high school, we ask this question: What were some of the enabling conditions that helped Michelle and Inara transition to postsecondary education when the majority of their peers did not?[32] While a number of factors certainly contributed, we consider how their after-school activities sustained and supported their postsecondary aspirations.

Michelle

Captain of the varsity basketball team, president of the school's Gay Straight Alliance (GSA), member of the National Honors Society, and more, Michelle was one busy student. She was also in the school's AVID college preparation program, helped with her parents' adult kickball league, and acted as an informal mentor to her friends and peers.

Michelle was one of the students in our study who invested meticulously in some of the more robust sources of social capital that Freeway was able to offer, namely, those that tracked her for admission to a selective college. She was a high academic achiever. But her success in the classroom was not guaranteed. When Michelle arrived at Freeway in her sophomore year, she did not know anything about higher education opportunities, what it took to get into college, or even how to apply. While not technically an after-school activity, the AVID program was an enrichment opportunity that led Michelle to meaningful social relationships and resources. The AVID program introduced Michelle to the school's transition counselor and, eventually, a university alumnus as part of a recruitment initiative that ended with her enrolling in an elite four-year university on a full academic scholarship.[33]

Michelle excelled in extracurricular activities. She skillfully leveraged after-school involvement to find leadership opportunities in varsity sports, Freeway's honors society, and the GSA. Her involvement in the extracurricular world at Freeway certainly buoyed her prospects for postsecondary opportunity. Michelle was extremely self-reflective and resilient, qualities that contributed to her ability to overcome the "at-risk" stigma and layers of structural disadvantage to pursue her educational goals and aspirations.

According to Bettie's ethnographic work on Latina youth, schools typically track minority girls like Michelle into noncollege preparatory classes. So Michelle's participation in AVID and AP classes was already aberrant in the context of the "at-risk" identity that schools typically impose on

Latina students. While most of the girls in Bettie's sample realized this bias too late in their high school education to change their track, Michelle, with the help of many adults, including her teachers, father, and coaches, was able to thrive in spite of the ways in which the system works against girls labeled as "at risk."

Through her participation in athletics and the GSA, Michelle continued to defy the "at-risk" narrative. She was strikingly visible in the Freeway community, took on leadership responsibilities, and demonstrated self-confidence in and out of the classroom. These qualities were complemented and magnified through her strong network of supportive adults, as noted in our field notes: "Part of the formula of Michelle's success at Freeway was a very robust set of relationships with adult mentors." School advisors, the principal of the school, adults in her parents' kickball league, and others became important figures in Michelle's life, helping her navigate an environment that could have easily held her down. Importantly, Michelle's investment in enrichment opportunities enhanced her social capital and the social resources that she was able to tap.

Michelle's leadership role (as captain) on Freeway's girls' varsity basketball team generated very specific forms of social capital. As varsity captain, Michelle was able to develop her leadership style, both for the team and in the larger Freeway community. Through this activity Michelle gained confidence and a strong identification with school that generated both social and educational benefits. Additionally, Michelle formed a close connection with her coach, which opened up life-changing opportunities. Her initial path to a university, an athletic scholarship to play at a tier-one public university in the Midwest, resulted from her coach's recommendation.

Michelle was a hard-working student who learned how to excel in her AP courses. Like students from more privileged circumstances, Michelle engaged in out-of-school activities that she found enriching and that also established her credentials as a top candidate for admission to selective colleges. As we see in the other cases in this chapter, Michelle's participation in extracurricular activities raised her social standing in school and established access to a host of resources, including leadership roles, college preparation mentoring, and personal introductions to college recruiters. In short, Michelle's investment in after-school activities opened up new frontiers of opportunity that transformed her life chances.

Inara

If there is one word to describe Inara, it would be "fashion." More precisely, fashion and design were an intimate part of Inara's early child-hood. She watched in amazement as her grandmother and mother crafted beautiful pieces of clothing with a sewing machine in their home. After noticing Inara's fascination with sewing, her grandmother began teaching her the craft and, thus, passed on an important family tradition to this second-generation Latina. Though they would not describe themselves this way, Inara's grandmother and mother were *makers*. They had developed a set of skills—designing and sewing—that were a skillful response to their family's economic situation. Inara, in contrast, would learn to sew not necessarily as a way to save her family money but rather to express her individuality and creativity, and eventually guide her toward a career path utilizing these skills. It is quite likely that making clothes for the family was an expression of creativity for her grandmother and mother. However, it was also a skill they developed as a means of economic ingenuity and survival.

Inara maintained some diverse friendship groups. Bettie notes in her ethnography of Latino girls that they found opportunities to gain skills (extrapolated here to those stemming from extracurricular involvement) while keeping their ethnic identity especially useful.[34] This creates what Bettie calls a "racial alliance," which Inara had within her network of Latina friends. These friends were a source of comfort, community, and caring. They hung out together and sometimes shared conversations in Spanish. Inara was also a member of the drill team, an extracurricular activity that generated school visibility and prestige for the dancers. The connections that she maintained in the drill team were ethnically diverse. The drill team also provided opportunities for Inara to engage her interests in fashion and design. For example, during the school year she would make small designs for her peers to accessorize their dance uniforms.

Inara was not the most academically driven student. In fact, she often found herself in credit recovery and was falling behind in several courses during our fieldwork. Our field notes reflect that she "passed her classes, but only through monumental last-minute efforts." Even so, Inara defied the "at-risk" girl label. Bettie notes that Latina females in a high school setting face layers of discourse surrounding their identity that originate from school and society. In Bettie's work, Latina girls were expected to perform worse in school than their white counterparts, an expectation that made it difficult to achieve academically.[35] Unlike many Latino youth who believe that college is important in life but do not pursue that path themselves, Inara went on to enroll in a higher-education institution.[36]

Academic achievement is one obvious way to gain access to the social resources available in schools. Inara was not a high academic performer but she did find other ways to support her ability to cultivate social capital and improve her access to school-based social resources. Inara's efforts to work around the "at-risk" stigma are reflected in her pursuit of an after-school activity that had an interest-driven focus in fashion. At school Inara pursued her passion for fashion, in part, through invention. Here we focus on one particular inventive pathway, Inara's founding of a fashion club.

When Inara spoke about postsecondary education, her interests in fashion were clearly apparent. "I see myself going to college, something I want to do, probably somewhere outside of Texas because I really want to travel and I feel like if I go somewhere I want to see and maybe live there, maybe it will be fun, maybe it won't." Inara adds, "I've always been interested in going [to Los Angeles or New York City], even if I wasn't going for modeling or anything. The fashion industry is in both of those states." When we met her, Inara was beginning to articulate professional aspirations.

"I'll hopefully study business and start owning my own stores, owning my own clothing line, doing what I want to do," she said during an interview. "Not just clothing stuff, but I want to own hotels and restaurants and things."

Inara sustained her interest in fashion by studying the sector and turning an extracurricular interest into an opportunity to cultivate a variety of design, art, and entrepreneurial skills that influenced her postsecondary trajectory. Not surprisingly, many of Inara's favorite online destinations reflected her interest in fashion, including style and fashion-oriented websites and blogs as well as Facebook and Stumble-Upon. The latter, StumbleUpon is a discovery engine that allows users to find photos and videos that are personalized to their interests through, for example, peer-sourcing. Inara explained how she uses Stumble-Upon for fashion purposes: "I think to myself that Facebook and StumbleUpon, the only ones that I have. It's really the only two social things that I have. StumbleUpon is not really social, you're just finding new websites on the Internet. . . . So you find like stuff like clothing, like finding new styles of clothing, you stumble, stumble, until you stumble into something you really like. Then that's it. You like it, so you can save it, and you can check it out later on, that's about it."

We were especially struck by Inara's decision to start a fashion club at Freeway and, moreover, what it reveals about the school culture and her sense of agency. The club was born out of Inara's decision to enroll in a home economics class. Freeway requires many of its students to take what is in essence a vocational course. Some of the other vocational courses included culinary arts, video production, technology applications, and business administration. In theory, courses like these are designed to help students, especially underachieving and/or low-track students, gain real-world skills that can translate into employment. As we discuss in chapter seven, the history and implementation of vocational education in the United States is intertwined with the histories of racial and class inequalities in education.

For all of the problems that we observed regarding the vocational courses at Freeway, one aspect about them impressed us: some of the courses allowed students to bring their outside interests to school, thus enabling some students to take on the role of connected learner.[37] As connected learners, students were able to link their engagement and learning across multiple settings, including school, after school, peer culture, and pop culture. As codesigners of their learning experience, students helped shape the classroom and learning activities they participated in.

In Inara's case, a relationship with her home economics teacher facilitated the launch of the fashion club and certainly strengthened her desire to apply and eventually enroll in a Los Angeles fashion and design school after graduation. The teacher was a key source of social capital, allowing Inara space at school to explore her passion and launch a leadership endeavor—the fashion club. The main project that the fashion club focused on was an annual fashion show that also functioned as a fundraiser. Inara led most of the planning and made the flyers, while other members of the club were responsible for soliciting donations from local businesses.

In school, Inara was an average student at best. After school, she was a self-starter, leader, and connected learner. Needless to say, the opportunity to initiate and execute an after-school activity like the fashion club transformed her social standing at Freeway, established a unique tie to an institutional agent (her home economics teacher), and redefined what school meant to her personal and educational development. Finally, the fashion club was an excellent example of how Freeway's creative approach to after-school enrichment established opportunities for students to launch school clubs that bore the mark of their interests and ingenuity.

Conclusion: Michelle and Inara

Despite their obvious differences, Michelle's and Inara's investments in the after-school world at Freeway were significant. Their navigation along different pathways compels a serious reconsideration of the influence of extracurricular activities in the lives of students. Both students made substantive investments in after-school activities and social relationships that forged open access to potentially life-changing resources and opportunities. An important takeaway from these two cases is that the after-school terrain offers multiple and inventive ways to work around the "at-risk" stigma that nondominant youth face. By exploring the after-school experiences of students like Michelle and Inara, we seek to illuminate the importance of after-school activities among places and people who are labeled "at risk" and often undervalued by our schools and society.

Case Study Three: Doing "After School"

Our final case study turns to another student that we spent tens of hours with—Diego. Born to Mexican immigrant parents, Diego was a junior when we met him. During his sophomore year Diego was enrolled in AP courses. His enrollment in the AP track turned out to be, in his words, "one of the worst experiences of my life." The homework load, demands, and hypercompetitive nature of AP coursework diminished his interest in academics. When his sophomore year ended, Diego informed his parents that he did not want to take any more AP classes. They accepted his decision. At this point in his academic life Diego had more schooling than either of his parents, and they often deferred to him when it came to decisions about school.

But Diego did not retreat from school. Instead, he charted a path that aligned with his interests and learning disposition. He enjoyed some of his classes, maintained a productive relationship with several of his peers, and was actively involved in various school-supported extracurricular activities. As we began to map Diego's after-school profile we noticed the sheer amount of activity. He was a member of the school's marching band and jazz orchestra—two relatively traditional school-base extracurricular activities that are time-intensive due to regularly scheduled practices, travel, and competitions. But what really captured our attention was the vibrant hub of enrichment activities and relationships that Diego built around his interests in games. The dynamic social ecosystem that Diego built wonderfully animates how some students turned Freeway into a unique space to "do after school" by deepening their interests-driven learning and participate in creative projects that were personally meaningful.

Creating an Interest-Powered Social and Learning Ecology

Diego's participation in Freeway's after-school world was shaped by a strong desire to connect his interests and informal learning with that of his peers. His game-based activities involved interactions with peers that were conspicuously different from the peer interactions situated during in-school class time. Whereas students are often discouraged from using each other as a source of knowledge and expertise in the classroom (i.e., this is often considered cheating), they are encouraged to engage each other as they pursue interest-driven endeavors in the after-school setting. These interactions are vigorously social as students routinely talk with, share with, and learn from each other.

In Diego's after-school practices, peers were a source of engagement, support, and knowledge—that is, social capital.[38] Diego often relied on them as a crucial information channel that supported his quest to develop his literacy in game-making practices. Take, for instance, the method that Diego employed to learn how to build a gaming computer.

When he began pursuing the idea of building a gaming computer, Diego had no previous experience or knowledge of how to build one. He also lacked the proper tools. Diego was literally starting from scratch.

One of the first things that he did was consult a peer who had built a gaming computer. Diego would meet with his friend after school and at home to grow his knowledge *and* hands-on expertise. As a result of this relationship, Diego was able to learn about the toolkit and range of hands-on skills that were required to build the computer. Diego worked on the computer in his bedroom at home, but it was the social relations that he built in the after-school setting that sustained his tenacity. The fact that his friend had built a gaming computer was a source of inspiration ("If he can make a computer, I can too") and perspiration ("I must work hard to make the computer").

Stanton-Salazar and Dornbusch consider the role of peers as sources of social capital.[39] In their study of low-income youth from Mexican origins, they suggest that diverse friendship ties across class and linguistic lines can be pivotal sources of social capital for low-income youth. The authors focus on what they call student social support networks with a specific emphasis on "informational support," including things such as personal advice on academic decisions, personal advice and guidance regarding future educational and occupational plans, advice on nonacademic matters, and information regarding current job opportunities.

We expand Stanton-Salazar and Dornbusch's notions of diversity in student networks and informational support. In the after-school environments that we studied, students encountered some degree of racial and ethnic diversity. The students that Diego encountered in his games-based enrichment activities were Latino, white, black, and Asian. Most importantly, the students reflected a diversity of interests, skills, and aspirations. Students who were interested in developing greater proficiency in digital media—graphic art, editing, design, audio—certainly benefited from sharing a space in which their peers could introduce them to new software, information, and technical skills.

In school, Diego had opted out of AP courses that, in his words, "demanded too much of my time." But from our perspective, the effort required to build the computer was no less demanding than the AP courses. Among other things this endeavor required independent research, identifying and assembling the right tools, hands-on techniques, talent to execute his goal, and persistence. The key difference, of course, was the sense of agency and creativity that he experienced in the pursuit of this interest-driven activity.

During an interview, Diego explained how the gaming computer that he built opened up a whole new window of possibilities in terms of his postsecondary and career aspirations. "I know that I want to work with computers after I graduate," Diego told one of our researchers. "I like the idea of working with my hands and learning about the things that make computers work." This experience specifically and the after-school ecology that he built around games more generally were consequential. When we spoke to Diego more than a year later and shortly after graduating high school, he was preparing to enroll in community college to continue pursuing his desire to work with computers.

Diego's games-based after-school activities were also an opportunity to grow his leadership skills. He was one of the organizers of the Yu-Gi-Oh! tournament discussed in chapter five. Among other things he coordinated the matches and closely monitored the execution of the tournament. Similar to Inara's creation of the school's very first fashion club, the creation of this tournament was a testament to how Freeway offered students the opportunity to show initiative and assert an extraordinary degree of influence in the design of its after-school culture. Diego recognized that the tournament was not only a source of recreation for the participants; it was also a great opportunity to cultivate relationships that deepened his engagement with games.

Also, Diego was handpicked by Mr. Warren to participate in a games-based after-school program that involved mentoring middle school students. More specifically, Diego and his peers were expected to teach middle school students how to use Gamestar Mechanic, a drag-and-drop game creation application that was developed to spark greater awareness for game development among elementary and middle school students. In this activity, Diego and his peers took on a decidedly leadership role, as they were responsible for helping middle school students gain firsthand experience in some of the most rudimentary aspects of game design. For students who may have never experienced formal leadership roles in school, this after-school opportunity was especially valuable.

Investing in School-Based Social Capital

Diego was not a top academic performer at Freeway, but in the after-school game-based environment that he built he worked as tirelessly as any of the school's top-ranking students did in their college-track courses. His focus on and diligence in after-school activities enhanced his social capital by strengthening his structural position within the school. This enhanced position also established access to better social resources, namely those dispensed by Mr. Warren.

In chapter four we noted that Mr. Warren was limited when it came to teaching his students game design principles and techniques. But Mr. Warren worked hard to build connections with game studios and the tech sector. Mr. Warren was also open to collaborating with surrounding universities (including our team), thus expanding his own personal networks, which could then be made available to his students.

Mr. Warren's relative advantaged position in the school's social hierarchy as an institutional agent was marked by his control of resources that had the power to influence the lives of students who developed ties to him. Along with Mr. Lopez, Mr. Warren had more control over the tech resources that some students coveted, such as laptops, software, and cameras, than anyone else in the school. In addition to sharing these resources with students in class, both teachers were willing to share these resources after school. Moreover, Mr. Warren and Mr. Lopez allowed students to turn their classrooms into peer-driven spaces of creativity and exploration during after-school hours.

While Diego's investment in his peers, for example, was a crucial aspect of the social and learning ecology that he fashioned during after-school time, his investment in Mr. Warren generated a host of resources that further enriched his education at Freeway. This is what Lin refers to as *differential influence* among social ties.[40]

Among other things, the link to Mr. Warren gave Diego access to high-powered computers and software. Equally important was the opportunity to routinely access a physical space—Mr. Warren's classroom—to explore his passion for games, build an interest-driven community, and pursue projects that reflected his interests. Mr. Warren's ability to network meant that he could broker for his students some degree of access to people in Austin's rapidly evolving innovation economy. Some of the activities that Mr. Warren supervised linked Diego to income-earning opportunities through summer internships and after-school partnerships with local tech companies and educational organizations.

The resources, activities, social relations, and sense of agency that Diego experienced in the after-school space were simply not available through the in-school regimen that typified life at Freeway. While these resources were available to all Freeway students, none of them would have materialized for Diego without effort on his part. It is one thing for resources to be available to students and another thing for students to, first, identify the available resources and, second, maneuver to access and catalyze the resources in ways that are purposeful. This is social capital in action.

Our fieldwork suggests that many students at Freeway made choices about the kinds of people and resources that they tapped, or what we refer to as "social investments." But the returns on these social investments vary. Diego's social investment in Mr. Warren generated access to resources that were quite different from the resources his peers could supply. In his case, both contributed to the formation of a vibrant informal learning ecology. As a result of the investments that he made in his peers, Diego gained access to informal channels of knowledge exchange, social support for things like building a gaming computer, the opportunity to exercise his leadership skills, and in-group prestige and recognition. His investment in Mr. Warren favorably positioned him to access an array of resources (e.g., technology, an interest-driven community, summer enrichment opportunities) that made his after-school activities remarkably rich and, in our view, consequential.

Why What Students Do after School Matters

After extensive observations of the after-school activities discussed in this chapter and conversations with teachers and administrators, we surmise that the after-school activities at Freeway were a deliberate attempt to address the enrichment opportunity gap. Mr. Lopez and Mr. Warren understood that after-school activities that were creative, powered by student interests, and relevant were absolutely essential to engaging students who found themselves on the academic margins. The examples profiled in this chapter illuminate the ways that schools can address the out-of-school learning gaps that contribute to academic achievement gaps and, by extension, broader forms of social and economic inequality.

School-based extracurricular activities are positively associated with higher grades, higher self-esteem in general, and higher educational aspirations. Some researchers hypothesize that participation in exciting after-school programs can even reduce academic inequality. This is referred to as the *social inequality gap reduction model*.[41] More specifically, the model predicts that while after-school activities will have positive benefits for all students, the benefits can be greater for socioeconomically disadvantaged students. For example, Herbert Marsh and Sabina Kleitman contend that school-supported extracurricular activities might be especially beneficial to disadvantaged students.[42] They conclude their study with the following statement: "Importantly, the development of an exciting program of extracurricular activities is likely to benefit all students, but particularly marginal, at-risk, and disadvantaged students who are least well served by traditional educational programs."[43]

We propose a slight modification that suggests that the benefits of extracurricular activities to students from lower-income households almost certainly vary from the benefits accrued by students from higher-income households. There are at least two reasons for this.

First, youth from lower-income homes are less likely than their higher-income counterparts to identify with school. Therefore, they may have less of a commitment to an institution that can often be hostile or indifferent to their development. Black and Latino students are significantly more likely than their white and Asian counterparts to face school discipline and be sorted into classes that underserve their academic development.[44] Second, because these students seldom experience achievement in school, the experience of opportunity and affirmation in the after-school setting may produce some spillover benefits in the form of greater identification with school. Students who participate in after-school activities are less likely to drop out of school.[45] Mahoney and Cairns conclude that students from resource-constrained homes and communities are more likely to benefit from extracurricular activities because they have limited sources with which to identify with school.

Studies show that extracurricular activities can strengthen student identification with school. In scenarios like these, school becomes a much more inviting place for students who struggle to find their voice and their place. After-school activities can enhance school identification and involvement in ways that positively support academic (i.e., higher grades) and nonacademic outcomes (i.e., persistence).[46] When students are actively involved in an after-school activity, the likelihood that they feel a greater sense of connection or belonging to school increases.[47] We see evidence of this in our fieldwork.

Many of the students in our study openly acknowledged their frustration with school. For students who have been labeled "at risk" or tracked in low-performing or English language learner courses, school can be an inhospitable place. Academic struggles in the primary schooling years often translate into more struggles in the secondary schooling years and, ultimately, disengagement and dis-identification with school. Moreover, researchers who subscribe to the *identification/commitment* model believe that any activity that keeps students coming to school is significant.[48]

Even though schools may be limited when it comes to boosting the academic performance of lower-income students, one thing is clear: being in school leads to better outcomes than not being in school.[49] Students who drop out of high school are more likely than their higher-educated counterparts to live in poverty, be unemployed, and end up in prison.[50] In short, the benefits of robust after-school programs are substantial if they make school a more attractive place for students who struggle academically or may be on the brink of dropping out.

In a context in which almost half of African American students, nearly 40 percent of Latino students, and only 11 percent of white students attend high schools in which graduation is not the norm, the potential impact of vibrant after-school opportunities for low-opportunity youth is significant.[51] Sergio, Antonio, Inara, and Diego accrued academic and nonacademic benefits in the after-school social and learning settings that they codesigned. It was in the after-school setting that these students were able to express their creativity, cultivate their leadership skills, and engage in more relevant forms of learning. Consequently, they experienced a higher internal locus of control, suggesting that engagement in after-school activities made them more in control of their lives in school.[52]

Data from the Austin MASD confirm that black and Latino students are significantly more likely than their white and Asian counterparts to leave Freeway without a high school diploma in hand. There are many reasons for this, including a greater likelihood that these students feel alienated from school. We believe that some students who struggled or did not identify with school maintained an interest in Freeway, in part, because of the opportunities that were available to them after school. For these students the after-school world at Freeway was more than a supplementary opportunity; it was, for all practical purposes, the most meaningful part of their experience at school.

7

Dissonant Futures

Alexander Cho, Vivian Shaw, and S. Craig Watkins

Prologue: "I Want to Be a Boss"

It is May, which means the school year is near the end. Amina is a graduating senior at Freeway. She is a second-generation immigrant from East Africa who lives with her mother and younger brother in a small one-bedroom apartment. The apartment is in a building that is part of a large residential complex, located alongside a major highway that bisects the city of Austin. The afternoon that we visit Amina is one of the few days that she is not scheduled for her after-school restaurant service job. Her mother is at work, and she and her friend Cassandra are watching hip-hop and comedy videos on YouTube while baby-sitting her brother. They are eager to show us funny videos by black performers on YouTube: a parody rap by two young men in their car and a young woman's acerbic dissection of a music video by pop performer Kesha. When conversation shifts to the topic of Amina's and Cassandra's plans after their upcoming graduation from Freeway, the atmosphere takes on a noticeably serious shift. Each student expresses varying degrees of uncertainty, excitement, and restlessness about her future.

Amina has figured out her new life plan: she is going to become a hospital administrator. The idea is the brainchild of her econom-ics class and popular culture. In class, Amina has recently completed a career-survey assignment, combing through information on various occupations, corresponding salaries, and the levels of education and work experience required to obtain each position. The character of Lisa Cuddy, a dean of medicine on the medical drama *House, M.D.*, is an-other source of inspiration. When asked about the appeal of becoming a hospital administrator, Amina speaks with a matter-of-fact assurance: "Being the boss of everybody." She explains: "I want to be a boss. 'Cause bosses don't technically have to know everything. They just have to know what's important and how to prioritize. And I feel like I know how to do that. I'm logical."

With a sense of pride, Amina narrates the details of each step leading to her dream of running a hospital in a small town in New England. She will be living in a scenic landscape, one removed from the cutthroat competition of a large city. In her story she is rising through the hospital ranks. She starts in her immediate future by enrolling at a local community college. There she will take phlebotomy classes, transferring to a four-year state university after her first year. Afterward, she will get hired as a lab technician and either gain enough experience to get promoted within the hospital or return to higher education for master's and doctoral degrees.

Yet, despite the apparent care and specificity of this plan, it also encapsulates many of the concessions Amina has already made in charting her future. We have known Amina for almost the entire school year. During this time she has taken AP courses, participated in an after-school college access program, applied for competitive scholarships, and successfully petitioned a rejection from her top school, while receiving an acceptance from another. By the end of the year, she has received offers from two state universities. At the time of our interview she has already rejected both of them, forfeiting her plans of attending a four-year university. There has been no word on financial aid, and she can no longer put off the mounting concerns immediately in front of her: obtaining a summer job, paying for school, contributing to her family's household expenses, securing an apartment for the fall, and transitioning out of a precarious home life. She has just recently returned to living with her mother after spending several months living with friends, including Cassandra. She is weary of being the primary earner for her family. Amina is eager for a change.

Dissonant Futures

The participants in our study come from a variety of backgrounds. They come from families with vastly different levels of income and educational history, have different attitudes toward school, and have different levels of achievement. Some have been taking advanced academic classes since middle school; others are barely squeaking by in general curriculum classes. Still, they all have articulated to us at one point or another their desires, wants, and hopes for the future, such as Amina's wish to be "a boss," Sergio's dream to attend film school at the University of Southern California, Jack's turning away from arts toward a career in finance and a life of "making a lot of money," and Caroline's desire to "create her own anime show for television."

Through our year spent with these teens it became clear that certain students were better positioned for the transition to young adulthood than others. These disparities became especially conspicuous in our follow-up meetings with graduates the summer after commencement and, particularly, when we compared their expectations voiced to us at the beginning of the school year with the realities they faced in the real world. Some students had laid a solid groundwork for their future trajectory; others saw their wishes dissolve once they left the walls of Freeway and were confronted with uncertain job prospects and familial financial obligations.

These observations opened up a new set of questions. First, we were concerned with disparities in students' abilities to access and actualize future opportunities. What were these disparities rooted in, and how did they take shape in our participants' daily lives? Also, what, if anything, was the role of the school—and especially the potential intervention of the formal and informal digital media production spaces we studied—in shaping students' abilities to articulate next steps? How were students' own visions of better futures matched to their effort and ability to realistically achieve these goals?

We realized that this was a set of questions that reached far back into the history of the American educational system while at the same time they were embellished with a contemporary set of circumstances. These factors are all important in painting a holistic picture of the challenges that youth in the digital edge face when trying to connect their learning and interests to opportunity. Key concepts that resonate for us here are school tracking and the role of the family as well as institutional agents in providing and growing the social capital assets of students. In this chapter, we outline some of the factors that have shaped our participants' future orientations and put them in conversation with these theoretical concepts to illuminate how deep structural forces are at work in the way that students in the digital edge are able to articulate, develop, and pursue better futures.

As we explained in detail earlier in this book, our immersion into daily life at Freeway introduced us to several formal and informal digital media learning environments. Through our ethnographic work, we observed the many different methods that students employed to capitalize on the connected learning opportunities generated through the digital media production settings at Freeway. As elective classes and after-school spaces, these environments were separate from and ancillary to a simple "academic track" of formal classwork. More specifically, these spaces provided an unusual window into how *heterogeneously grouped* students experienced formal and informal digital media production environments. These classes and extracurricular environments drew students from the different academic tracks at Freeway—those who were tracked into AP and college-readiness courses as well as those who were in general education and had little to no college plans. These spaces became common ground for students with disparate academic dispositions and orientations—and as such, they provided a common vantage point from which we could observe students moving through the same environment to drastically different futures.

Unfortunately, the picture is somewhat checkered. Though it is clear that many of the students in our study who participated in these informal learning spaces benefited from them, we also found that students who enter these spaces with more diverse forms of capital—especially social—were more favorably positioned to use them to articulate future pathways than students with less diverse forms of capital. The teachers in these spaces acted as institutional agents of social capital, often leveraging personal industry contacts, staying late after class, and creating rich opportunities for their students in the local media community. However, without a rich curriculum and in-school scaffolding to prepare these students for either entry into college or some other community or vocation-based plan, many were left floundering.

Freeway participates in "de facto" or "laissez-faire" tracking—that is, the grouping of students into homogeneous ability groups.[1] It is "de facto" or "laissez-faire" because, as opposed to the overdetermined vocational and academic tracks of late nineteenth-century and early twentieth-century public schools, students ostensibly have the option to choose classes in whichever track they wish. However, research over the past two decades has revealed that, far from being a voluntary arrangement, these new forms of tracking echo and reinforce long-standing class and race divisions in opportunity in American public schools. Factors such as parent involvement and counselor bias often conspire to place otherwise capable students on unequal paths.[2] Since tracking is a way that future opportunities are realized and next steps are articulated, we assert that diverse forms of social capital are necessary to cultivate and curate high school experiences that prepare students for life after the primary and secondary years of schooling.

Despite the best efforts of institutional agents such as teachers, counselors, and technology-rich formal and informal learning environments, both in-school and out-of-school factors stymied the transition to young adulthood for several students. For example, stubbornly ingrained de facto tracking in school and familial environments that did not offer a college-going tradition made it hard for some students to effectively pursue their future aspirations. We close this chapter with an explanation of what we call a *trajectory multiplier effect*—wherein digital media and learning environments generate benefits for almost all students involved in them. However, those who enter these spaces already enriched with social capital and "higher" academic tracking were better positioned to leverage the school's resources in the pursuit of their future plans.

Tracking: Context and Implications

Put succinctly, "tracking" is a way that students are homogeneously grouped and placed into different courses in school. It has existed in many forms in secondary schools in the United States for more than a century, and it is a practice that has profound consequences for a student's future trajectory. Education researcher Jeannie Oakes defines tracking as follows: "The process whereby students are divided into categories so that they can be assigned in groups to various kinds of classes. Sometimes students are classified as fast, average, or slow learners and placed into fast, average, or slow classes on the basis of their scores on achievement or ability tests. Often teachers' estimates of what students have already learned or their potential for learning more determine how students are identified or placed."[3] In its most traditional iterations, tracking is built around the assumption that certain future opportunities are better "fits" for some students than others. This practice is commonplace in Europe, for example, where students are often compelled to choose from or are assigned to a number of different tracks that emphasize vocational/technical career opportunities or prepare students for university.

The practice of tracking students has been commonplace in American high schools since at least the late nineteenth century. However, the practice has looked drastically different in different eras of our history. The history of educational tracking in the United States began in 1867 as a result of industrialists' clamor for large masses of workers to enter into the manual labor force.[4] Tracking had several functions, not the least of which was to figure out how best to "Americanize" the waves of immigrants from southern and eastern Europe in the late nineteenth century as well as "vocationalize" them, while maintaining high-level curricula for "native" born white Americans and their eventual path to a baccalaureate.[5] Oakes cites, for example, Boston's superintendent of schools in 1893: "The systematic introduction of Manual Training appears to be the only remedy for this enervated condition of our city population; the only universal stimulus to ambition and original effort on the part of our children."[6] According to Oakes, these initial forms of tracking were heavily influenced by ethnocentric theories of social Darwinism and the mechanization of the labor force.

Tracking, after a waning period in the early twentieth century, was used by southern schools as a way to segregate students after forced integration in the wake of the *Brown* decision in 1954.[7] Indeed, de facto segregation in schools as a result of racist tracking procedures has a history of litigation in the U.S. legal system, resulting in several Supreme Court cases.[8] Twala Grant also cites the post-Sputnik space race as the beginning of the impetus to select out "gifted" students for their own tracked curricular offerings.[9]

According to Lucas, the period from the mid-1960s through the early 1980s saw a drastic change in the way that schools grouped students.[10] After a series of influential publications in the late 1980s and early 1990s, the practice of overt tracking became anathema. A 1990 report by the National Education Association seriously questioned the practice and its future implications.[11] Most schools today do not have formal tracks, and most high school students may choose which classes they want to take, which sometimes results in disparate levels of course offerings on any one student's course schedule. However, Lucas concludes: "Despite the plethora of opportunities created by these changes, the change in school practice I have called the unremarked revolution appears to have failed. That is not to say that the previous regime is in some sense preferable. It is to say, however, that students now encounter a more hidden in school stratification system."[12] The persistent informal or nonexplicit grouping of students through seemingly disparate course level offerings is what Lucas calls "de facto tracking," and this system is still with us today. "Achievement trajectories" that reproduce social inequity are laid out as early as elementary school, effectively sealing the fates of low-tracked students as they progress through the system.[13] Lucas locates the "proactive behavior of middle class parents" as the main force in this early school sorting.[14]

These unequal opportunities often play out over the terrain of race. Writing at the height of the tracking debate, Wheelock explained that "African-American, Latino, Native American, and low-income eighth graders are twice as likely as white or upper-income eighth graders to be in remedial math courses,"[15] adding, "[Tracking] allocates the most valuable school experiences—including challenging and meaningful curricula, top-quality instruction, and high teacher expectations—to students who already have the greatest academic, economic, and social advantages."[16] In this way, tracking is a self-fulfilling prophecy, one that evades its own stated goal of distribution of opportunity.

The very nature of the process of tracking selection is inconsistent and beholden to the social norms that it aims to reform. According to Oakes, "It is important to realize that tracking students in schools is *not* an orderly phenomenon in which practices, even within a single school, are consistent or even reflective of clearly stated school or district policies."[17]

Students from all tracks at Freeway enrolled in the technology courses that our research team observed. Further, students from high and low tracks could participate in the digital media after-school activities. Throughout our study, we generally found that students were directed into two areas of future orientation: higher education and postgraduation employment. Graduating seniors in our study usually elected to attend a four-year university, a two-year college, or a trade school, or enter the job market after their graduation. However, it is critical to note that students who ended up entering the job market after high school did not necessarily lack ambitions for educational and career advancement. Rather, many of them struggled to access higher-education pathways despite expressing ambitious dreams of careers in the film industry, games industry, and other creative sectors.

Our emphasis on the informality of this tracking is to underscore that while students at Freeway are not explicitly "tracked" by the school, many of them still report the experiences of being sorted into different pathways as learners. Echoing findings discussed in earlier chapters, our analysis makes note of the ways in which a number of students in our study report feeling uninspired by the core academic curriculum at Freeway. Still, several students emphasized their emotional and social investment in creative careers, including STEM, fashion, and culinary arts. For these students, the excitement present during their participation, for instance, in courses and extracurricular activities related to games, digital story-telling, or design was a stark contrast to their experiences of boredom and frustration within core academic classrooms.

In this chapter we raise the question of what it means for students involved in the school's creative offerings to be de facto tracked outside of academic curricula and what the implications of this sorting suggest for students' pursuits of opportunity in the creative sector. Moreover, in examining how this de facto tracking occurs, we look at the mechanisms through which creative arts practices are mapped as "vocational" at Freeway, rather than as part of the core academic curriculum.

Community College as Ambiguous Next Step

Among the students in our study who chose the postsecondary path, many elected to attend a two-year community college rather than a four-year college. As we talked with them throughout the year, and as their outlook and circumstances changed from fall to spring, we began to realize that community college played an important, if ambiguous, role in their postsecondary decision-making process. This was influenced by a number of factors, including the presence of a well-regarded community college in the area as well as family and financial constraints.

For Amina, two-year community colleges were an academic concession, offering a way to offset the costs of education en route to a bachelor's degree. As we have already discussed, Amina's decision to attend the local community college was greatly influenced by the instability of her home life. As she saw it, four-year universities required a luxury of both money *and* time. After enrolling in the local community college, she planned to begin summer courses and quickly move into her own apartment.

Gabriela, however, appeared to be less strategic in her rationale for attending community college. In discussing her views on higher education, Gabriela overlooked the differential benefits of obtaining a bachelor's degree versus an associate's degree, describing four-year degrees as purposeless. When asked if she viewed four years of college as a waste, Gabriela answered:

> Not a waste, but it's, like, I don't see the point of it. Like, I'm pretty sure you can have, like, a two-year college and still get a good job. Also what confirms my mind that I'm not going to a four-year college is the executive producer that I followed [on social media], she went to college to be a nonfictional writer, or a fictional-science writer, and she became, like, the executive producer. And so she's, like, on top. And then also somebody else that I met [at a local ad agency that she toured], he didn't go to school for advertising. He only went for two years for graphic design, and he's, like, the head of the creative side. And so that really surprised me.

Gabriela's focus on the number of years required to complete degrees in her comparison of community colleges and universities suggests a lack of awareness of the secondary benefits of pursuing higher education, including social experiences, intellectual exploration, and career networking opportunities. Moreover, research suggests that black and Latino students who attend select four-year colleges are more likely to earn a degree and find employment than those who attend two-year or less select colleges.[18]

It is important to note that Gabriela did not suffer from a lack of ambition. Gabriela was, in fact, creatively driven and passionate about digital photography. Throughout the school year, she consistently articulated a desire to pursue a career in advertising. Instead, Gabriela's views about higher education might be better understood in relation to her ongoing frustrations with the academic environment at Freeway. Gabriela seemed to envision college as an extension of high school, saying that she preferred the shortened two-year length of an associate's degree to a four-year university degree: "I cannot do four years again. It's not that I never found the point of it, but it's, like, I don't want to waste my life in school." The greater source of Gabriela's academic disconnect, in this case, was not the degree of her intellectual interests or academic abilities but a misinformed impression of the benefits of higher education and the ways that college might translate to professional pathways that could support her desire to work in the creative sector.

Other students, such as Cassandra, reflected a more complicated view of two-year community colleges. Throughout our interviews, Cassandra expressed significant frustration with the school environment at Freeway. With many of her friends having dropped out from high school and moving on to different plans, Cassandra was eager to leave what she considered an immature and understimulating school environment. Cassandra also recalled confusion in understanding how the first few years of high school would affect her grade point average. She compared her own performance with that of other students who were higher academic achievers throughout high school. Cassandra's plans were to attend a two-year community college and then transfer to a four-year university.

> I'm going to probably graduate still in the third quartile is what the college career counselor told me. She [her school counselor] said even if I make all A's—she said it might look good—it'll look better than slacking off my whole senior year, but she said people who have been making all A's freshman, sophomore, junior, and senior year—they are going to stay in the first and second quartile. But people that didn't do so hot their first three years and now they're trying to improve—she said that . . . it'll be better than nothing to see that, but she said the people that tried hard all four years are still going to be above me just because—that's the order it will go in. I wouldn't be put before someone who's been working their butt off all four years and I just am barely trying to get my stuff together.

Cassandra's predicament is emblematic of the de facto tracking that occurred at Freeway, and particularly how important the influence of external capital is in shaping how students navigate the course offerings at Freeway. The fact that she spent the first three years of high school enrolled and underperforming in classes that were not oriented toward postsecondary opportunity is an example of how a substantial portion of Freeway students simply fell through the cracks and into what could only be described as uncertain futures.

What Is Vocational about Creativity?

While some students in our study went on to attend two-year community colleges, other students ended up not attending college at all. In the case of Sergio, who did not have immediate plans to enroll in college, this discrepancy was particularly striking given his excitement about film school that he discussed in the fall. In some of our first interviews, Sergio presented a list of potential college options, prestigious private universities that specialize in filmmaking. However, by the end of the school year, Sergio no longer envisioned himself attending these universities and instead was planning to find a job after high school. He described feeling lost in his attempts to navigate the college admissions process: "I don't have a plan on how to get in. I mean, I'm just trying to build up a portfolio because I know they ask for a short film along with the résumé."

Antonio experienced a similar situation. Like Sergio, Antonio dreamed of a career in film production. In our interviews, he described his experience with the CAP as a fertile ground for a future career in media (see chapter six). He credited the CAP as the reason he was hired for an editing internship for a local Spanish-language television station, which he began in his last semester. In a focus group we conducted with graduating seniors, Antonio expressed gratitude for Freeway's digital media classes and after-school programs for giving him a job. However, when we followed up with him several months later, he was struggling to find employment in low-wage service sector jobs. In his words, he came to the realization that creative-sector media industries "don't want to hire a freshly-out-of-high-school student."

Antonio elaborated: "I can't find a job. I'm calling Target, Walmart, stuff like that. I don't want to work at Walmart, though. I don't want to work in fast food either. I haven't applied to those. They probably have jobs, but I don't want to go into them, because my sister and brother, they've been in there, and I don't want to go into that, because they said that it sucks. I'm just trying to find a job somewhere where I actually like it. Anywhere which is not just video and work."

In a powerfully disappointing irony, Antonio described his job search as particularly difficult despite a paid internship with the local Spanish-language TV station during his last semester of high school. When asked what other skills he could use from his experiences to relate to other jobs, few ideas came to mind. Moreover, apart from the video editing experience, he felt that he did not have any other job experience. He concluded, "For me, it's kind of hard."

Antonio's precarious situation is especially distressing in light of the persistent vocational discourses surrounding the digital media and learning endeavors at Freeway. He essentially discovered that the tech skills he cultivated in Freeway's formal and informal learning settings were limited when it came to his job search. Without more robust education and technology training, the only jobs available to him were low-skill, low-wage service sector jobs. In our view, Antonio did not lack ambition; rather, he lacked access to the educational and learning experiences and social networks that are the crucial pathways to opportunity in the creative sector.

We consistently heard teachers rely on a rhetoric of vocational preparation as a way to promote and justify the existence of the digital media classes and clubs. Student participation in these spaces was framed as a way to get real-life job skills. In the absence of other scaffolding for postsecondary education, especially for students who were not de facto tracked to college prep courses, the actual opportunity to develop and transfer knowledge and technology skills into bona fide employment after high school was slim.

To be sure, digital media and other extra-academic classes offered a way of involving students who might otherwise not be invested in school. However, we noticed that despite this opportunity for engagement, students' expectations for what they may extract from participation in these programs ultimately led to feelings of career frustration and disappointment. We note the trend in which students' interests in creative industry work such as digital media production, game design, and fashion are tracked as "vocational" rather than "academic."

Straightforward vocational approaches toward digital media curricula and vocational discourses about extracurricular activities ("These skills will get you a job") mask the underlying system of gatekeeping and badging that is required to gain entry into the creative sector, including college degrees, even for entry-level positions. Furthermore, these discourses oriented toward immediate vocation miss the opportunity to clarify how the skills students have tinkered with in digital media production could translate to higher education. In light of the long history of biased school tracking in the United States, the categorization of Freeway students' creative interests as primarily vocational reflects a troubling legacy of racial and class stratification.

Social Capital and Institutional Agents

What is the link between our students' vision of better futures and their ability to actually forge pathways to make their vision a reality? The answer to this question is a complicated one, and combines our earlier discussion of tracking, social capital, and the role of influencers in and outside the family. For students in the digital edge, the accumulation of capitals does not necessarily begin or end with the home environment. Several of our students from working-class backgrounds and nontraditional family structures proved quite adept at accruing social capital at Freeway through their inventiveness, grit, and the intervention of what Stanton-Salazar and Dornbusch term "institutional agents."[19]

By "institutional agents," Stanton-Salazar and Dornbusch mean "those individuals who have the capacity and commitment to transmit directly or to negotiate the transmission of institutional resources and opportunities (such as information about school programs, academic tutoring and mentorship, college admission, and assistance with career decision making)."[20] While institutional agents can include adult family members, Stanton-Salazar and Dornbusch are generally referring "to such people as teachers and counselors, social service workers, clergy, community leaders, college-going youths in the community, and the like." Peers may also act as institutional agents when students obtain informational resources from other students.

As Watkins, Lombana-Bermudez, and Weinzimmer note in chapter six, most of the parents that we interviewed during our research were limited in their ability to invest time and money in their children's educational development, thus widening the enrichment opportunity gap. Further, they explain how several students in our study made strategic investments in school-based resources such as peers, institutional agents, and digital media–making projects. Our research shows that, in some cases, these institutional agents intervene in meaningful ways that help students forge a path to future opportunity—whether it's admission to a prestigious East Coast private four-year college or being the first in their family to graduate from high school. But our research also suggests that students with more diverse sources of social capital—school, after school, nonschool, home, peers—were able to leverage connections to institutional agents for greater benefit than those with less diverse sources of social capital.

Students from more resource-rich homes are more likely than their resource-constrained counterparts to have greater variety in their social networks, leading to notable advantages in resources and opportunities. Indeed, as one sociologist explains, network diversity—having a variety of contacts—may actually be more useful in life than simply having a lot of contacts.[21] In the case of teens, network variety might consist of nonfamilial institutional agents such as mentors, teachers, community figures, or extended family members. This dynamic was evident among our study participants.

Many students realized in their final year of school that they may have been better positioned for opportunities after graduation had they been more academically engaged and better directed in their first few years. But as many of the chapters in this book illustrate, the struggles that students encountered academically and in the transition to young adulthood were largely societal and institutional, not individual. A combination of social, economic, and educational factors converged to begin shaping the life chances of Freeway students in early childhood. It is also apparent that many of the students in our study did not receive the type of structured guidance—at home or in school—that could have helped them identify and navigate their prospects for better futures. The limited guidance at home reflects the challenges many lower-income parents face in navigating institutions like schools for the educational and personal benefit of their children.[22] The limited guidance from school illuminates the challenges school administrators face in designing systems—curricula, enrichment programs, and counseling services—that prepare students for a rapidly evolving society and economy.

Jada and Cassandra, both graduating seniors at the time of our study, discussed similar experiences of independently discovering the importance of academic achievement despite limited input from family, peers, or even teachers and administrators. While Cassandra described her orientation to school as premature "senioritis," Jada's description of thinking like a senior does not simply correspond to a disinterest in schoolwork. It also demonstrates how important adult scaffolding—teachers, counselors, parents—is in the education sphere. Early in her academic career at Freeway, Jada treated school primarily as a place to socialize. However, by her sophomore year Jada began to understand the repercussions of her grades on her future. She said, "I don't know how it changed, I just thought about, 'Oh, like, this stuff got to average up by the time I graduate,' like, my grades. And if I don't turn to a certain way I may not get accepted into the college that I want to." Still, she was unable to identify what caused the change in this attitude and was ambiguous and unclear about the role of her teachers, parents, and friends in helping her revise these priorities. We could not pinpoint exactly what shifted, but she developed an understanding of the importance of academic achievement early enough so that her parents did not have to intervene.

In contrast to Jada, Cassandra's testimony reflects deeper regrets and feelings of institutional neglect with regard to her academic performance and future trajectories. Comparing her academic disposition as a graduating senior with her attitude a year prior, Cassandra described herself as "taking school more seriously now" amid discussion of a series of "mistakes" throughout her high school career. In her senior year she turned around her grade point average by earning straight A's, which was a contrast to her first three years.

Despite this effort, however, Cassandra described serious repercussions for the mistakes she made in the first years of high school. That spring, she graduated in the lowest seventy-fifth percentile of her class, and, unfortunately, it appeared "too late" to turn things around. Cassandra described the damage incurred as a result of feeling lost and directionless during many of her high school years:

All my low grades from previous years ruined my GPA for my senior year and I didn't know it was gonna do that—no one really had sat down and talked to me and was like, "Your first three years of high school are the most important"—senior year, your GPA is pretty much gonna stay the same but freshman and sophomore and junior year you have to try hard to get your GPA high and then keep it like that your senior year but I can't— but my case is, my GPA is so low, and now that I'm turning over a new leaf and I'm trying to get my grades high and GPA high—it's really not possible.

Cassandra's situation was common at Freeway. In our year at the school, we observed a myopic institutional focus toward simply pushing students through to graduation. It was up to self-motivated students and the very small administrative counseling staff to articulate a viable four-year college pathway; college was not "in the air" at Freeway. Many students simply had no understanding of what it takes to attend college, and the learning climate for the majority of students was not focused toward this goal. Many students, besides the few who were determined to obtain and maintain a standing in the top 10 percent of their class, were connected to a network of peers who were not necessarily resistant to attending college, but rather lacked a genuine understanding of what it means to be "college ready" in terms of course selection, academic performance, and résumé building.

As others in this book have stated, the academic experiences of many students at Freeway remind us of a key claim made by education scholar Angel Harris.[23] Virtually all of the students that we met wanted to achieve in school, but they did not always know how. This strongly suggests that high academic performance is at least partially related to social capital—that is, the kinds of social ties and social resources that help students cultivate greater awareness of what it takes to transition successfully from secondary to postsecondary opportunities. Rather than think about the college-going ethos as individually determined, we believe it is socially determined. Thus, growing up in families, communities, and schools in which going to college is a norm produces a kind of contagion effect.[24] This is, quite frankly, the power of social networks and how the social ties in which we are embedded influence not only our behaviors but also the underlying norms that often lead to specific social and behavioral patterns.

Echoing the experiences of Cassandra and Jada, students such as Sergio and Antonio offered more detailed insights into familial influences on academic achievement. Their stories point to structural considerations, rather than emotional neglect or apathy, in parents' struggles to guide their children's postsecondary trajectories. Sergio, for example, pointed out that he did not have a family model for going to college. His brother had enrolled in community college for about one year, but soon dropped out. When asked if anyone in his family would be able to give him advice on college, he said, "No one. I'm going to be the first one if I do go." Antonio attributes his parents' long working hours to their distance from his academic experience. While describing the challenges of lacking this guidance, he also recognized their busy schedules and personal sacrifices: "They have other priorities. I know my parents, they work late. They really can't participate in, like, PTA—I think it's called. They've never participated in that in my life. Only time they came back to school is if I ask them to come to a play when I was maybe 3rd grade. That's it."

Indeed, in the absence of the social capital that comes with a familial college-going legacy and without external agents to provide the infrastructure to support social and educational mobility, some of the students we followed had unclear ideas about their future. Jasmine, already a senior, described a dramatically broad range of dreams following graduation—from studying film to leaving the state and moving overseas to study in southern Europe. Yet at the same time, Jasmine revealed no plans for making these dreams a reality. She had not thought about which colleges she would like to attend, nor had she discussed these goals with her grandparents, her legal guardians. Instead, academic achievement seemed to operate amorphously within her family, an idea untethered to clear signposts or goals. In reference to her grandparents, Jasmine explained that "he [grandfather] just wants me to get my education. And my grandma just kind of wants me to stay close." Apart from the statement of these dreams, however, Jasmine received little other guidance about academics and college.

According to the "network orientation" framework outlined by Stanton-Salazar and Dornbusch, Jasmine may have had a hard time accessing the social capital provided by the institutional agents in her school and community for two reasons. First, she may not have had "a high level of trust in society's gatekeepers and agents." Second, institutional agents may not have identified her as an "attractive and worthy candidate for institutional mentorship and promotion."[25]

There were some exceptions among the families that we studied. Michelle's family's outlook on her education was prominent in her pathway to an elite four-year university. Although neither of her parents finished college, they both count "some college" experience. When Michelle was in middle school, her father had asked her if she was being challenged academically. Recounting the conversation to us, she explained that she told him: "Well, I'm learning, I just get it fast and easy, and right where I can just finish anything within the period or the class time. It's easy to me, Dad, it's easy to me." Her father's response, she explained: "You're going to take all AP classes, and I'm changing you [to more advanced classes]." Uncertain about the workload, Michelle initially argued with her father. "I've seen these kids, with this stack of books and work and you see me in my regular classes, all you need is a notebook and a pencil," she told us. She admitted, "I was worried about how much work; I wasn't worried about how hard it would be."

In her general track classes, Michelle rarely had homework because she usually finished all of her assignments in class. In her first week of AP classes it was clear that she would be challenged academically, a fact that did not gain her immediate approval. Despite her early misgivings, when Michelle reflected back on that pivotal decision during her middle school years, she explained, "Now I'm good and I know that it was a good decision for my purpose."

The experiences of students appear to uphold Lucas's assertion that "the proactive behavior of middle class parents" offers the likeliest explanation of their children's transition into higher education.[26] Jack, Inara, Gabriela, and Michael appeared to have a significant level of mentorship and guidance from their immediate family in terms of how to best articulate a path toward future opportunity. In contrast, the cases of Amina, Cassandra, Jasmine, Sergio, and Antonio often display a reversal of roles—with the child demonstrating greater influence in the navigation of academic life at Freeway.

Amina described tensions with her mother about her plans to first enroll in a community college and then transfer to a four-year university. Concerned about Amina's likelihood of transferring out of a community college to complete her bachelor's degree, her mother frequently encouraged Amina to enroll directly at one of the four-year universities that had already admitted her. Despite this discomfort, however, her mother ultimately deferred to Amina's decision: "I keep telling her what my plans are. And then she's just, like, 'Well you know best, I guess.' But, like, she's just not. . . . She knows my decision but she's not too okay with it." This stark testimony reveals a troubling truth: it is hard to believe a student from a resource-rich family, one with a strong college-going tradition, would be in this situation, with parents deferring to the child, assuming the child "knows best" about deciding not to enroll in a four-year college.

The significance of external institutional agents is immense in these circumstances. Like other students in our study, Michelle came from a family with modest economic means. Her father did not finish his associate's degree. However, because of active involvement from institutional agents, Michelle cultivated diverse sources of social and cultural capital that prepared her for the college application process. She also benefited from the aforementioned strong parental involvement in her curricular choices.

In contrast to Cassandra, Michelle was identified as a potential college-bound student by the teacher who ran Freeway's AVID program, a nationwide initiative that teaches students the skills and know-how to apply to college. Michelle had a great relationship with the school principal, and as reported in chapter six, she smartly leveraged extra-curricular activities to strengthen her leadership skills and connections to resource-rich institutional agents. In short, Michelle had a cadre of institutional agents in her social network as she ventured into the uncharted territory of college applications, which she admits she had no understanding of prior to her involvement with AVID, the school counselor, and a college recruiter.

Michelle's investment in these relationships paid huge dividends. She received a full scholarship to a prestigious East Coast private university whose diversity recruitment program was introduced to her by Freeway's college counselor. Michelle's college application choices were tellingly stilted, revealing a poor understanding of her college choices. More specifically, her college choices consisted of a few second-tier Texas schools that many Freeway students applied to; a small, low-profile university in Kansas that was recruiting her for the basketball team; and this seemingly random, prestigious East Coast private university that outreached to Freeway through its diversity recruitment program. Despite her reluctance to leave Texas and her family, Michelle ended up enrolling in this East Coast university and relocating to the New England area. The connection to her high school counselor and a subsequent introduction to a college recruiter changed the trajectory of her life. Many at Freeway were not so fortunate.

Social Capital as Trajectory Multiplier

The CAP was a pivotal source of capital—social, cultural, and human— for the students who made significant investments in the project. We maintain that the CAP produced real value for students in terms of their experience at Freeway. Students were able to cutivate social identities, social relationships, and digital media literacies that enhanced the quality of their schooling experience. Next, we consider another potential feature of the CAP: the degree to which it supported the ability of students to access opportunities that extended beyond high school.

One way to think about these informal learning environments is as a *multiplier, that is, a resource that increases the chances of a student to connect to richer resources and opportunities.* As our colleagues contend in chapter five, the life chances of students from affluent households not only benefit from richer in-school learning opportunities; they also benefit from richer out-of-school learning opportunities. These out-of-school activities can multiply the academic (i.e., higher grades) and non-academic (i.e., leadership skills) benefits available to affluent students, thus widening the achievement gap with their less affluent counterparts.[27] This is what is referred to as the "enrichment opportunity gap."[28]

Most of the students in our study cultivated important social ties through their after-school activities. The CAP, for example, introduced students to a more dynamic set of social relations with peers and the faculty sponsor (Mr. Lopez) that proved to be personally meaningful and beneficial. But not all social networks and the ties they afford are equal. Consequently, not all of the resources mobilized from social ties are equal. At this point we consider another feature of social network theory, what Nan Lin calls the *extensity-of-ties proposition* or "the more extensive the networks, the better social resources to be accessed and mobilized."[29] The extensity-of-ties proposition suggests that the value of social networks is not necessarily the size (knowing a lot of people) but rather the variety (knowing a diversity of people).

Writing about the value of extensive ties, Lin says, "Extensive ties afford better opportunities for individuals to locate the resources useful for instrumental actions."[30] Thus, the more extensive or diverse the ties are in a social network, the better the social resources one can likely access.

One way to think about this dynamic is to wrap back to the concept of tracking and its attendant concerns and structural inequities related to social capital and future-oriented trajectories. Students who have been identified as worthy of investment by institutional agents for higher tracks are better positioned to strategically leverage school for opportunities after graduation. In contrast, general track students receive conflicting messages from institutional agents and even family members regarding their direction and potential opportunities, often defaulting to a vocational orientation that does not prepare them for entry into a rapidly evolving educational or job market.

We contend that the students without extensive social ties did not gain as much from these informal learning environments as students who maintained a greater variety of social connections in their social networks. To illustrate this theoretical claim we consider the way two students—Alberto and Sergio—catalyzed their participation in the CAP for instrumental actions, or in this case transitioning from Freeway to the beginning stages of young adulthood.

Alberto and Sergio were both seniors. Additionally, both were actively involved in the informal learning environment established by the CAP.

Alberto was part of the team that was invited to screen their short feature at a prestigious European film festival. He was also a high-track student, was enrolled in AP classes, and possessed knowledge about college-bound steps. His knowledge about and preparation for college were enhanced by the diversity of his social ties. His older sister, a Freeway graduate, attended the University of Texas at Austin, the state's flagship university. She was a constant source of informal knowledge and inspiration. His parents graduated from college in Mexico. He also cultivated a rich set of ties through his participation in the National Latino

Institute debate league, which allowed him to develop connections to mentors, program coordinators, and students who provided formal and informal knowledge related to the college admissions process.

When we caught up with Alberto roughly a year after graduation he was enrolled at the University of Texas. In fact, he had gained admission into the business school, one of the most competitive majors at the university.

Alberto and Sergio had enriching experiences through the CAP, but Alberto's investment in the program was clearly designed to make him a competitive college applicant. He viewed his experience in the CAP as an opportunity to build his skills and a portfolio—just one piece of many that would help pave the way to college and, in his mind, future opportunity. Whereas Alberto and Sergio demonstrated deep commitment to the CAP, sometimes sacrificing sleep and academic assignments in service of the project, Alberto's participation in the project was only in his junior year.

Explaining why he elected not to participate in the club in his senior year, Alberto said, "It seemed interesting, but I felt like I got out of it what I needed to get out of it. I wanted to try different things." Alberto credited the CAP with giving him a rare "outlandish" opportunity to travel to Europe but also approached these experiences practically, explaining how he translated the skills he learned from the film project into a broader skill set that helped him in composing his college application essays.

Alberto's recollection of his high school career was peppered with notes of confidence, resourcefulness, and resilience. "My résumé is beautiful," he told us, explaining how his extracurricular experiences taught him important skills such as "time management" and "leadership." Moreover, Alberto, while narrating the process of writing his college application essays, demonstrated an ability to market himself and anticipate the desires of universities and employers:

> [The topic of the essay was] something that hindered you during high school, benefited you during high school, something impactful. So what I did was three things that greatly impacted my high school life, that turned me into a leader. The National Latino Institute, the Cinematic

Arts Project, and being the leader of a band. And all of those three things cultivated me into becoming the leader that I am. And what's funny is that I didn't even know that's what the business school is all about. Like, "Oh, like, we built leaders in the business school." So I think that might be one of the reasons why they were, like, "Oh, we need this kid in the business school."

When we met with Sergio several months after graduating Freeway, his path was notably different from Alberto's. For example, Sergio was struggling to find low-wage service sector employment. Sergio had vague plans to attend Austin Community College at some point in the future. His parents' highest level of education was middle school in Mexico, and he was not placed in a high-achieving track at Freeway. Sergio did accumulate many benefits from the CAP. Mr. Lopez acted as a strong institutional agent and mentor. Sergio even leveraged this experience for a paying gig at a local Spanish-language TV affiliate during his senior year. Still, he seemed uninformed, and uncertain about next steps beyond Freeway.

In the fall semester of his senior year, Sergio expressed an interest in attending a prestigious film school and even to double major. However, by the following spring he had no college plans in place. From our vantage point, Sergio struggled to catalyze his participation in the CAP into opportunities beyond high school.

Sergio, unlike Alberto, did not have a strong college profile, a concrete plan, or the social connections and resources to support his postsecondary aspirations. He had not created a reel or creative portfolio. He seemed unaware that the film schools in Texas would be far less expensive than those in California and that he would qualify for in-state tuition. Additionally, he seemed unaware that many students do not transfer from community college to the University of Texas at Austin, but rather from a satellite UT System campus, such as San Antonio or Arlington.

The gaps in knowledge between Alberto and Sergio are best considered through a consideration of social capital. Relegated to a low-achieving track at Freeway, Sergio was not embedded in social relations that supplied the social capital needed for instrumental actions related to attending film school. For example, he did not come from a family tradition of higher education that could informally impart knowledge about the college-going process. Sergio's mediocre academic standing did not lend itself to meaningful social relations with teachers or the school's transition counselor.

Sergio's primary after-school activity was the CAP. The ties that he cultivated in the CAP enriched his access to informal and peer-driven knowledge related to digital media production (see chapter six) and enhanced his social standing with a capital-rich institutional agent (see chapter six). These ties were meaningful, but they were also principally contained within the school. In other words, the social ties were not necessarily extensive.

Sergio could very well realize his goal of going to community college and transferring to a prestigious film program. He certainly is talented enough, and he has the stunning accolade of having a film he helped create already screened at one of the world's most prestigious student film festivals. What Sergio needed was a more extensive set of social ties—that is, connection to a diversity of capital-rich agents such as teachers, counselors, family members, peers, and out-of-school institutional agents who could support his higher-education aspirations.

Importantly, we contend that it is not just access to enrichment opportunities that matters in young people's lives, but the degree to which those opportunities are enveloped in capital-enhancing social relations. The CAP clearly benefited Sergio and Alberto. We have strong reasons to believe that Sergio's participation in this extracurricular activity was a motivator for his engagement with school in general and journey to becoming the first in his family to earn a high school diploma. Alberto, in his own words, benefited from his participation in the CAP as well. However, his ties to family with collegiate experience and resource-rich institutional agents in school and out of school strengthened Alberto's ability to leverage his experience in the CAP to map a trajectory that produced exponential benefits—media production skills, leadership, persistence, global travel, and a competitive college application.

The CAP was, indeed, an important source of social capital for Sergio and Alberto. However, if Alberto's and Sergio's experiences are any indication, the CAP was especially beneficial to those students who combined the connections made through participation in the project with a more diverse network of institutional agents, peers and resources.

Finally, Alberto's and Sergio's CAP stories highlight the so-called Matthew Effect, the idea that the "rich get richer."[31] In the case of our analysis, the students who benefited from a more diverse and, therefore, richer set of connections in their social network accrued more diverse gains from their participation in extracurricular activities like the CAP. Crucially, these gains propelled them toward more promising opportunities in the transition to young adulthood.

Conclusion

Future Ready: Preparing Young People for Tomorrow's World

S. Craig Watkins

Like most ethnographic inquiries, our fieldwork at Freeway High School generated more questions than answers. In the pages of this book we have presented only a small sample of the data, stories, and profiles collected from our study. Still, we think that the accounts and analysis offer an in-depth and even unique perspective on the life of a school that typifies many of the transformations that are under way nationwide.

Freeway is similar to a growing number of schools in the United States in several ways. First, the school has a majority-minority student population. Second, it suffers from deeply entrenched racial academic achievement gaps. Finally, Freeway struggles to prepare its students for postsecondary education and life beyond high school. From our perspective, the teachers, administrators, parents, and certainly students at Freeway labored to build better futures. But they did so in the face of stiff circumstances—social and spatial isolation, economic inequality, and resource-constrained schools and families—not of their own making.

Freeway makes for an interesting case study precisely because it illuminates one of the most urgent challenges facing the United States today: preparing the most diverse student population in the nation's history for a world marked by rapid social, technological, and economic change. In 2000 whites made up 59 percent of the students enrolled in U.S. public schools compared with 17 percent for Latinos.[1] By 2014 white enrollment had decreased to 50 percent, whereas Latino enrollment had increased to 25 percent.[2] Black enrollment between 2000 and 2014 remained basically unchanged, going from 17 to 16 percent. Historically, youth from Latino and African American mixed-race households have been referred to as minorities, but they now represent the majority of school-aged children and teens in the United States.[3] Consequently, the societal stakes for not properly educating them are higher than ever.

If it is true that the road to building better social, civic, and economic futures includes creating more equitable educational outcomes, then schools like Freeway must become a national priority. Ask any K–12 educator what the goal of education is today, and you are likely to hear some version of this: "Upon graduation, our students should be career ready or college ready." During our time at Freeway we constantly heard the "career or college ready" mantra. This is the twenty-first-century battle cry in education. However, just a cursory glance at education data suggests that a majority of U.S. students, especially Latino, African American, and lower-income, are not college ready. Moreover, as we reflect on our fieldwork we believe that schools should rethink what it means to be career ready. In fact, the very notion of career ready strikes us as increasingly anachronistic in a world in which the idea of a career as we understood it in the twentieth century seems less and less applicable in the twenty-first century.

We suggest that, rather than develop career-ready skills and dispositions, schools begin to think about what it means to be "future ready." "Career ready" implies preparing students for a world in which work is stable, linear, and secure. Alternatively, "future ready" implies preparing students for a world in which work is in flux, non-linear, and insecure. In the economy of tomorrow, jobs will be anything but stable and predictable, which means that workers must learn to be flexible earners *and* flexible learners. And while some students will have access to the schools and learning opportunities that will prepare them for a rapidly evolving society and economy, most will not. Equipping our most vulnerable schools with the resources to develop future-ready students must be a prominent component of any effort to make our schools more relevant.

The College Readiness Crisis

Midway through the fall term, Freeway's principal, Mr. Gomez, summoned all of the seniors and their teachers to a special assembly. He warned them that more than half of the senior class was in danger of not passing their final year of high school. A number of students were not submitting homework or attending their classes. Senioritis had come early at Freeway, and now the school was potentially facing what could only be described as a serious embarrassment. Improving the high school graduation rates of lower-income students has become a national goal. It was, arguably, the main goal at Freeway. School officials engaged in a variety of creative techniques to make sure that students who suffered from chronic absenteeism or failed to submit homework stayed on track for graduation.

The National Center for Education Statistics reports that the graduation rate in 2014-15 for American Indian/Alaska Native (72 percent), black (75 percent), and Hispanic (78 percent) students was below the national average of 83 percent.[4] By contrast, the graduation rates for Asian/Pacific Islander (90) and white (88 percent) were above the national average.[5] Texas was the only state in which the graduation rate for black students was higher than the overall national rate. In addition, the percentage of Latino students graduating high school in Texas has also increased sharply. [6] Still, the state's success in driving up high school graduation rates has not translated to the postsecondary level, especially among students from lower-income households. When State District Court judge John Dietz of Austin ruled that the manner in which Texas funds public education is unconstitutional, he also issued this harsh rebuke of the educational inequities in the state: "An alarming percentage of Texas students graduate high school without the necessary knowledge and skills to perform well in college."[7]

There is a growing recognition that the relaxation of standards and the new policies that make it easier for students to overcome chronic absenteeism, poor literacy skills, and less than stellar academic work to meet graduation requirements may be coming at a cost: the production of a generation of graduates who are not adequately prepared for postsecondary education or the rapidly evolving workforce.

According to the state's metrics, the vast majority of Latino and black graduates at Freeway are not adequately prepared for college. Take two measures—enrollment in AP courses and college readiness.[8] Roughly 40 percent of Asian American and 36 percent of white students were enrolled and received credit in at least one AP course. By comparison, 21 percent of Latino and 20 percent of black students were enrolled in academically advanced classes. A similarly low percentage of economically disadvantaged students (21 percent) and English language learners (19 percent) were enrolled in Freeway's most rigorous courses. The enrollment disparities in advanced coursetaking drive the racial and ethnic disparities in college-readiness.

According to the Texas Education Agency, in order to be a college-ready graduate, a student must have met or exceeded the college-ready criteria in the state assessment exit exam or the SAT or ACT test in English language arts or mathematics. Among white and Asian graduates, 71 percent and 66 percent, respectively, met this college-ready graduate standard. The percentages of Latino (39 percent) and black (38 percent) college-ready graduates were considerably lower. Less than half of the students, 43 percent, designated by the district as "economically disadvantaged" were college-ready graduates. Students classified as English language learners were the least likely (11 percent) to be college ready by graduation.[9]

The education story in the United States is remarkably complex. For example, since 2000 the rate of black and Latino enrollment in college has actually increased more than that of whites.[10] This is partially attributable to the fact that more black and Latino students are graduating high school than ever before. Also, black and Latino students represent a greater share of the student-age population than at any other time in U.S. history. However, growth in college enrollment has not closed the college degree attainment gap.[11]

If enrolling black and Latino students in college has been a challenge, earning a degree once enrolled in college has been even more daunting. Despite the greater number of black and Latino students enrolling in college, they are much less likely than their white and Asian counterparts to graduate. The National Center for Education Statistics found that 62 percent of whites earned a bachelor's degree within six years of enrolling in college. By comparison, 51 percent of Latinos and 40 percent of blacks earned a bachelor's degree within six years of enrollment.[12] Even though record high numbers are entering college, black and Latino students are three times more likely to leave college without a degree in hand than their white or Asian counterparts.

Along with getting more underrepresented students into college, an equal challenge is getting them out with the credentials and skills to navigate our rapidly evolving knowledge economy. But even when young African Americans earn a college degree, they are more likely than their white counterparts to be unemployed or underemployed.[13]

The High Cost of the College Readiness and Affordability Crisis

Virtually all of the students that participated in the in-depth portion of our study had no intentions of attending a four-year college. And in our informal conversations with other students, it was clear that a significant portion of the general track students—the majority of Freeway students—were not planning to enroll in a postsecondary institution. There were two primary reasons, academic and financial, why a four-year degree was not a viable option for many Freeway students.

A great number of Freeway students were simply not prepared academically for college. In many instances they lacked the proper course work, grades, and academic training to succeed at the collegiate level. College readiness begins long before students enter high school and reflects the extent to which both schools and the home environment can supply the resources that support the development of a college-going disposition. As we note in chapter five it is likely that a majority of the students who enter Freeway fell behind the college readiness standards as early as the elementary and middle school years. The state's college readiness metrics noted above suggest that getting these students college ready in the four years of high school is a formidable task.

Most of the participants in the in-depth portion of our study were general track students. The general track courses met the state's requirement for graduation but fell short of what was expected for college preparation. Some of the students that we followed contended with alienation from school and struggled to meet graduation requirements. But many also had college potential. Students such as Diego and Sergio were clearly capable of doing college preparatory work, but declined. As a result, their academic training was not oriented to enrolling in a four-year college.

Affordability was another main reason Freeway students cited for not attending a four-year college.[14] Many students explained that their families simply could not afford the high cost of a four-year college. Minh, a precocious student from a Vietnamese immigrant household, was strongly committed to enrolling in a four-year college, but his dad discouraged him largely due to concerns about cost. Even though Amina (profiled in chapters two and seven) was admitted to a four-year college, she elected not to enroll, citing concerns about financial and familial instability. Nelson, a young African American student at Freeway, experienced firsthand the steep economic barriers lower-income families face to send their children to college. His story is revealing.

Nelson was one of the more promising students that we met during our time at Freeway. His big smile was matched only by his ambitions to become a filmmaker. Nelson was a founding member of the digital media club at Freeway. The after-school club was an alternative space for students like Nelson who otherwise struggled in school. His engagement in the digital media club presented the opportunity to craft a distinct identity and practice his digital media making skills, and provided the motivation to stay in school and earn his diploma.

In addition to enrolling in technology classes and participating in the activities available through the digital media club, Nelson studied online tutorials and films to sharpen his technical skills and creative vision. The music library on his laptop was filled with musical scores from his favorite films. After graduating from high school, Nelson created his own media production company, began making short films, and built a social media presence. The short films that he made were smart, expertly edited, and wonderfully immersive. Members of our research team were impressed by the quality of his storytelling. Nelson had real talent.

But Nelson did not have strong grades, which blocked a fluid transition to college after graduation. Like most high school only graduates, Nelson struggled to find employment.[15] Still, he continued to keep his passion for the digital media arts and film alive. For example, he volunteered to be a mentor for the students who participated in Freeway's CAP (see chapter five for a description of the project). Serving as a mentor kept his mind and creative inclinations engaged. During this period Nelson submitted one of his short films to a prestigious European student film festival competition. When the film was accepted, he raised money to help finance his trip to Europe. The experience confirmed his desire to make films.

Nelson's grades were not necessarily competitive, but his portfolio of creative work offered a glimpse into his potential as a filmmaker and helped earn him admission into a film school in Chicago. Nelson's friends and family were ecstatic. He was set to become the first member in his family to attend a four-year college. Attending film school in Chicago promised to expand his social network, introduce him to new opportunities, and strengthen his skills as a media maker and storyteller. A couple of weeks before the start of classes, Nelson announced via Twitter that he would not be moving to Chicago to pursue the study of film. The high cost of tuition was simply too prohibitive and the amount of loans too debilitating. Several of his friends expressed collective grief via Twitter that offered some degree of solace. Roughly one year later, Nelson maintained dreams of making digital media content for a living but struggled to secure full-time employment as a high school graduate.

There are tens of thousands of stories like Nelson's, and they are spurring concern that, as the price tag of a four-year degree continues to escalate, many students are simply priced out of the college-going market and, consequently, a chance to earn the education and credentialing necessary in a skills-based economy. While the high cost of college kept Nelson from enrolling in film school, the cost of not going extended beyond his own personal circumstances. There was, we argue, a cost to his community too.

Many of Nelson's peers at Freeway knew that he had been admitted to a four-year college. He was a source of inspiration, an example that someone with a modest academic record could still gain admission to a four-year college. It is easy to overlook how an act like going to college is a social contagion.[16] Many students go to college partly because it is a norm, something that family members, teachers, and peers expect. Nelson was not the only one to suffer when he decided that college was too expensive. Freeway and his community suffered also as his inability to afford college reproduced a devastating norm—not pursuing a postsecondary credential—that undermines the social and economic security of communities like the one Nelson belonged to.

Educational Equity: The College Wage Premium

The racial disparities in college readiness and completion have serious social and economic implications. In an economy in which high levels of educational attainment closely correspond to meaningful employment, the under-education of so many Latino, African American, and lower-income youth poses long-term concerns. A report by the Pew Research Center titled *The Rising Cost of Not Going to College* presents data that strongly make the case that the current educational achievement gaps in the United States are the civil rights issue of our time.[17] The college readiness gap is steadily rolling back many of the social, educational, and economic gains made by Latino and African Americans in the period that followed the struggle for civil and economic rights in the 1950s, 1960s, and 1970s.

While college graduates from previous generations have long faced economic futures that were brighter than those of their counterparts who did not attend college, the employment and economic well-being gap between graduates and nongraduates is greater today than at any other time in U.S. history. According to the Pew Research Center, the pay gap between a college graduate and someone with just a high school diploma was $7,449 in 1965. By 2014 the pay gap between these two groups was $17,500.

On every measure of economic performance and well-being, college-educated millennials far outperform their non-college-educated counterparts. For example, when compared with their non-college-educated counterparts, college-educated millennials earn more, are significantly more likely to be employed, and are far less likely to live in poverty. Economic inequality among millennials is fueled in large part by unequal educational outcomes and, more specifically, the attainment of a college degree. This is what economists refer to as the "college wage premium."[18]

A key factor in the rising inequality among college-educated and non-college-educated millennials is the declining value of a high school diploma in today's economy. Whereas the earnings of college graduates have increased over the last half century, the reverse is true for those with only a high school diploma. Rising poverty rates among millennials underscore the diminishing value of having only a high school diploma. Since 1979 poverty rates among twenty-five- to thirty-two-year-olds with only a high school education have tripled.[19] The life chances of persons with only a high school diploma in hand have sharply declined over the last half century.

These trends, from our perspective, raise serious concerns about the kinds of futures the majority of Freeway students are likely to encounter in their transition to young adulthood without the adequate preparation to earn a postsecondary credential. In the world that students are transitioning into today, having only a high school diploma is an almost certain path to living at or below the nation's poverty line.

From Career Ready to Future Ready

In addition to producing students that are college ready, there is a strong emphasis across the nation to ensure that students are career ready. But the very notion of career readiness seems anachronistic in a world in which the nature of work is undergoing a profound transformation. More specifically, the likelihood of having a "traditional career" is not very good for persons entering the workforce in the twenty-first century. Therefore, we encourage schools to develop students who are future ready rather than career ready. What does it mean to be future ready in today's knowledge-driven economy?

Any valid future-ready curriculum must take a serious look at the economy and society students are transitioning into. It is a world marked by striking changes and uncertainty.

As we have suggested throughout this book, technology is a dominant trope in discourses about the future of learning. In addition to acquiring a wide range of technology—hardware and software—schools are offering a mix of tech-oriented courses including game development, video production, graphic arts, robotics, and computer science. While the massive financial investment in technology is a common practice among schools, the design of curriculum-rich classrooms and learning opportunities that cultivate the skills that are aligned with a steadily evolving knowledge economy remains elusive.[20] The main challenge to building a future-ready curriculum is that the skills required for meaningful and sustainable employment are in a constant state of flux. The school-to-work transition has never been more complex than it is today, which makes the work of education and future preparation especially daunting.

No Work or New Work?

Among the many factors that are driving change in the U.S. economy, none is more hotly debated than the presumed impact of technology.

There are, broadly speaking, two competing perspectives. One commonly held view is that technological advances—robots, intelligent machines, and advanced computing—have rendered many jobs obsolete. The other view asserts that technological advances do not eliminate work but rather increase the need for higher-skilled workers.

Human labor, the first perspective asserts, is being replaced by smart machines and, thus, leads to what some call the "post-market" society or "jobless future."[21] Martin Ford maintains that steady progress in software automation and predictive algorithms has pushed technology into a new frontier. Computerized technologies are no longer mere tools; they are capable of becoming autonomous workers. Ford maintains that the rising capacity of smart technologies will render a variety of jobs, lower skill and higher skill, obsolete. The tech industry, known for its appetite for disruption, may be provoking the biggest disruption of all—forcing workers across the United States out of the labor market or into lower-skill jobs that place an enormous amount of stress on society and the economy.

A second and competing view is that technological advances will lead to new forms of work rather than the demise of work.[22] According to this perspective, new technologies increase the demand for higher-skilled workers who can, for example, design, manage, and secure the operations and performance of smart machines. Writing for *Wired*, Kevin Kelley notes that robots inevitably take over most of the jobs and tasks that humans do, including both manual and cognitive labor.[23] But rather than become idle, humans, Kelley claims, will do what they have always done in the face of technological advances: create new tasks to execute.

In this bold new future, Kelley asserts that "the postindustrial economy will keep expanding, even though most of the work is done by bots, because your task tomorrow will be to find, make, and complete new things to do." The idea is simple and radical at the same time. To paraphrase Erik Brynjolfsson and Andrew McAfee, humans are not in a race against machines—a race that we would lose—but rather a race with the machines.[24]

Advocates of this perspective do not fear that smart machines will render humans useless in a soon to arrive jobless future. Rather, the rise of smart machines will forge extraordinary creative, civic, and economic opportunities for those who learn how to work with them. In the current era of innovation there is a rising premium on the ability to use smart machines to do smart, creative, useful, and novel things.

Perspectives like these illuminate the degree to which the development of innovation skills should matter more than ever for schools seeking to nurture future-ready students. Further, this perspective highlights one of our key claims: the innovation economy is not about technology but rather about the ability to leverage technology and other resources to innovate and intervene in the world in ways that are both original and valuable. Much of the energy and creativity happening across America's innovation hubs involves the smart application of smart technologies. Rather than building the Internet's infrastructure or hardware, innovators are using smart technologies to disrupt the services and products offered in traditional industries such as media, finance, fashion, health, transportation, and education.[25] Today's knowledge economy is driven by good ideas, not technology.

Raising the Cognitive Bar

One of the big challenges facing Freeway is helping students develop the skills and disposition that matter most in a society and economy undergoing rapid change. Most economists believe that one of the more significant impacts of technological innovation is the degree to which it increases the demand for skilled laborers. This, more specifically, is called *skill-biased technological change.*[26]

Claudia Golding and Lawrence Katz find a turning point in the late nineteenth century when technological changes became, generally speaking, skill biased.[27] Golding and Katz maintain that the rise in economic inequality over the past three decades is due, in large measure, to a slowing rate of educational attainment that has not kept pace with technological change and the surging demand for more high-skilled workers. They characterize this dynamic as "the race between education and technology." The most noticeable losers in this race typically resemble the young students who populated the classrooms at Freeway—poor, Latino, black, and immigrant.

As the skill requirements in our rapidly evolving economy are rising, the cognitive bar that schools must meet is also rising. What future-ready skills should schools be cultivating?

Frank Levy and Richard J. Murnane argue that the steady rise of computers has reorganized America's occupational structure.[28] More specifically, the growing presence of smart machines in the economy renders a growing inventory of jobs, manual and cognitive, obsolete. Analysts have long maintained that those tasks—manual or cognitive—that are predictable and repetitive and that computers can be programmed to execute by following specific rules will be automated. The tasks, manual or cognitive, that are more insulated from automation require skills like flexibility, complex thinking, solving uncharted problems, managing people, or social interactions.

The rise of smart machines, according to Levy and Murnane, has provoked a new division of labor, one that, broadly speaking, creates two classes of workers: those who can perform valued work in a world filled with computers and those who cannot. From their perspective, schools should be cultivating a repertoire of skills that are difficult for smart machines to perform by themselves.

In addition to expert technical knowledge, what these tasks require is the ability to grapple with novelty and complexity and also see opportunity where others do not. Some skills, no matter what the economy or jobs landscape looks like, are likely best performed by humans. Here we focus on two skills that any future-ready curriculum should be seeking to nourish, what Levy and Murnane refer to as *expert thinking* and *complex communication*.

Expert thinking reflects the ability to identify and solve problems for which there are no routine solutions. One example of expert thinking is pattern recognition. This particular skill reflects the ability of humans to understand the data-driven world around them and, importantly, discern change and distinct patterns. It is one thing for a computer to run algorithms that produce big data capable of mapping the spread of the Ebola virus. It is another thing to be able to recognize and analyze correlations, patterns, and causal insights that understand the geographical, sociological, and biological characteristics of the virus. Humans are better suited to ask the kinds of questions that will strengthen the algorithms' ability to generate data that support human creativity in the form of intervention and proactive problem solving.

Building on the research of Levy and Murnane, economists Brynjolfsson and McAfee posit that the human ability to ask novel questions will remain highly valuable even in the "second machine age," a period characterized by rapid computerization and automation.[29] Brynjolfsson and McAfee contend that ideation skills are an example of expert thinking, or the ability to grapple with complex problems for which there are no routine solutions. Computers may be powerful tools in the effort to raise money from millions of people distributed across the world, crowdfunding, but are not very good at knowing that they could be used this way. Humans are much more likely to ask "what if?" or "how can we?" Brynjolfsson and McAfee write, "We predict that people who are good at idea creation will continue to have a comparative advantage over digital labor for some time to come, and will find themselves in demand.[30]

And then there is what Levy and Murnane call complex communication skills. More generally, communication skills embody the prehistoric inclination among humans to tell stories that give meaning to human experience. In the age of big data, there is growing demand for analysts who can smartly and persuasively interpret the deluge of information generated through rising computing power and massive data networks. Complex communication, according to Levy and Murnane, involves the ability to convey not just information but a particular interpretation of information.[31] Transforming the world's information into complex forms of communication via policy, organizational strategy, a compelling ad campaign, or a stirring novel will continue to be an important human skill.

Expert thinking and complex communication involve the ability to grapple with some of the defining features of our time, such as complexity, uncertainty, and diversity. We believe that the knowledge and competencies associated with expert thinking and complex communication skills are poised to grapple with a steadily evolving society and economy. These are future-ready skills—that is, skills that are not simply focused on getting a job today but rather cultivating the competencies and dispositions to effectively navigate the world of tomorrow. But these are also skills that will be the primary domain of those who cultivate a questioning, risk-taking, and innovative disposition. If our fieldwork at Freeway is any indication, our schools are not properly designed, resourced, or incentivized to cultivate the skills that embody future readiness.

The Future of Work

Any future-ready curriculum must reflect a sharp understanding of the society and economy that young people are transitioning into. Levy and Murnane's thesis that the world of work is splitting into two classes—those who work with computers and those who do not—is provocative, but it requires some modifications. Technology is not the only driving force in the future jobs economy. The nation's growing racial and ethnic diversity, economic polarization, and aging population, for example, will have as much of a long-term impact on the economy as any other phenomenon, including technology. This is especially clear when you look at the U.S. Bureau of Labor Statistics (BLS) occupational employment projections over the 2016–2026 period.[32] The BLS expects overall occupational employment to increase by 7.4 percent between 2016 and 2026. These five occupational groups are projected to grow even more, according to the BLS:

- Healthcare support occupations (23 percent)
- Personal care and service occupations (18 percent)
- Healthcare practitioners and technical occupations (15 percent)
- Community and social service occupations (14 percent)
- Computer and mathematical occupations (14 percent)

While technology is driving changes in each of these occupational categories, these projections are driven as much by social transformations as they are technological transformations. For example, the much-faster-than-average growth in healthcare-related occupations is shaped by an aging baby-boom population, longer life expectancies, and anticipated increases in chronic diseases that have links to widening social and economic inequality. Despite our fascination with the "new digital economy," one of the BLS's assertions about the future jobs landscape is eye-opening: "Of the 30 fastest growing detailed occupations, 19 typically require some level of postsecondary for entry."[33] With the exception of computer and mathematical occupations, most jobs in the fastest-growing occupational categories listed above do not require a four-year college degree, contradicting widespread notions about education and future employment.

The BLS employment projections raise questions about the actual demand for knowledge-based work. Economists Paul Beaudry, David A. Green, and Ben Sand point to employment patterns and wage data that suggest that, after years of steady growth, the demand for cognitive labor began declining around 2000.[34] They identify trends that suggest that during this time college graduates began moving out of high-wage occupations and toward lower-paying occupations. Other studies suggest that young college graduates are increasingly more likely than previous generations of college graduates to be underemployed—that is, working in jobs that do not require their college degree.[35]

In his book *Rise of the Robots*, Martin Ford challenges the basic premise developed by Levy and Murnane that the employment prospects of those with high levels of education will be protected from the rise of smart machines. Ford maintains that the advances in software automation and predictive algorithms are gradually replacing white-collar jobs in a number of sectors, including medicine, journalism, and the law. As the learning and predictive capabilities of these technologies improve, the impact on white-collar workers, Ford argues, will be catastrophic. He writes, "The unfortunate reality is that a great many people will do everything right—at least in terms of pursuing higher education and acquiring skills—and yet still will fail to find a solid foothold in the new economy."[36] Ford points to data that suggest that opportunities for college graduates in the labor market as well as their earnings are already being limited by the ability of advanced technologies to do entry-level, knowledge-based work.[37]

Further, not all knowledge work is equal or fulfilling, as is evident with the rise of "white collar sweatshops," precarious white-collar labor, and cognitive stratification.[38] While some of the jobs projected to grow between 2016 and 2026 will require advanced cognitive skills that complement smart technologies, most will not. In the United States, virtually all of the major industry job growth in the forthcoming decade will be in service provision industries. Additionally, the organization of the service-base economy into low-skill/low-wage labor and high-skill/high-wage labor suggests that some workers will experience unprecedented economic opportunities and prosperity while others will experience shrinking economic opportunities and uncertainty. The former are the winners and the latter are the losers in what has become a winner-take-all economy.

Sadly, under these conditions a growing share of workers will be losers. Since the start of the Great Recession in 2007, lower-wage occupations have grown at a much faster rate than their mid-wage and higher-wage occupation counterparts.[39] The spread between the high-skill workers (e.g., managers, professionals) and low-skill workers (e.g., retail, food preparation) is widening and reflects the acute social and economic inequalities that are a striking feature of the new economy. Daniel Bell's assertions in the 1970s that the coming of a postindustrial society would lead to a revolution not only in the occupational structure in the United States but also in the class structure has come to pass.[40]

Levy and Murnane's thesis about being able to work with smart machines is instructive. However, the reality is that the majority of jobs do not require one to work with smart machines. Moreover, these jobs are likely to be lower-skill and lower-paying jobs that offer few opportunities for upward mobility and economic security.

The bridge to economic opportunity in tomorrow's economy appears especially weak in light of what we witnessed at Freeway and what we surmise may be going on in other schools similarly challenged by social, demographic, and economic change. At Freeway the primary goal was training students well enough to meet the minimum state standards for graduation that have dumbed down education and driven much of the life out of schools.[41] The emphasis on being obedient, compliant, and quiet and memorizing facts runs counter to the skills and dispositions that the current era of innovation demands, such as risk taking, assertiveness, curiosity, and out-of-the-box thinking. At Freeway, the intense pressure to get bodies in seats, cram for state exams, and grapple with state-driven teacher accountability mandates precluded any real opportunity to think about a future beyond simply getting students to the finish line of graduation.

Freeway students were seldom exposed to learning opportunities that cultivated future readiness. Consequently, learning at Freeway rarely involved asking novel questions, solving uncharted problems, or conveying a particular interpretation of information. What kind of future were Freeway students being prepared for?

School was essentially preparing students for a world that no longer exists, an era described by economist Tyler Cowen as "the age of average."[42] "Average" in this case refers to the period when individuals with only minimal levels of educational attainment (say, a high school diploma) could still secure meaningful employment, namely, in the middle-skill industrial sector. But as Cowen and others argue, the age of average is over.

Most schools struggle to design curricula and classrooms that engage the decisive shifts driving the new division of labor. The jobs projections over the next two decades, the expanding capacity and impact of smart technologies, and the skill-biased technical change make for a radically different world that demands that schools think and act differently. So much of the schooling at Freeway is premised on the notion that passing students through secondary school and into the workforce is the school's principal task. But the influence of automation and innovation in tomorrow's economy renders schools like Freeway dangerously out of touch with the world its students will encounter upon graduation.

A 2017 report by the McKinsey Global Institute finds that as early as 2030 about one-third of the American workforce may have to find new work as a result of automation. These changes, the report asserts, "imply substantial workplace transformations and changes for all workers."[43] McKinsey adds that if historical trends are a guide, 8–9 percent of 2030 labor demand will be in occupations that have not existed before. Some of these new occupations will almost certainly be related to technological transformation (i.e., artificial intelligence) and social transformation (i.e., a more diverse and aging population). One of the big challenges, and the one that we have focused on in this book, is the preparation of young people for a world in which work—what people do and how they do it—will continue to look much different compared with previous decades. This is true for all workers, including human experts and professionals.[44]

Current economic data and future employment projections suggest that the majority of Freeway students will enter a labor market that will offer them few, if any, opportunities for meaningful employment and economic mobility. Young people with only a high school diploma are extremely vulnerable, as their wages and prospects for employment continue to decline. The cost of not being future ready will be extraordinarily high as lower-income and undereducated youth continue to face daunting odds of climbing out of the lower rungs of America's stratified economic order.[45]

Future Ready or Not

If the future of work is at least partially about reimagining the work that we do, an important question emerges: Who is best prepared and positioned to thrive in that future? In other words, who is most likely to be future ready? The question brings schools and the growing educational disparities in the United States squarely into view. Unfortunately, the skills and disposition required for future readiness illuminate the current limitations in education and the crisis that challenges our ability to prepare the nation's most diverse student population in history for a school-to-work transition that is more daunting than ever.

Like many of their peers across the nation, the educators and district leaders at Freeway emphasize the acquisition of technology as an indicator of investing in better learning futures. Our fieldwork suggests that the most urgent challenge in education is not making sure that all students have equal access to technology but rather that all students have equal access to high-quality learning opportunities that prepare them for a world marked by complexity, uncertainty, and diversity. Latino, black, immigrant, and poor youth make up majorities of our school-aged population, and yet they are the least likely to receive a future-ready education. This was certainly the case with the majority of the students at Freeway. Further, many of them did not have plans to attend college after high school. Instead, they intended to go directly into the paid labor force. When we followed up with a sample of these students, their prospects for opportunity were predictable. They struggled to find work that was stable and financially and personally rewarding. For the few who did find employment, it was typically in the sectors associated with retail and food preparation.

We spent more than a year with these students and knew that many of them harbored aspirations of entry into Austin's expanding creative economy. They spent an extraordinary amount of time in school, after school, and with their peers cultivating their interests in digital media and the creative arts. Despite these efforts, pathways to careers in tech and media were simply not accessible to many of them. Freeway students typically suffered from two things. First, most did not have the human capital—that is, the education, training, and experience that typically facilitate entry into high-skilled and creative labor sectors. Second, most did not have the social capital—that is, the social networks and rich information channels that are also essential to finding good work.[46]

In addition to the skills identified above—expert thinking, ideation, complex communication—schools should labor to cultivate what might be called a "future-oriented disposition." This includes, for example, the ability to grapple smartly with uncharted problems and leverage technology to do novel things that are responsive to the shifting currents in society. Rather than develop the skills to find a job today, students will be better served cultivating a way of thinking and being that navigates the uncertainties *and* opportunities of tomorrow. Skills like these—design, problem solving, entrepreneurship, civic-mindedness—cannot be overestimated in a world shaped by accelerating changes and uncertainty. Finally, notice anything about these skills? Notably, these are not technology skills; they are thinking skills or skills that require cognitive nuance and the ability to create and apply ideas in novel ways.

Today's tech- and service-driven economy has been more than a century in the making. A presidential committee assigned by Lyndon B. Johnson in 1964 produced a memo that stated, in part, that the combination of computers and automated self-regulating machines would one day lead to mass unemployment. For more than fifty years social scientists have been examining social and economic trends as they forecast the "coming of postindustrial society," the reorganization of the occupational structure, and what this all means for the future of work, opportunity, mobility, and equity.[47] Still, schools have remained largely resistant to or incapable of designing classrooms, curricula, and learning experiences that are aligned with an economy that has developed a strong bias toward those persons that possess the skills to ask novel questions, engage in expert thinking, or master more complex forms of analysis and communication.

This is precisely the challenge that faces Freeway specifically and our nation's schools more generally. It is not simply that we have been unable to redesign education in alignment with a rapidly evolving world. There is no sustained effort to establish a new paradigm for schooling that effectively recalibrates what it means to be a learner, worker, or citizen in the world today.

As a result of our fieldwork and involvement with the MacArthur Foundation's Digital Media and Learning initiative, we are frequently asked what we would recommend to educators. Upon reflection, we would encourage educators to ask themselves these questions: Are we preparing our students to perform tasks in which humans maintain a distinct advantage over intelligent machines? Are we designing learning environments that encourage students to grapple with and solve uncharted problems? Are we training our students to ask novel questions? Are our students being taught to work with data, analyze data, recognize patterns, and interpret them in particular ways? Does our school understand that technology is a tool for solving problems and not the solution?

If the answer to these questions is no, then educators should begin rethinking their learning goals and curriculum. In short, they should begin to think carefully about what it means for students to be future ready.

Appendix

Design of the Study

Alexander Cho, Jacqueline Ryan Vickery,
Andres Lombana-Bermudez, and
S. Craig Watkins

When our Austin research team was initially designing the plan for the Digital Edge project as part of the MacArthur Foundation's Connected Learning Research Network, we considered this question: What would be the best way to produce an analysis of the daily lives, learning practices, and media behaviors of teens from resourced-constrained communities that was as comprehensive as possible? We were intrigued, for example, by a number of studies from the Kaiser Family Foundation, the Pew Research Center, and others that showed, for example, that black and Latino youth were *more* likely than their white counterparts to use the mobile Internet. Many of these were provocative survey-based quantitative information, but it left us wondering—what was the quality and character of this type of access? Far from celebrating the bridging of the digital divide, was it possible that this was, in fact, a new dimension of social, economic, and digital disparities? This was just one of many questions that we felt quantitative data on youth digital media practices left unanswered. And if we were going to marry youth digital media practices with their potential for rich informal and connected learning experiences, we were going to have to figure out how to understand and describe these practices in much greater detail.

We realized that two facets of the traditional ethnographic method would be invaluable to us: long time on task and nuanced qualitative data gathering. We wanted to pick up where the quantitative data left off. What were black, Latino, and lower-income teens doing with digital media, and how did the rapidly evolving world around them—widening social inequality, the new geography of poverty, and the spread of

Internet-enabled technologies—work to situate their engagement with digital media technologies? How did the precarious conditions of poverty and geographically induced racial and social isolation influence their schooling experiences, opportunities to learn, and acquisition of social capital? How did students navigate economic uncertainty (a parent losing a job) or a lifeline slipping away (a student forgoing college because it was too expensive)? Could we paint a picture of the daily lives, practices, opportunities, and challenges that youth in the digital edge experience in life and at school? And what, if any, is the potential or affordance of digital technology for these young people to create social and educational environments that develop the skills and literacies necessary to thrive in their transition to young adulthood?

Recruitment of Participants

One obvious question for our team is, how did we choose our sample? The short answer is that we do not necessarily have a sample; in fact, ethnography resists the idea of the "sample." Instead of speaking generally, ethnography generates specific stories that help us understand the lived experiences of certain people in a certain population, through nuance, detail, and time on task. In this way, we were able to gain insight into practices, spaces, and meanings that may help us understand how, in this instance, technology, digital participation, and learning are related in complex ways.

Mr. Lopez, the tech apps teacher and head of the digital media club and the CAP, initially helped us recruit participants. He introduced us to students from his classes who he thought might be interested in the project. We also held two recruitment meetings after school to explain the project goals and expected time commitment. We asked interested students to return the consent and assent forms (signed by a legal guardian) to Mr. Lopez. We also used a snowball approach wherein we asked students if they had any friends who they thought would like to participate. This allowed us to recruit more participants, some of whom were directly connected to the digital media classes and clubs, as well as friends who were less interested in digital media production. Because we expected access to students for the entire school year and beyond, we offered compensation as an incentive.

The participants included a total of nineteen students between the ages of fourteen and nineteen years old. We worked with nine female participants: Gabriela (sophomore, Mexican American), Jada (junior, black), Selena (senior, Mexican American), Jasmine (junior, black, white, and Native American), Amina (senior, east African), Cassandra (senior, black and white), Anna (senior, Mexican American), Inara (senior, Mexican American), and Michelle (senior, black and white). We worked with ten male students: Javier (senior, Mexican), Sergio, (senior, Mexican American), identical twins Miguel and Marcus (freshmen, Mexican American), Kyle (senior, white), Michael (senior, black), Antonio (senior, Mexican American), Diego (junior, Mexican American), and Alberto (senior, Mexican American). We also worked with an alumnus of Freeway who served as a mentor in the CAP, Nelson (twenty years old, black).

We also conducted interviews with the principal, school personnel, school district administrators, and school board members but worked most closely with Mr. Lopez, the head of the digital media club and the CAP, and Mr. Warren, the game design teacher.

Doing Ethnography

Classic ethnography involves participant observation and qualitative interviewing over a lengthy time period. In many respects, then, our approach certainly reflects elements of classic ethnography. We spent about a year and half at Freeway High School, hanging out and participating extensively in three classes, an after-school program designed to foster digital media production skills, and summer enrichment activities. As part of our fieldwork we engaged various aspects of school life. For instance, we attended sports events, music concerts, public-facing events like fund-raisers, and even graduation ceremonies. Our initial introduction to the school and its students was through a summer enrichment program that involved students making simple video games for a tech company.

Study participants were matched with a member of our research team based on common interests and similar demographics. For example, we matched female students with female researchers and when possible paired researchers and participants of similar ethnic identities.

Participants met one-on-one with a member from the research team on a weekly basis. The weekly meetings lasted anywhere from thirty minutes to an hour. Meetings usually took place in a school classroom, hallway, or lab after school. However, some weeks it was more convenient for students to meet us at a coffee shop, their home, or a restaurant. Because of transportation and time constraints for some students, we were flexible to meet them in a space that was accessible and comfortable for them. We conducted formal follow-up interviews with study participants through the summer and continue to be in touch with some through social media networks. S. Craig Watkins continues to be in touch with both Mr. Lopez and Mr. Warren.

One female participant dropped out of the study, and one male participant joined the study during the school year. However, all other participants met with their respective team members on a regular weekly basis for seven months. This allowed us time to build trust and a rapport with students.

With permission from the students and a legal guardian, all interviews were recorded for the purpose of transcriptions and data analysis. Initial interviews were informal and unstructured; they provided us opportunities to get to know students' interests and identities. However, over the course of several months, we developed twelve semistructured thematic interview protocols: (1) home life and routines, (2) school and learning, (3) peers and social groups, (4) social influence of adults, (5) risk, rules, and privacy, (6) pop culture and media, (7) mobile technologies, (8) social media, (9) experiences with the international film club (conducted only with students involved in the club), (10) online information seeking practices, (11) civic engagement, and (12) future plans and goals. Based on the goals of the project, some initial protocols were developed around specific overarching objectives (e.g., technology use, home life, educational goals and interests). Other protocols were developed as themes emerged over the course of the fieldwork (e.g., civic engagement, influential adults, future trajectories). The interviews were mostly semistructured conversations, and our primary goal was to listen and probe carefully.

The protocols provided topical organization for the researcher conducting the interview and ensured some thread of consistency for the purpose of analysis. However, all of the interviews were designed to be open-ended conversations with participants. This allowed all researchers the opportunity to tailor follow-up questions to students' interests, experiences, and answers. Additionally, there were weeks when we met with participants merely to catch up on their lives or follow up on earlier topics; these meetings were unstructured and individualized to each participant.

In total we conducted more than 230 interviews with students, teachers, administrators, and parents. This number does not include countless informal conversations we had with participants while we were in the after-school club or informally meeting with students and their friends before or after organized interviews. Because we spent a significant amount of time with students one-on-one, we feel confident that we built trusting and honest relationships with participants. This is also evidenced by their commitment to us; participants rarely canceled meetings and demonstrated deep levels of commitment to our research team. Some have even continued to stay in touch with us in the years following the initial fieldwork to update us on their lives, seek advice, or ask for a reference letter.

Focus Groups

We conducted three organized focus groups with some of the participants. Jacqueline Ryan Vickery coordinated the very first interview that we conducted during the school year, a focus group session in a computer lab after school. We provided paper, pens, and markers and asked participants to draw their favorite technology at that time (see chapter three). After they drew their favorite technology, the participants were asked to share their drawing with the group and talk about what they had selected and what it meant to them. In our second organized focus group we asked students to map the technology in their home. We drew samples of our own homes and technology to demonstrate what we meant by mapping technology in the home. Some participants drew only their bedroom, while others drew the entire house. After they finished their maps we asked questions about what media were included or not, who primarily used it, how long they had had it, and so on. The maps continued to evolve as students got ideas from other students while they shared their maps with everyone. Jacqueline Ryan Vickery and Vivian Shaw organized our final organized focus group, which was conducted with graduating seniors at the end of the school year. We asked them about their future goals and plans. They also reflected on their time at Freeway and the extent to which they felt prepared for life after high school. Several students brought friends along for this focus group session as well.

In addition to the organized focus groups, we met informally with participants and their friends after school. These meetings were typically not recorded (and thus not transcribed), but were captured through field notes. Meeting participants' friends provided additional insight into their peer groups, interests, personalities, and networks.

Participant-Generated Data

In an effort to empower the voices and contributions of our participants, we provided them with disposable cameras. We asked the teens to take pictures of anything they wanted throughout the week, explaining that we were particularly interested in life outside school, so time at home, with their friends, at work, using technology, and so on. Some students chose to use their camera phones in lieu of the disposable camera. After the photos were developed (or the participants sent us digital photos), we met one-on-one with our respective participants to discuss the photos. They told us what the photo was of, why they took it, what was going on that day, and so on. This provided another way for us to understand the nuances of their day-to-day lives beyond the walls of Freeway.

One of the interview themes was social media. During this meeting we asked students to provide us a glimpse of the social media platforms that they use. This was at the discretion of the students, but the majority felt comfortable showing us their profiles and networks. Because school policies blocked most social media sites, many of these interviews were conducted off campus at nearby coffee shops or restaurants. Some participants bypassed the school's filter on their phones or used proxy servers in the computer labs. The interviews were tailored to the specific platforms students used and provided a way for us to gain a more nuanced perspective of their peers, media culture, and networks.

While the drawing, mapping, photograph, and social media meetings were successful (that is, participants openly shared information and data with us), we attempted one strategy that largely failed. We asked students to maintain a journal about their technology use for one week. A few participants generated some notes, but the overwhelming majority did not complete this part of our project. Reflecting on this, we recognized that the assignment felt too much like homework and thus students resisted sharing information in this format.

In-Home Interviews

We also conducted at least one in-home interview with a parent, grandparent, or legal guardian for seventeen of the nineteen student participants. The purpose was twofold. First, we wanted to gain a richer understanding of the students' home lives. Second, we believed that it was important to include the perspectives of parents/guardians. The majority of the in-home interviews took place at the end of the fall semester and were conducted in English. Three of the in-home interviews were conducted in Spanish (Miguel and Marcus's parents, Antonio's parents, and Sergio's mother). The Spanish interviews were later translated and transcribed in English. The coordination of our Spanish interviews was led by Andres Lombana-Bermudez and Alexander Cho. In situations in which the student did not live with his or her parents or the parents were separated, we let the student choose which parent or guardian they wanted us to meet. While most interviews were conducted in the home of a parent(s), a small number of interviews were conducted at the home of a grandparent or legal guardian instead.

At the discretion of the interviewer and the parent, we were given a tour of the home. We were primarily interested in assessing the accessibility of media and technology available in the home. For example, were there computers and Internet access in the home? If so, where were computers located and how current was the hardware, software, and Internet connection? Were there televisions, books, video game consoles, and so on? Who had access to these goods, where were they located in the home, what condition were the items in, and did they appear to be used by parents or their kids? This information provided nuance and context to our interpretations and understandings of participants' media and literacy environments.

The interviews with the parent(s) or guardian(s) were typically 60–120 minutes. Some parent(s) and guardian(s) were more talkative and willing to share information than others. The interview protocol primarily focused on parents'/guardians' education, career, and familiarity with technology, perspectives about Freeway and education more generally, and their hopes and concerns for their child.

Transcriptions and Analysis

In most cases, interviews were recorded on mini digital recorders and then transcribed and uploaded to a cloud-based qualitative analysis program called Dedoose. Analysis involved reading and coding initial interviews and field notes to identify emergent themes and trends. The team often went back to participants to test hypotheses—that is, to check that what we observed matched participants' perspectives.

We created and coded excerpts according to a code tree developed by the team. This code tree was a result of multiple team meetings wherein we developed a hierarchical structure, including big-picture thematics such as "future orientation" or "learning," as well as finer-grained nested codes such as "peer learning" or "inequality." Often, excerpts were coded with more than one code, as they touched on many topics simultaneously, to facilitate ease in finding relevant data across different potential search queries. The coding process was iterative and required adjustments along the way, as data were continually collected over the course of the year at Freeway and as we began coding. The codes rendered data searchable and also allowed for the identification of trends and themes. From the more than 215 interviews, our team coded over 4,700 excerpts and applied codes to those excerpts over 17,000 times.

The team also developed an internal-facing Wordpress blog to house our own field notes. Team members posted a brief summary of each interview with their paired participant(s) on the blog as they went along, as well as posted free-form thoughts and field notes of spaces they observed and in which they participated. These blog posts were tagged by interview protocol as well as participant name. Because team members interviewed only their own paired students, this blog became crucial during the analysis phase of our work. More specifically, it allowed team members who were not familiar with other participants to get a picture of their lives and the context of each interview as a cross-reference to our interview data in Dedoose. Further, we used the blog to produce biographical sketches of each participant to further acquaint team members with study participants. After our initial data collection phase, we used the blog to write up short briefs that summarized specific interview protocols (such as "mobile" or "civic engagement") horizontally across all participants for easy reference and knowledge building.

The team employed a number of design-thinking techniques to help facilitate brainstorming, data analysis, and insight building. Exercises such as affinity mapping, stakeholder mapping, persona profiles, and concept posters deepened our learning and capacity to think critically and creatively.

The iterative design of the study and the data analysis was enhanced by a team that reflected a range of research and academic interests, including media studies, youth culture, race and ethnicity, queer studies, digital media, and social inequality. The team consisted of the following individuals:

Alexander Cho (Communication)
Bailey Cool (Communication)
Andres Lombana-Bermudez (Communication)
Jennifer Noble (School of Information)
Vivian Shaw (Sociology)
Jacqueline Ryan Vickery (Communication)
S. Craig Watkins (Communication)
Lauren Weinzimmer (Communication)
Adam Williams (Communication)

Participant Observation in the Classroom

We also spent considerable time in three technology classes. During the fall term (September–December) we closely observed and participated in the two advanced game design classes. In the spring term (January–June) we observed one of the advanced game design classes and Mr. Lopez's technology applications class. Data collection in each class consisted of mixed methods. For example, we routinely conducted observations of the students, teachers, practices, and learning environment. Two members of our research team, S. Craig Watkins and Jennifer Noble, conducted these observations.

After each class Watkins and Noble contributed field notes to a password-protected Google document. The notes were a combination of observations and reflections. For example, the researchers generated notes about some of the interactions that took place during each class. This included conversations between students, teacher and students, researchers and teachers, and researchers and students. These observations inspired reflections too. Thus, analysis was happening alongside data collection.

It was also common for Watkins and Noble to stay after class and compare notes and reflect on the day's class. The researchers also conducted formal and informal interviews with several students from the classes. Watkins and Noble began the interviews after they had been in the class and had the benefit of establishing a good rapport with students. These interviews often followed the protocols that we used for the students in the in-depth portion of the study. Thus, we spoke with students about a range of topics, including their academic disposition, social networks, and social media adoption and practices. Because of their deep embedment in the course, Watkins and Noble had access to ongoing informal conversations and quasi interviews that could range from a task that a student was working on to how a student felt about school or home life on a particular day. The researchers were quite intentional about observing the learning practices of students, degrees of academic engagement, and creative work performed in class. For example, when a student was working on character art for the game, Noble might sit next to him and observe his work flow. Along the way she might ask questions regarding the software he was using and his method for achieving a specific task.

The most instructive part of the classroom data collection came from the implementation of design-thinking principles with the students. As we note in chapter five, this approached dramatically altered our presence in the classroom and to some degree our involvement in the story that we tell. The project allowed us to work side by side with students. Rather than assuming a fly-on-the-wall status, we were intimately involved in the day-to-day life of the class. This generated several advantages. First, it broke down the researcher–study participant barrier that precludes the opportunity to connect in a more personal way. We worked with students by creating many of the design techniques used in class. This gave us a chance to see up close the potential power and influence of design thinking in secondary education.

Second, because we worked so closely with students we were able to connect with them in a more substantive way. Conversations about games, the class, or their project oftentimes bled into conversations about their lives at school and beyond. Consequently, it invited a deeper connection to students that transformed our insights and perspectives. Third, we gained a real perspective on the challenges that teachers and students face on the ground. Immersion into the life of these three classes taught us things that we never could have learned otherwise. Finally, our approach also meant that we were contributing to the environment by sharing our resources, which included, for example, expertise, technology, and support for the effort that the students demonstrated.

Participant Observation in the After-School Setting

During the period of the fieldwork, researchers conducted approximately seventy-plus hours of fieldwork in the after-school setting. One of the qualitative data collection methods used by the Digital Edge research team in the after-school setting was participant observation. The bulk of the data collection for the after-school activities was conducted by Andres Lombana-Bermudez and Adam Williams. Following the traditional stages of participant observation (Howell 1973), researchers first established rapport with the participants of the study, then immersed themselves in the field, recorded observations as field notes, and finally analyzed and organized the information gathered.[1] According to the types of participant observation described by James P. Spradley, the role of our researchers in the after-school setting was one of passive participants who functioned primarily as bystanders immersed in the spaces inhabited by students.[2] The main activities of the researchers included observations of the creative and digital media practices and social interactions among the students.

Researchers did not actively participate in the after-school activities, nor did they become members of the community. The students and the supervisors in the after-school setting recognized them as researchers from the University of Texas.

Because the CAP was so ambitious, the fieldwork stretched across multiple spaces. For instance, inside the school building the after-school program was split between two computer lab classrooms. Researchers spent time observing the activities in each classroom and also examined after-school activities in the cafeteria, the theater, the second floor hall, and two adjacent rooms to Mr. Lopez's classroom. The CAP also established opportunities to observe a variety of activities including film shoots, rehearsals, casting sessions, and film screenings. Some of the after-school activities took place in several locations around the Austin metropolitan area where students had the opportunity to shoot scenes, do public presentations, organize fund-raising events, and participate in educational conferences and local film industry events. Some members of the research team followed the participants of the study as they continued their after-school activities out of the school setting and were able to observe them in other locations.

The interviews conducted in the after-school setting were usually either informal or semistructured. On the one hand, informal interviews were conducted with the students who participated in the after-school activities.[3] The questions asked during these casual interviews were specifically related to the practices that students were doing in situ, did not follow a structured protocol, and were not audio recorded. The main purpose was to clarify some of the actions observed during fieldwork. The majority of these informal interviews happened inside the school, with few exceptions when researchers had the opportunity to observe after-school activities that developed outside of the school setting.

Researchers also conducted semistructured interviews in the two computer labs associated with the digital media after-school programs.[4] When conducting these interviews, researchers used the structured protocols discussed above that addressed specific topics. Researchers followed the protocols, but they also had the option of straying from the interview guide to engage in deeper conversations to develop a better understanding of the students' lives, learning ecologies, and media practices.

Ethnography in the Digital Edge

The abundance of good quantitative data about Freeway, the school district, this specific suburb, and the broader Austin metropolitan map paints a bleak picture for many of the students in our study. Indeed, as we found through our interactions with several students and the adults in their lives, Freeway students face obstacles that students from more resourced environments do not. However, were we to rely on only quantitative data, we would have surely missed the more subtle and dynamic aspects of life in the digital edge. Instead of viewing Freeway as a "low-performing" school that was "economically disadvantaged," we began to understand, instead, how the school setting and the resources available there—peers, relationships with adults, access to technology and creative informal learning ecologies—serve a critical and powerful role in the lives of students. For all of the problems with Freeway, one thing was clear from our time in the field: the school was the last, best chance for many students.

Ultimately, though the quantitative "big picture" may be somewhat bleak, ethnography, through long time on task and nuanced qualitative data gathering, allowed us the on-the-ground specificity that was necessary to understand the lived experience and contours of our young learners' lives with greater nuance. The statistics and predictive analytics that stigmatize some young people as "at-risk," "suspicious," or "oppositional to learning" miss the grit, ingenuity, and expertise that we regularly witnessed among Freeway students and their families.

Finally, it is our hope that richer ethnographic portraits of life in the digital edge can lead to greater insights, empathy, and purpose in the design of learning opportunities that are meaningful, relevant, and connected to our rapidly evolving world. Communities like Freeway deserve nothing less than that.

Notes

Foreword
1 President's Council of Advisors on Science and Technology (2010:p.10).
2 Ibid.
3 Ibid., p.80.

Introduction
1 Cowen (2013b).
2 Frey (2011).
3 Straubhaar et al. (2012).
4 Rideout, Foehr, and Roberts (2010); Lenhart (2015).
5 For more on the growing economic inequality in the United States, see, for example, Stiglitz (2012) and Shapiro (2017).
6 For an analysis of the relationship between geography and occupational opportunity, see, for example, Moretti (2012).
7 Straubhaar et al. (2012); Long (2010).
8 Chetty et al. (2014).
9 Ibid.
10 The researchers also compare intergenerational mobility patterns across the one hundred largest counties in the United States. How did Austin rank? When compared with a counterpart growing up in one of the hundred largest counties in the United States, a child growing up in a lower-income family in the Austin area has a relatively small chance of moving out of poverty. More precisely, Austin ranks in the lower third among the top one hundred counties on this metric. In the Austin area, a child growing up in a low-income family (twenty-fifth percentile) would earn 7.5 percent less by age twenty-six than a child growing up outside the Austin area in a household with a similar income.
11 Kneebone and Berube (2013).
12 Ibid. p.35.
13 During this period, the population in Austin increased 43 percent, making it one of the fastest-growing cities in the United States. To put that number in perspective, the U.S. population during the same span increased by less than 10 percent. However, the population in Austin's suburbs grew at a rate faster than that of the city. Whereas the city grew by 18 percent, the suburbs grew by 57 percent. The number of Austin's poor increased by 77 percent in the city and 143 percent in the suburbs. Roughly one-fifth of Austin's suburban poor population was foreign-born, suggesting greater racial and ethnic diversity and economic instability

too. According to the data compiled by Brookings, Atlanta was the only city that experienced more growth in suburban poverty than Austin during this period (Castillo 2013a; Castillo 2013b).

14 Frey (2014).

15 Austin Metro Area School District is a pseudonym.

16 The Austin Independent School District (AISD) saw its Asian/Pacific Islander and Latino student populations increase 59 percent and 40 percent, respectively. By contrast, the percentages of black and white students in the AISD decreased during this period, 26 percent and 19 percent, respectively.

17 Tang (2014).

18 The Texas Education Agency (2015) developed a formula for assessing the percentage of at-risk students who drop out of school. At-risk students include, for example, those who did not advance from one grade level to the next for one or more school years; did not perform well on an assessment instrument; are in pre-K, kindergarten, or grades 1, 2, or 3 and did not perform satisfactorily on a readiness test; are pregnant or are a parent; and are of limited English proficiency.

19 Carter (2005).

20 Massey and Denton (1993); Rothstein (2017).

21 Tyson (2011).

22 Musu-Gillette et al. (2016).

23 Houston Endowment (2012).

24 Wells and Lewis (2006).

25 Ibid.

26 U.S. Department of Commerce (1999).

27 Rideout, Foehr, and Roberts (2010); Watkins (2012); Lenhart (2015).

28 Rideout, Foehr, and Roberts (2010); Lenhart (2015).

29 Rideout, Foehr, and Roberts (2010).

30 For a consideration of the "participation gap" see Jenkins et al. (2009). For a consideration of both the "participation gap" and "digital literacy gap" see, Watkins (2012).

31 Warschauer (2003).

32 For more on the theory of racial formation, see Omi and Winant (2015). For more on the role of schools in reproducing social and economic inequality, see, for example, Bowles and Gintis (2011).

33 Pope (2001).

34 Fordham and Ogbu (1986).

35 For more on how black student expressions of cultural capital lead to discipline and low academic performance, see, for example, Carter (2005). For an examination of the racial disparities in how schools discipline students, see, for example, U.S. Department of Commerce (2014).

36 Tyson (2011).

37 Angel Harris (2011).

38 Ito et al. (2013).

39 Ibid.
40 Kaushal, Magnuson, and Waldfogel (2011).
41 Rideout, Foehr, and Roberts (2010); Lenhart (2015).
42 Kantor and Tyack (1982).
43 Tyner (1998).
44 U.S. Department of Commerce (2014).
45 Barron et al. 2014.
46 Partnership for 21st Century Skills (2008); Jenkins et al. (2009).

Chapter 1. How Black and Latino Youth Are Remaking the Digital Divide

1 See, for example, Rideout, Foehr, and Roberts (2010); Lenhart (2015).
2 Rideout (2015).
3 U.S. Department of Commerce (1999).
4 Pew Research Center (2015).
5 For more on the condition of poverty in suburban communities, see, for example, Kneebone and Berube (2013).
6 Ito et al. (2010).
7 For a study of teens and instant messaging, see Stern (2007). For an examination of teens and their adoption of social media, see, for example, Watkins (2009); Ito et al. (2010); and Boyd (2014).
8 Jenkins et al. (2016) consider how the terrain of youth political practice is evolving in relation to a changing media and technology landscape. Their case studies examine how young people are using a mix of media, participatory culture, and content creation practices to produce political media, mobilize for political action, and remake the civic imagination. Jenkins et al. (2016) counter the shortsighted view that political acts that leverage social media are largely passive, soft, low-risk, and disengaged (Gladwell 2010). In a survey of nearly three thousand young people ages fifteen to twenty-five, political scientists Cathy Cohen and Joseph Kahne (2012) found that a surging number of young people are engaging in what they call "participatory politics." This includes, for example, writing a blog, using networked technologies to reach and mobilize large audiences, and producing content (e.g., blogs, video) and creative opportunities (e.g., poetry slams) that engage issues of public concern. Among other things, participatory politics are driven by the creative use of technology to circumvent traditional political influencers including the news media and political parties. Further, the use of networked technologies has the potential to scale the communication and mobilization efforts of individuals and communities in unprecedented ways (e.g., #BlackLivesMatter).
9 Rideout and Watkins (Forthcoming).
10 For more on "tool literacy," see Tyner (1998).
11 Kress (2003), Hargittai and Hinnant (2008).
12 For a mix of perspectives on information literacy and its relationship to digital media and digital literacy, see, for example, Lankshear Knobel (2008).

13 U.S. Department of Commerce (2014).
14 Ibid., 16.
15 Brown and Thomas (2006).
16 Wells and Lewis (2006).
17 Ibid., 2.
18 Ibid., 16.
19 Ibid.
20 EducationSuperHighway (2015).
21 U.S. Department of Education (2013).
22 A. Smith (2012).
23 Ibid., 5.
24 Pew Latino Center 2009.
25 Lenhart (2015).
26 Watkins (2009); Ito et al. (2010); boyd (2014).
27 Lenhart (2015).
28 Jenkins et al. (2009, 3).
29 For a social-scientific exploration of teens and popular music, see, for example, Christenson and Roberts (1998).
30 For a consideration of the creative interactions between digital technologies and hip hop culture, see, for example, Watkins (2005).
31 Sisario (2014).
32 For more on youth, music, and subcultural capital, see, for example, Thornton (1996).
33 Straubhaar et al. (2012).
34 Madden et al. (2013, 21–22).
35 Ibid.
36 Ibid.
37 Rogers (1995).
38 For perspectives on Black Twitter as a pop culture and political force, see, for example, Watkins (2017).
39 For a discussion of social media and ambient awareness, see, for example, Thompson (2008); for the role of social media in maintaining social ties, see, for example, Ellison, Steinfield, and Lampe (2009).
40 Lopez, Gonzalez-Barrera, and Patten (2013).
41 For more on how Latino children use technology to broker familial engagement with the outside world, see, for example, Katz (2014).
42 Ibid.
43 Rideoout (2015).

Chapter 2. The Mobile Paradox
 1 For more on mobile phones as a source of status, personal expression, and identity construction, see Ling (2004).

2 Between 1999 and 2010 the Kaiser Family Foundation conducted three national surveys (Roberts, Foher, and Rideout 1999), (Roberts, Foher, and Rideout 2005), (Rideout, Foher, and Roberts 2010) that tracked the media environment of children eight to eighteen years old in the United States. While virtually all forms of media consumption increased between 1999 and 2010, young people's shift to mobile devices was both historical and decisive. In 1999 Kaiser did not track young people's ownership of personal devices and handhelds, likely because it was not common for a ten-year-old in the United States to own a phone or an iPod. In 2004, 18 percent of young people surveyed by Kaiser owned an iPod/MP3 player compared with 76 percent in 2009. Whereas 12 percent of youth owned a laptop in 2004, nearly 30 percent (29 percent) owned one in 2009. And in that five-year period, mobile phone ownership among teens grew from four in ten (39 percent) to nearly two-thirds (66 percent).

3 Lenhart (2009).

4 Lenhart (2015).

5 Lenhart et al. (2010).

6 Madden et al. (2013, 7).

7 Ibid.

8 Ibid., 9.

9 For research on how teens use mobile to negotiate the spatial dynamics and their relationship to adults, see, for example, Ito and Matsuda (2005); for teen mobile global adoption trends, see, for example, Castells et al. (2007), Ling and Bertel (2013); for a consideration of teen identity practices and mobile, see, for example, Ling (2008); for teen mobile phone practices and gender, see, for example, Ling et al. (2014).

10 Watkins (2012).

11 Madden et al. (2013, 4).

12 Ibid.

13 Horrigan (2009).

14 Ibid., 16.

15 Ibid., 19.

16 Madden et al. (2013, 6).

17 U.S. Department of Commerce (2014, 11).

18 Horrigan (2009, 33).

19 Ibid., 35.

20 Ibid.

21 U.S. Department of Commerce (2014).

22 Crawford (2013).

23 Roberts et al. (1999).

24 Rideout (2015).

25 Rideout, Foehr, and Roberts (2010, 2).

26 Rideout (2015, p. 18).

27 Rideout, Foehr, and Roberts (2010).

28 Ibid., 18.

29 Ibid., 19.

30 Nielsen Media Research (2013).

31 Bourdieu (1984).

32 Ling (2004).

33 For instance, owing to intense academic pressures and workloads, participation in various extracurricular activities, and the hypercompetitive race for admissions into select colleges and universities, youth in higher-income households have very little free or unstructured time in their daily schedules. This is the "overscheduled" syndrome that has been a source of increased public debate. For more on the disparities in enrichment activities between youth from lower-income families and youth from higher-income families, see, for example, Kaushal, Magnuson, and Waldfogel (2011). The lower levels of mobile media consumption among youth in higher-income households compared with youth in lower-income households are not because of disinterest. Rather, they simply may not have significant blocks of time to devote to media consumption. By contrast, many youth in lower-income households are less likely to face heavy academic loads or overscheduled lives outside of school, thus creating more free and leisure time in their daily schedules.

34 Greenberg and Dominick (1969).

35 Watkins (2009).

36 Johnson, Adams, and Cummins (2012, 16).

37 Johnson, Adams, and Haywood (2011).

38 Lenhart et al. (2008).

39 For examples of how the poor leverage social networks and design informal economies in the face of social and economic inequalities, see Stack (1974); R. Kelley (1997); Venkatesh (2006).

40 Stack (1974).

41 Ibid., 43.

42 Ibid., 44.

43 Madden et al. (2013).

Chapter 3. Technology on the Edge of Formal Education

1 Murphy and Lebans (2008); Kalmus, Runnel, and Siibak (2009); Watkins (2009); Livingstone (2009); Lange and Ito (2010).

2 Finkelhor (2011); Livingstone (2009); Vickery (2017).

3 Van't Hooft (2007).

4 Vickery (2012, 2017).

5 Livingstone (2009); Marwick (2008); Vickery (2017).

6 Katz (2006); Kolb (2008).

7 Taylor (2005, 163).

8 De Certeau (1984); O'Brien (2009, 34).

9 O'Brien (2009, 38).

10 Jenkins (2006); Lessig (2008).
11 Ison et al. (2004); Parker (2010).
12 Dourish et al. (1996).
13 Feldman (1984, 47).
14 Cramer and Hayes (2010).
15 Rheingold (2012).
16 Fabos (2004, 95).
17 Schofield and Davidson (2002).
18 Hobbs (2017).
19 Rheingold (2012).
20 Frechette (2006, 170).
21 Achterman (2005); Morrissette (2008).
22 Sormunen, Lehtio, and Heinstrom (2011, 1).
23 Glott, Schmidt, and Ghosh (2010).
24 Lavin (2016).
25 Fabos (2004).
26 Hammond and Lee (2009).
27 Jones and Cuthrell (2011).
28 Ally (2009, 1).
29 Jenkins (2009).
30 Chau (2010).
31 During a home interview with Selena she played several songs on her keyboard, which she had taught herself to play by watching YouTube videos of other people playing the songs.

Chapter 4. The STEM Crisis in Education

1 Seely-Brown (2012).
2 Oakes (2005).
3 Ibid., 94.
4 Ibid., 94.
5 During our fieldwork the Texas Education Agency (2012) used the Texas Essential Knowledge and Skills system for Technology Applications to establish a set of uniform standards to guide education and classroom instruction for courses related to game design.
6 Margolis et al. (2008).
7 Several states including Texas, Montana, New Mexico, Kentucky, Florida, and Michigan have considered bills that would let credits from computer coding courses count as a foreign language requirement (Zubrzycki 2016).
8 For more on the low number of black and Latino students taking the AP exam in computer science, see, for example, Ericson (2017); Watkins and Vasudevan (2017).
9 Time-on-task is influenced by several factors, including, for instance, instructional time in the classroom, time to work on tasks that support proficiency, and attendance.

10 Oakes (2005, 94).

11 For an examination of "out-of-field teaching," see, for example, Ingersoll (2003).

12 Naruto is a Japanese manga series about an adolescent ninja seeking recognition from his peers.

13 Hidi and Renninger (2006, 12).

14 Ibid., 14.

15 Hidi and Renninger (2006) cite several studies that consider the relationship between a well-developed individual interest and modeling, innovative task organization, and expert or peer feedback that encourages students to maintain attention and grow more curious and competent about an interest.

16 Ibid., 115.

17 Ibid., 112.

18 Jenkins et al. (2009).

19 Ibid., 19.

20 Ibid.

21 Schell (2015).

22 For more on the role of social capital and social networking in creative economies, see, for example, Currid (2007); Neff (2012).

23 See Fayer, Lacey, and Watson (2017, 6); Langdon et al. (2011).

24 Langdon et al. (2011).

25 Fayer, Lacey, and Watson (2017, 10).

26 Ibid.

27 Langdon et al. (2011, 1).

28 Ibid., 5.

29 Levy and Murnane (2004).

30 Ibid.

31 Levy and Murnane (2013).

32 Xue and Larson (2015).

33 Langdon et al. (2011, 6).

34 Rothwell (2013).

35 Ibid.

36 Central Texas Middle School is a pseudonym.

37 These college- and career-ready statistics were based on ACT's extensive database of course grade and test score data from a sizable number of first-year students and across a wide range of postsecondary schools. These data, ACT posits, provide a strong measure of what it takes to be successful in selected first-year college courses.

38 West Hills is a pseudonym, although the data describing the school are real.

39 After examining the 2010 Census data, the *Washington Post* did an analysis of the country's highest-income and highest-educated zip codes (Mellnik and Morello 2013). The *Post*'s analysis shows intense segmentation as the residential concentration of income wealth and high educational attainment increases.

40 Attending a school in which more than three-quarters of the students meet college- and career-readiness benchmarks in STEM-related disciplines has many advantages. First, it means that the percentage of students who can potentially pursue postsecondary education in a STEM field is notably higher compared with schools with a low percentage of students who meet college- and career-readiness benchmarks. Second, West Hills is marked, more generally, by high academic achievement, which is a basic requisite for future opportunity at the four-year college level. In contrast, students at Central Texas Middle School were much more likely to attend a school in which only a small percentage of students were on track to pursue a four-year college degree.

41 Garcia (2015).

42 Yeung and Pfeiffer (2009).

43 Golding and Katz (2008) maintain that the rise in economic inequality over the last three decades or so is due, in large measure, to a slowing rate of educational attainment that has not kept pace with technological change and the surging demand for more high-skilled workers.

44 Kena et al. (2016, 179)

45 Ibid.

46 National Student Clearinghouse (2016).

47 For more on the racial disparities in STEM degree attainment, see Rodriguez et al. (2012). Moreover, the low number of STEM degrees awarded to Latino, black, and American Indian students is even more troubling when you consider the rising number of these students enrolling in postsecondary education. In 1980, roughly 30 percent of Latino students were enrolled in college compared with 46 percent in 2012. About 28 percent of black students were enrolled in college in 1980. By 2012 this percentage grew to 43 percent. Between 2006 and 2012 the percentage of students enrolled in college grew substantially for Latinos and marginally for blacks, while declining for whites.

48 In 1971 there was a sizable gap in STEM aspirations between white students and their black and Latino counterparts. In the late 1980s trends in STEM aspiration by race and ethnicity began to converge. By 2009, underrepresented minorities were just as likely as whites and Asian Americans to aspire to major in STEM (Higher Education Research Institute 2010).

49 Papastergiou (2008).

50 Watkins (2014).

51 Hickey (2018). After the success of the movie and the comments referencing the portrayal of a black woman in STEM the film's distributor, Disney, announced that it was donating $1 million of the box office receipts to support STEM education in underrepresented communities Bromwich (2018).

52 The reasons for the low representation of blacks and Latinos in the technology sector are, not surprisingly, multifaceted and complex and can be best explained by a combination of factors that are internal and external to tech companies.

Internally, for example, tech companies have practiced limited recruiting, which influences the type of tech talent they are most likely to hire. Since the release of their workforce data, companies like Google and Facebook have extended their recruitment of STEM talent to historically black colleges and universities. Another internal factor is the practice of unconscious bias, which often influences who is hired and promoted. Externally, the biggest challenge is the inadequate academic preparation among lower-income students. For an exploration of how these and other factors contribute to the diversity crisis in tech, see, for example, Watkins and Vasudevan (2017).

53 Wacquant and Wilson (1989).

54 For more on the role of social networks and occupational mobility, see, for example, Granovetter (1995); DiTomaso (2013).

55 Levy and Murnane (2004).

56 Cuban (1986).

Chapter 5. Gaming School

1 Institute of Play (2014).

2 For examples of the research on games and violence, see Kutner and Olson (2008); Anderson, Gentile, and Buckley (2007); for games and racism see Everett and Watkins (2008); for games and sexism see Dill (2007); Dill, Brown, and Collins (2008).

3 Granic, Lobel, and Engels (2014).

4 For games and experiential learning, see Gee (2007b for problem solving, see Adachi and Willoughby (2013); for creativity, see Jackson et al. (2012); for persistence, see Ventura, Shute, and Zhao (2013); for cooperation, support, and helping behaviors, see Ewoldsen et al. (2012), and for Motivation, see Barab et al. (2005); Yee (2007).

5 Kahne, Middaugh, and Evans (2009).

6 For more on the exploration of play, see Salen and Zimmerman (2003); Jenkins et al. (2009).

7 Partnership for 21st Century Skills (2008); Gee and Hayes (2010).

8 Gee, Hull, and Lankshear (1996).

9 Gee (2007a, 207); diSessa (2000).

10 Bogost (2011, 7).

11 Ibid., 8.

12 Ito et al. (2013, 74).

13 Hutchins (1996).

14 Jenkins et al. (2009).

15 Ibid.

16 Levy (2000).

17 Katz and Wagner (2014).

18 Barker and Aspray (2006); Blickenstaff (2005).

19 Indeed, many designers make the case that design—a term used to describe the process of inquiry lead problem solving and innovation—is too important of a skill to be left to designers. The design consultancy IDEO (2012) has been working with educators to integrate design thinking in ways that reimagine how teachers teach and students learn. Emily Pilloton's Project H introduces socially engaged design thinking to high school students. For more on her work, see Pilloton (2010).

20 Pacione (2010, 11).

21 Centers for Disease Control and Prevention (2013).

22 Hart and Kirshner (2009, 107).

23 Pacione (2010).

24 Facer (2011).

25 Texas Education Agency (2012).

26 Ibid.

27 Ibid.

28 Ibid.

29 The initial business strategy followed the "Freemium" model, which is a popular form of Internet commerce. GameSalad allowed users to download the platform for free, which also provided access to its game making software. The company's vision was to convert users who wanted to publish their games on Apple's operating system into paying customers. To grow its revenue, the company changed its model and now offers different tiers of service, including a basic software package, a professional version, and different packages for educators.

30 In addition to Apple's iOS, the update of the GameSalad platform allows game makers to publish to a variety of operating systems including Google's Android, Microsoft, and Amazon Prime.

31 Boekaerts, Pintrich, and Zeidner (2000); Pintrich and Zusho (2002).

32 Zumbrunn, Tadlock, and Roberts (2011).

33 Ibid.

34 Ibid., 5.

35 Labuhn, Zimmerman, and Hasselhorn (2010).

36 Clarebout, Horz, and Schnotz (2010).

37 Harris (2011).

Chapter 6. After the Bell

1 Jencks and Phillips (1998); Rothstein (2004); Barton and Coley (2010); Harris (2011).

2 For research on the effects of early childhood learning gaps, see Duncan and Magnuson (2011). For the lack of resources or quality of instruction in low-performing schools, see Oakes (2005). For the legacy of tracking in schools see Oakes (2005); Tyson (2011).

3 Kaushal, Magnuson, and Waldfogel (2011).

4 Ibid. From 1972 to 1973, for instance, affluent families spent roughly $2,700 more per year on enrichment opportunities for their children than their low-income counterparts. By 2005 the expenditure gap had virtually tripled as high-income families spent about $7,500 more per year than lower-income families (Duncan and Murnane 2011, 11).

5 Kaushal, Magnuson, and Waldfogel (2011).

6 Ibid.

7 Garey Ramey and Valerie A. Ramey (2010) found that while both college-educated and non-college-educated parents, especially mothers, have increased the amount of time that they devote to child care, the increases among college-educated parents are more than double that of non-college-educated parents. Most of the added time spent on child care was devoted to chauffeuring or driving kids from one extracurricular activity to the next. The two researchers write, "It appears that college-educated parents with children aged 5 or over spend a good deal of their time on education and on children's organized activities" (143).

8 Ibid.

9 Friedman (2013).

10 One of the more notable investments that we noticed among nearly all of the parents in our sample was the decision to move their families into the Austin MASD. They viewed this as an opportunity to expose their children to better educational opportunities.

11 Alexander, Entwisle, and Olson (2001).

12 In her study of childhood inequality, Lareau (2003) argues that children who have access to enrichment activities gain noteworthy benefits through their engagement with adult forms of institutional authority.

13 For the students interested in digital media production, the CAP and games-based activities provided an opportunity to tinker with technology in more creative and interest-powered ways. Moreover, the after-school activities that we observed established a rich context for developing the kinds of skills and dispositions that are rarely developed in the traditional school setting, including, for example, leadership, communication, independent thinking, and self-regulation.

14 Halpern (2003).

15 Lin (2001).

16 Lin (2001, 43).

17 Portes (1998, 7).

18 Stanton-Salazar and Dornbusch (1995).

19 Lin (2001).

20 Schools occupy very different social positions according to geography, recruitment and maintenance of experienced teachers, and social, curricular, and financial resources. Further, the resources of the wider community—most notably the parents, families, and institutions associated with the school—may provide access to additional assets.

21 Lin (2001).

22 Lin (2001, 95).

23 Stanton-Salazar and Dornbusch (1995).

24 Lin (2001, 65).

25 These two elements reflect the ongoing debates about school-based extracurricular activities and the extent to which these should be spaces that are primarily powered by student interests and peer-to-peer relations or an activity that generates some noteworthy academic/vocational outcomes that are at least partially shaped by the vision that adults set for after-school experience (Halpern 2003).

26 The lab also had an equipment room with lighting kits, green screens, tripods, microphones, boom poles, sound recorders, midi keyboards, headphones, laptops, and several HD video and digital single-lens reflex cameras. Furthermore, and specifically for the activities of the CAP, the lab was upgraded with professional filmmaking gear, such as a dolly, a jib, and a fake rig, donated by a local media company.

27 For more on the theory of constructionism, see, for example, Harel and Papert (1991).

28 It is notable here as well that both girls share Latino ethnicity and went on to a postsecondary institution after graduating high school. According to a Pew Latino Center's study (Fry and Taylor 2013 a milestone was reached in 2012. The study reports that: "A record seven-in-ten (69%) Latino high school graduates in the class of 2012 enrolled in college that fall, two percentage points higher than the rate (67%) among their white counterparts" (Fry and Taylor 2013, 4). This enrollment in higher education for Latino youth (though not broken down by gender) is notable, but the report also notes: "Young Latino college students are less likely than their white counterparts to enroll in a four-year college (56% versus 72%), they are less likely to attend a selective college, less likely to be enrolled in college full time, and less likely to complete a bachelor's degree" (Fry and Taylor 2012, 4–5).

29 According to the Texas Education Agency (2008), students who are at risk for dropping out are those who have limited English proficiency, have been expelled during the previous or current year, are pregnant or a parent, were not advanced from one grade level to the next for one or more school years, have been placed in an alternative education program, or are homeless.

30 Latina young adults have come far in the past four decades. "In 1970, 77% of Latinos ages 16 to 25 were either working, going to school or serving in the military; by 2007, 86% of Latinos in this coming-of-age group were taking part in these skill-building endeavors" (Fry 2009, i). Even so, "nearly one-in-five (19%) female Latino young adults in 2007 were not in school or in the work force" (Fry 2009, ii). Part of this 19 percent can be accounted for by teen pregnancy. "Birthrates among young Latino women are higher than those of whites or blacks, but these rates have been falling for decades" (Fry 2009, ii).

31 Anita Harris (2004, 15).

32 Bettie (2003).

33 Research suggests that high-performing, lower-income students are significantly less likely to enroll in a selective college or university compared with their high-performing, higher-income counterparts. These students have performed well in school, test well, and show signs of leadership and initiative. Still, when it comes to the recruitment process, elite colleges and universities often overlook or simply are unable to reliably find these students. For more on this topic, see, for example, Hoxby and Avery (2012).

34 Bettie (2003).

35 Over the course of our study, several Latino students noted that teachers and schools held low academic expectations for them dating back to their initial entry into public schooling. These low expectations and poor academic outcomes are compounded by statistics that consistently report that Latino youth are more likely than other students to drop out of high school: "The high school dropout rate among Latino youths (17%) is nearly three times as high as it is among white youths (6%) and nearly double the rate among blacks (9%). Rates for all groups have been declining for decades" (Pew Latino Center 2009).

36 The most common reason why Latino youth note that they do not pursue higher education is that they need to support their families (Pew Latino Center 2009b). Inara is privileged in that this common cause for not pursuing postsecondary education was not an intervening factor in her life, though the financial implications of her decision to move to Los Angeles did affect her family and her personal financial situation via the debt she incurred.

37 For more on the concept of connected learning, see Ito et al. (2013).

38 Stanton-Salazar and Dornbusch (1995).

39 Ibid.

40 Lin (2001).

41 Marsh and Kleitman (2002).

42 Ibid.

43 Ibid., 508.

44 U.S. Department of Education Office for Civil Rights (2014).

45 Mahoney and Cairns (1997).

46 Marsh (1992).

47 Fin (1989).

48 Marsh and Kleitman (2002).

49 Alexander, Entwisle, and Olson (2001).

50 Sum et al. (2009).

51 Balfanz and Legters (2004).

52 Marsh (1992).

Chapter 7. Dissonant Futures

1 For a discussion of "de facto" tracking, see Lucas (1999); for "laissez-faire" tracking, see Tyson (2011).

2 See Oakes (2005).

3 Ibid., 3.

4 Grant (1991).

5 For more on the origins of tracking, see Oakes (2005); Lucas (1999).

6 Oakes (2005, 31).

7 Grant (1991); Dickens (1995).

8 Grant (1991).

9 Ibid., 299.

10 Lucas (1999).

11 National Education Association (1990).

12 Lucas (1999, 131).

13 Tyson (2011).

14 Lucas (1999, 132).

15 Wheelock and Massachusetts Advocacy Center (1992, 9).

16 Ibid. (1992, 6).

17 Oakes (2005, 43).

18 Horn and Carroll (2006); Carnevale and Strohl (2013).

19 Stanton-Salazar and Dornbusch (1995).

20 Stanton-Salazar and Dornbusch (1995, 117).

21 Erickson (2003).

22 Lareau (2000).

23 Harris (2011).

24 See Christakis and Fowler (2009) for a data-driven analysis of the social contagion aspects of social networks.

25 Stanton-Salazar and Dornbusch (1995, 117).

26 Lucas (1999, 132).

27 Alexander, Entwisle, and Olson (2001).

28 Kaushal, Magnuson, and Waldfogel (2011).

29 Lin (1999, 483).

30 Ibid.

31 Merton (1968).

Conclusion

1 Aud, Fox, and KewalRamani (2010).

2 McFarland et al. (2017).

3 Frey (2011).

4 McFarland (2017).

5 Ibid.

6 For example, between 2007 and 2013, the high school graduation rates in Texas
increased significantly. In 2007, the graduation rate was 78 percent compared
with 88 percent in 2013. The graduation rate for black students improved to 84
percent from 71 percent during that same period. Among Latino students, the rate
improved from 69 percent in 2007 to 85 percent in 2013. While the rates improved

for all racial and ethnic groups, Asian (94 percent) and white (93 percent) graduation rates remained higher. Texas Education Agency (2014).

7   Dietz (2014); M. Smith (2014).

8   AP courses are expected to provide advanced academic instruction beyond or
in greater depth than the essential knowledge and skills required for the equiva-
lent high school courses in subjects such as math, English language arts, and
science. The state defines college-ready graduates as meeting or exceeding the
college-ready criteria on the Texas Assessment of Knowledge and Skills exit-level
test, the SAT test, or the ACT test. For more details on how the state measures
college readiness, see Texas Education Agency (2015).

9   While we do not have specific data on the college attainment rates of Freeway
students, a study of statewide higher-education credentialing patterns offers some
insight. In 2012 the Houston Endowment, a philanthropic foundation committed to supporting education, examined statewide data to determine how many
of Texas's eighth-grade students achieved a postsecondary certificate or degree
within six years of their expected high school completion date. The study notes
that it "provides a straightforward measure of Texas' success in producing well-
educated young people" (Houston Endowment 2012, 1). Specifically, researchers
looked at 883,260 public school students who started eighth grade between 1996
and 1998. Only one out of five eighth-grade students, or 19 percent, achieved a
postsecondary credential within six years of finishing high school. There were
sharp gender and racial disparities in higher-education achievement. For example, female eighth-grade students in Texas were much more likely than their
male counterparts to have earned a higher-education credential within six years
of completing high school. Twenty-four percent of female students earned a
credential compared with 16 percent of male eighth graders. The racial disparities
were even more pronounced. Forty-one percent of Asian American students and
28 percent of white students earned a credential. Native American (14 percent),
Latino (12 percent), and black students (11 percent) were much less likely to earn a
higher-education credential.

When researchers disaggregated the data, the racial and gender disparities
were especially alarming for Latino and black males. Among all eighth-grade
students in the state of Texas, Latino (9 percent) and black (8 percent) males are
the least likely to earn a postsecondary credential after high school completion.
The researchers write, "In light of the tremendous growth in Texas' young Latino
population, it will be difficult for the state's overall completion rates to improve
without special efforts to elevate the success rates of all students and of these boys
in particular" (Houston Endowment 2012, 6).

10 During that period, college enrollment among those aged eighteen to twenty-four
increased 240 percent among Latinos, 72 percent among blacks, and 12 percent
among whites. The census did not publish Asian college enrollment figures before
1999 (Krogstad and Fry 2014).

11   To get a perspective on how wide the racial gap is in terms of college degree at-
     tainment, consider the following trends reported by the Musu-Gillette et al. (2016).
     Between 2002–2003 and 2012–2013, bachelor's degrees awarded to Latinos and
     blacks increased, respectively, 110 and 54 percent. By contrast, bachelor's degrees
     awarded to Asian/Pacific Islanders increased by 48 percent, while degrees
     awarded to whites increased by 23 percent. However, the total share of bachelor's
     degrees awarded to whites was 69 percent compared with 11 percent for both
     Latinos and blacks. Latinos and African Americans make up about 17 and 13 per-
     cent, respectively, of the total U.S. population. Though they represent only about
     6 percent of the total population, Asian/Pacific Islanders were awarded 7 percent
     of the share of bachelor's degrees. Even as the pace of black and Latino college
     degree attainment increased during the first decade of the new millennium, their
     rates still fell far below the attainment rates of whites. See also Casselman (2014).

12   Casselman (2014).

13   Jones and Schmitt (2014).

14   Bureau of Labor Statistics (2016).

15   For comparisons in rates of employment by education, see, for example, Taylor,
     Fry, and Oates (2014).

16   For more on social networks and social contagion, see Christakis and Fowler
     (2009).

17   Taylor, Fry, and Oates (2014).

18   James (2012).

19   In 1979, 7 percent of young adults with only a high school degree lived below the
     poverty line. In 2013, 22 percent of young adults with only a high school diploma
     in hand lived below the poverty line. See Taylor, Fry, and Oates (2014).

20   See Margolis et al. (2008).

21   Rifkin (1996).

22   The ability of technological advances to transform the work that people do is not
     unique to the new millennium. No technologically induced economic transfor-
     mation was more profound in U.S. history than the shift from a predominantly
     agricultural-based economy to an industrial-based economy (Bell 1973). In 1850
     more than six in ten U.S. workers (65 percent) were employed as farmers or farm
     laborers. Roughly one hundred years later, in 1952, more than half (53 percent) of
     U.S. workers were in service-producing industries, and about one in ten (11 percent)
     were in the agriculture sector. In less than half of a century, technological trans-
     formation—in this case the mechanization of farming—transformed the very
     core of American life by changing what people did for work (laboring on farms to
     laboring in factories) and where people worked (a move from rural areas to urban
     areas). Rather than put people out of work, technological advances transformed
     the kind of work that people did.

23   Kelley (2012).

24   Brynjolfsson and McAfee (2011).

25 Bowles and Giles (2012).

26 Autor, Katz, and Krueger (1997).

27 Golding and Katz (2008).

28 Levy and Murnane (2004).

29 Brynjolfsson and McAfee (2014).

30 Ibid, 192.

31 Levy and Murnane (2004).

32 U.S. Bureau of Labor Statistics (2017, 5).

33 Ibid, 5.

34 Beaudry, Green, and Sand (2016).

35 Sum et al. (2014).

36 Ford (2015, xvi).

37 Ford (2015).

38 For an exploration of white-collar sweatshops, see Fraser (2001); for precarious white-collar labor, see Ross (2009); and for cognitive stratification, see M. Crawford (2009).

39 For a more detailed analysis of the wage and job growth trend, see, for example, National Employment Law Project (2014).

40 Bell (1973).

41 Robinson and Aronica (2015).

42 Cowen (2013a).

43 McKinsey & Company (2017, 2).

44 Susskind and Susskind (2015).

45 For more on the relationship between social class, geography, and intergenerational mobility, see Chetty and Hendren (2017).

46 There is an extensive literature on the relationship between social networks and employment. Mark Granovetter's "strength of weak ties" argument is a widely cited example. For an extensive elaboration of this perspective, see Granovetter (1995).

47 Bell (1973); Harvey (1990).

Appendix. Design of the Study

1 Howell (1973).

2 Spradley (1980).

3 Bernard (1994).

4 Ibid.

References

Achterman, D. 2005. "Surviving Wikipedia: Improving Student Search Habits through Information Literacy and Teacher Collaboration." *Knowledge Quest* 33 (5): 38–40.

Adachi, Paul, and Teena Willoughby. 2013. "More Than Just Fun and Games: The Longitudinal Relationships between Strategic Video Games, Self-Reported Problem Solving Skills, and Academic Grades." *Journal of Youth and Adolescence* 42: 1041–1052.

Alexander, Karl L., Doris R. Entwisle, and Linda S. Olson. 2001. "Schools, Achievement, and Inequality: A Seasonal Perspective." *Educational Evaluation and Policy Analysis* 23, no. 2 (Summer): 171–191.

Ally, Mohamed. 2009. *Mobile Learning: Transforming the Delivery of Education and Training*. Edmonton, AB: AU Press.

Anderson, Craig A., Douglas A. Gentile, and Katherine E. Buckley. 2007. *Violent Video Game Effects on Children and Adolescents: Theory, Research, and Public Policy*. New York: Oxford University Press.

Aud, Susan, Mary Ann Fox, and Angelina KewalRamani. 2010. *Status and Trends in the Education of Racial and Ethnic Groups*. Washington, DC: National Center for Education Statistics, U.S. Department of Education.

Autor, David, Lawrence F. Katz, and Alan B. Krueger. 1997. "Computing Inequality: Have Computers Changed the Labor Market?" National Bureau of Economic Research Working Paper.

Balfanz, Robert, and Nettie Legters. 2004. *Locating the Dropout Crisis: Which High Schools Produce the Nation's Dropouts? Where Are They Located? Who Attends Them?* Baltimore: Johns Hopkins University Center for Social Organization of Schools. www.eric.ed.gov/ERICDocs/data/ericdocs2sql/content_storage_01/0000019b/80/1b/a3/a0.pdf.

Barab, Sasha et al. 2005. Making Learning Fun: Quest Atlantis, a Game Without Guns. Educational Technology Research and Development, 53(1):86-107.

Barker, L. J., and W. Aspray. 2006. "The State of Research on Girls and IT." In *Women and Information Technology: Research on Underrepresentation*, edited by J. M. Cohoon and W. Aspray. Cambridge, MA: MIT Press.:3-54.

Barron, Brigid, Kimberly Gomez, Nichole Pinkard, and Caitlin K. Martin. 2014. *The Digital Youth Network: Cultivating Digital Media Citizenship in Urban Communities*. Cambridge, MA: MIT Press.

Barton, Paul E., and Richard J. Coley. 2010. *The Black-White Achievement Gap: When Progress Stopped*. Princeton, NJ: Educational Testing Service.

Beaudry, Paul, David A. Green, and Benjamin M. Sand. 2016. "The Great Reversal in the Demand for Skill and Cognitive Tasks." *Journal of Labor Economics* 34 (S1): S199–S247.

Bell, Daniel. 1973. *The Coming of Post-Industrial Society: A Venture in Social Forecasting*. New York: Basic Books.

Bernard, H. Russell. 1994. *Research Methods in Anthropology: Qualitative and Quantitative Approaches*. Thousand Oaks, CA: Sage Publications.

Bettie, Julie. 2003. *Women without Class: Girls, Race, and Identity*. Berkeley and Los Angeles: University of California Press.

Blickenstaff, Jacob Clark. 2005. "Women and Science Careers: Leaky Pipeline or Gender Filter?" *Gender and Education* 17 (4): 369–386.

Boekaerts, Monique, Paul R. Pintrich, and Moshe Zeidner. 2000. *Handbook of Self-Regulation*. San Diego, CA: Academic Press.

Bogost, Ian. *How to Do Things with Video Games*. Minneapolis: University of Minnesota Press, 2011.

Bourdieu, Pierre. 1984. *Distinctions: A Social Critique of the Judgement of Taste*. Cambridge, MA: Harvard University Press.

Bowles, Jonathan, and David Giles. 2012. *New Tech City*. New York: Center for an Urban Future.

Bowles, Samuel, and Herbert Gintis. 2011. *Schooling in Capitalist America: Educational Reform and the Contradictions of Economic Life*. Chicago: Haymarket Books.

boyd, danah. 2014. *It's Complicated: The Social Lives of Networked Teens*. New Haven, CT: Yale University Press.

Bromwich, Jonah Engel. 2018. Disney to Donate $1 Million of 'Black Panther' Proceeds to Youth STEM Programs. New York Times, February 27. https://www.nytimes.com/2018/02/27/movies/disney-black-panther-stem.html.

Brown, John Seely, and Douglas Thomas. 2006. "You Play World of Warcraft? You're Hired!," *Wired*, April 1.

Brynjolfsson, Erik, and Andrew McAfee. 2011. *Race against the Machine: How the Digital Revolution Is Accelerating Innovation, Driving Productivity, and Irreversibly Transforming Employment and the Economy*. Lexington, MA: Digital Frontier Press.

———. 2014. *The Second Machine Age: Work, Progress, and Prosperity in a Time of Brilliant Technologies*. New York: W. W. Norton.

Bureau of Labor Statistics. 2016. "College Tuition and Fees Increase 63 Percent Since January 2006." August 30, 2016. www.bls.gov/opub/ted/2016/college-tuition-and-fees-increase-63-percent-since-january-2006.htm.

Carnevale, Anthony P., and Jeff Strohl. 2013. *Separate and Unequal: How Higher Education Reinforces the Intergenerational Reproduction of White Racial Privilege*. Washington, DC: Center on Education and the Workforce: Georgetown Public Policy Institute.

Carter, Prudence. 2005. *Keepin' It Real: School Success beyond Black and White*. London: Oxford University Press.

Casselman, Ben. 2014. "Race Gap Narrows in College Enrollment, but Not in Graduation." *FiveThirtyEight*, April 30, 2014. https://fivethirtyeight.com/features/race-gap-narrows-in-college-enrollment-but-not-in-graduation/.

Castells, Manuel, Mirela Fernandez-Ardevol, Jack Linchuan Qui, and Araba Sey. 2007. *Mobile Communication and Society: A Global Perspective.* Cambridge, MA: MIT Press.

Castillo, Juan. 2013a. Poverty Takes Root in Austin's Suburbs. Austin American-Statesman, May 19. https://www.mystatesman.com/news/local/poverty-takes-root-austin-suburbs /osUzE33wHfZVfKASJXs2ML/.

———. 2013b. As Austin and Most Suburbs Grow, So Does Poverty. Austin American-Statesman, November 13. https://www.mystatesman.com/news/austin-and-most -suburbs-grow-does-poverty/5NpkAaMx5S2sRNbiooECHP/.

Centers for Disease Control and Prevention. 2013. "Obesity—United States, 1999– 2010." *Morbidity and Mortality Weekly Report* 62 (3): 12–128.

Chau, Clement. 2010. "YouTube as a Participatory Culture." *New Directions for Youth Development* 2010 (128): 65–74.

Chetty, Raj, and Nathaniel Hendren. 2017. "The Impacts of Neighborhoods on Inter-generational Mobility: Childhood Exposure Effects." National Bureau of Economic Research Working Paper No. 23001, Revised Version, May.

Chetty, Raj, Nathaniel Hendren, Patrick Kline, and Emmanuel Saez. 2014. "Where Is the Land of Opportunity? The Geography of Intergenerational Mobility in the United States." *Quarterly Journal of Economics* 129 (4): 1553–1623.

Christakis, Nicholas A., and James H. Fowler. 2009. *Connected: The Surprising Power of Our Social Networks and How They Shape Our Lives.* New York: Little Brown.

Christenson, Peter G., and Donald F. Roberts. 1998. *It's Not Only Rock n' Roll: Popular Music in the Lives of Adolescents.* Cresskill, NJ: Hampton Press.

Clarebout, Geraldine, Holger Horz, and Wolfgang Schnotz. 2010. "The Relations between Self-Regulation and the Embedding of Support in Learning Environments." *Educational Technology Research and Development* 58 (5): 573–587.

Cohen, Cathy J., and Joseph Kahne. 2012. *Participatory Politics: New Media and Youth Political Action.* MacArthur Foundation Youth and Participatory Politics Research Network. https://ypp.dmlcentral.net/sites/default/files/publications/Participatory _Politics_Report.pdf.

Cowen, Tyler. 2013a. *Average Is Over: Powering America beyond the Age of the Great Stagnation.* New York: Dutton.

———. 2013b. Why Texas Is Our Future. *Time,* October 28, http://content.time.com/time /subscriber/article/0,33009,2154995-2,00.html.

Cramer, Meg, and Gillian R. Hayes. 2010. "Acceptable Use of Technology in School: Risks, Policies, and Promises." *Pervasive Computing* 9 (3): 37–44.

Crawford, Matthew B. 2009. *Shop Class as Soulcraft: An Inquiry into the Value of Work.* New York: Penguin Press.

Crawford, Susan. 2013. *Captive Audience: The Telecom Industry and Monopoly Power in the New Gilded Age.* New Haven, CT: Yale University Press.

Cuban, Larry. 1986. *Teachers and Machines: The Classroom Use of Technology Since 1920.* New York: Teachers College Press.

Currid, Elizabeth. 2007. *The Warhol Economy: How Fashion, Art, and Music Drive New York City*. Princeton, NJ: Princeton University Press.

De Certeau, Michel. 1984. *The Practice of Everyday Life*. Berkeley: University of California Press.

Dickens, Angelia. 1995. "Revisiting Brown v. Board of Education: How Tracking Has Resegregated America's Public Schools." *Columbia Journal of Law and Social Problems* 29: 469.

Dietz, John. 2014. Texas School Financing Ruling: Final Judgement. Austin, TX: District Court, Travis County, TX, 200th Judicial District, August 28.

Dill, Karen E. 2007. "Video Game Characters and the Socialization of Gender Roles: Young People's Perceptions Mirror Sexist Media Depictions." *Sex Roles* 57: 851–864.

Dill, Karen E., Brian P. Brown, Michael A. Collins. 2008. "Effects of Exposure to Sex-Stereotyped Video Game Characters on Tolerance of Sexual Harassment." *Journal of Experimental Social Psychology* 44 (5): 1402–1408.

diSessa, Andrea A. 2000. *Changing Minds: Computers, Learning, and Literacy*. Cambridge, MA: MIT Press.

DiTomaso, Nancy. 2013. *The American Non-dilemma: Racial Inequality without Racism*. New York: Russell Sage Foundation.

Dourish, Paul, Annette Adler, Victoria Bellotti, and Austin Henderson. 1996. "Your Place or Mine? Learning from Long-Term Use of Audio-Video Communication." *Computer Supported Cooperative Work (CSCW)* 5 (1): 33–62.

Duncan, Greg J., and Katherine Magnuson. 2011. "The Nature and Impact of Early Achievement Skills, Attention Skills, and Behavior Problems." In *Whither Opportunity? Rising Inequality, Schools, and Children's Life Chances*, edited by Greg J. Duncan and Richard J. Murnane. New York: Russell Sage Foundation.

Duncan, Greg J. and Richard J. Murnane. 2011. Introduction: The American Dream, Then and Now. In *Whither Opportunity? Rising Inequality, Schools, and Children's Life Chances*, edited by Greg J. Duncan and Richard J. Murnane. New York: Russell Sage Foundation: 3–26.

EducationSuperHighway. 2015. *2015 State of the States: A Report on the State of Broadband Connectivity in America's Public Schools*. http://stateofthestates2015.educationsuper highway.org/assets/sos/full_report-55ba0a64dcae0611b15ba9960429d323e2eadbac5 a67a0b369bedbb8cf15ddbb.pdf.

Ellison, Nicole, Charles Steinfield, and Cliff Lampe. 2009. "The Benefits of Facebook 'Friends': Social Capital and College Students' Use of Online Social Network Sites." *Journal of Computer-Mediated Communication* 12: 1143–1168.

Erickson, Bonnie. 2003. "Social Networks: The Value of Variety." *Contexts* 2 (1): 25–31.

Ericson, Barbara. 2017. "Detailed Race and Gender Information 2016." http://home.cc .gatech.edu/ice-gt/596.

Everett, Anna, and S. Craig Watkins. 2008. "The Power of Play: The Portrayal and Performance of Race in Video Games." In *The Ecology of Games: Connecting Youth, Games and Learning*, edited by Katie Salen, 141–166. Cambridge, MA: MIT Press.

Every, Vanessa, Gna Garcia, and Michael Young. 2010. "A Qualitative Study of Public Wiki Use in a Teacher Education Program." In *Proceedings of Society for Information Technology & Teacher Education International Conference 2010*, edited by D. Gibson and B. Dodge, 55–62. Chesapeake, VA: AACE.

Ewoldsen, David R., Cassie A. Eno, Bradley M. Okdie, John A. Velez, Rosanna E. Guadagno, and Jamie DeCoster. 2012. "Effect of Playing Violent Video Games Cooperatively or Competitively on Subsequent Cooperative Behavior." *Cyberpsychology, Behavior, and Social Networking* 15: 277–280.

Fabos, Bettina. 2004. *Wrong Turn on the Information Superhighway: Education and the Commercialization of the Internet*. New York: Teachers College Press.

Facer, Keri. 2011. *Learning Futures: Education, Technology and Social Change*. London: Routledge.

Fayer, Stella, Alan Lacey, and Audrey Watson. 2017. *STEM Occupations: Past, Present, and Future*. Washington, DC: U.S. Bureau of Labor Statistics.

Feldman, Daniel C. 1984. "The Development and Enforcement of Group Norms." *Academy of Management Review* 9: 47–53.

Finn, Jeremy D. 1989. "Withdrawing from School." *Review of Educational Research* 59: 117–142.

Finkelhor, David. 2011. *The Internet, Youth Safety, and the Problem of "Juvenoia."* Report published by the Crimes against Children Research Center. www.unh.edu/ccrc/pdf/Juvenoia%20paper.pdf.

Ford, Martin. 2015. *The Rise of the Robots: Technology and the Threat of Mass Unemployment*. New York: Basic Books.

Fordham, Signithia, and John Ogbu. 1986. "Black Students' School Success: Coping with the 'Burden of "Acting White."'" *Urban Review* 18 (3): 176–206.

Forte, Andrea, and Amy Bruckman. 2010. "Writing, Citing, and Participatory Media: Wikis as Learning Environments in the High School Classroom." *International Journal of Learning and Media* 1 (4): 23–44.

Fraser, Jill Andresky. 2001. *White Collar Sweatshop: The Deterioration of Work and Its Rewards in Corporate America*. New York: W. W. Norton.

Frechette, Julie. 2006. "Cyber-Censorship or Cyber-Literacy? Envisioning Cyber-Learning through Media Education." In *Digital Generations*, edited by David Buckingham and Rebekah Willett, 149–176. Mahwah, NJ: Lawrence Erlbaum Associates.

Frey, William. 2011. *America's Diverse Future: Initial Glimpse at the U.S. Child Population from the 2010 U.S. Census*. Washington, DC: Brookings Institution.

———. 2014. *Diversity Explosion: How New Racial Demographics Are Remaking America*. Washington, DC: Brookings Institution Press.

Friedman, Hilary Levey. 2013. *Playing to Win: Raising Children in a Competitive Culture*. Berkeley: University of California Press.

Fry, Richard. 2009. *The Changing Pathways of Latino Youths into Adulthood*. Washington, DC: Pew Latino Center.

Fry, Richard, and Paul Taylor. 2013. *Latino High School Graduates Pass Whites in Rate of College Enrollment*. Washington, DC: Pew Latino Center.

Garcia, Emma. 2015. *Inequalities at the Starting Gate: Cognitive and Noncognitive Skills Gaps between 2010–2011 Kindergarten Classmates*. Washington, DC: Economic Policy Institute.

Gee, James Paul. 2007a. "Learning Theory, Video Games, and Popular Culture." In *The International Handbook of Children, Media and Culture*, edited by Kristen Drotner and Sonia Livingstone. London: Sage Publications.

———. 2007b. *What Video Games Have to Teach Us about Learning and Literacy*. 2nd ed. New York: St. Martin's Griffin.

Gee, James Paul, and Elisabeth Hayes. 2010. *Women and Gaming: The Sims and 21st Century Learning*. New York: Palgrave Macmillan Press.

Gee, James Paul, Glynda Hull, and Colin Lankshear. 1996. *The New Work Order: Behind the Language of the New Capitalism*. Sydney, Australia: Allen & Unwin.

Gladwell, Malcom. 2010. "Small Change: Why the Revolution Will Not Be Tweeted." *New Yorker*, October 4.

Glott, Ruediger, Philipp Schmidt, and Rishab Ghosh. 2010. "Wikipedia Survey— Overview of Results." United Nations University Collaborative Creativity Group. www.wikipediasurvey.org/docs/Wikipedia_Overview_15March2010-FINAL.pdf.

Golding, Claudia, and Lawrence F. Katz. 2008. *The Race between Education and Technology*. Cambridge, MA: Harvard University Press.

Granic, Isabela, Adam Lobel, and Rutger C. M. E. Engels. 2014. "The Benefits of Playing Video Games." *American Psychologist* 69 (1): 66–78.

Granovetter, Mark. 1995. *Getting a Job: A Study of Contacts and Careers*. Chicago: University of Chicago Press.

Grant, Twala M. 1991. "Legal and Psychological Implications of Tracking in Education." *Law and Psychology Review* 15: 299.

Greenberg, Bradley S., and Joseph R. Dominick. 1969. "Racial and Social Class Differences in Teen-agers' Use of Television." *Journal of Broadcasting* 13, no. 4 (Fall): 331–344.

Halpern, Robert. 2003. *Making Play Work: The Promise of After School Programs for Low-Income Youth*. New York: Teachers College Press.

Hammond, T. C., and J. Lee. 2009. "From Watching Newsreels to Making Videos." *Learning & Leading with Technology* 36 (8): 32–33.

Harel, Idit, and Seymour Papert. 1991. *Constructionism: Research Reports & Essays, 1985–1990*. Norwood, NJ: Ablex Publishing.

Hargittai, Eszter and Amanda Hinnant. 2008. Digital Inequality: Differences in Young Adult's Use of the Internet. Communication Research. 35(5): 602-621.

Harris, Angel L. 2011. *Kids Don't Want to Fail: Oppositional Culture and the Black-White Achievement Gap*. Cambridge, MA: Harvard University Press.

Harris, Anita. 2004. *Future Girl: Young Women in the Twenty-First Century*. New York: Routledge.

Hart, Daniel, and Ben Kirshner. 2009. "Civic Participation and Development among Urban Adolescents." In *Engaging Young People in Civic Life*, edited by James Youniss and Peter Levine, 102–120. Nashville, TN: Vanderbilt University Press.

Harvey, David. 1990. *The Condition of Postmodernity: An Enquiry into the Origins of Social Change*. Malden, MA: Blackwell Press.

Hickey, Walt. 2018. 'Black Panther is Groundbreaking, But It's Shuri Who Could Change the World. FiveThirtyEight., February 18. https://fivethirtyeight.com/featuresblack -panther-is-groundbreaking-but-its-shuri-who-could-change-the-world/.

Hidi, Suzanne, and K. Ann Renninger. 2006. "The Four-Phase Model of Interest Development." *Educational Psychologists* 41 (2): 111–127.

Higher Education Research Institute. 2010. *Degrees of Success: Bachelor's Degree Completion Rates among Initial STEM Majors*. HERI Report Brief, January. www.heri .ucla.edu/nih/HERI_ResearchBrief_OL_2010_STEM.pdf.

Hobbs, Renee. 2017. "Hobbs Talks about Fake News in Italy" [video]. Media Education Lab. http://mediaeducationlab.com/hobbs-talks-about-fake-news-italy. Horn, L., and C. D. Carroll. 2006. *Placing College Graduation Rates in Context: How 4-Year College Graduation Rates Vary with Selectivity and the Size of Low-Income Enrollment*. Postsecondary Education Descriptive Analysis Report. Washington, DC: National Center for Education Statistics, U.S. Department of Education.

Horrigan, John. 2009. *Wireless Internet Use*. Washington, DC: Pew Research Center.

Houston Endowment. 2012. *A New Measure of Educational Success in Texas: Tracking the Success of 8th Graders into and through College*. Houston, TX: Houston Endowment.

Howell, Joseph T. 1973. *Hard Living on Clay Street: Portraits of Blue Collar Families*. Garden City, NY: Anchor Press.

Hoxby, Caroline, and Christopher Avery. 2012. "The Missing 'One-Offs': The Hidden Supply of High-Achieving, Low-Income Students." Working Paper 18586, National Bureau of Economic Research, Cambridge, MA.

Hutchins, Edwin. 1996. Cognition in the Wild. Cambridge, MA: MIT Press.

IDEO. 2012. *Design Thinking for Educators*. 2nd ed. Palo Alto, CA: IDEO.

Ingersoll, Richard M. 2003. *Out-of-Field Teaching and the Limits of Teacher Policy*. Report of the Center for the Study of Teaching and Policy and the Consortium for Policy Research in Education. http://repository.upenn.edu/cgi/viewcontent. cgi?article=1143&context=gse_pubs.

Institute of Play. 2014. "Glossary." www.instituteofplay.org/about/context/glossary/.

Ison, A., A. Hayes, S. Robinson, and J. Jamieson. 2004. "New Practices in Flexible Learning Txt Me: Supporting Disengaged Youth Using Mobile Phones." www.flexi bilelearning.net.au.

Ito, Mizuko, Kris Guitérrez, Sonia Livingstone, Bill Penuel, Jean Rhodes, Katie Salen, Juliet Schor, Julian Sefton-Green, and S. Craig Watkins. 2013. *Connected Learning: An Agenda for Research and Design*. Irvine, CA: Digital Media and Learning Research Hub.

Ito, M., H. Horst, M. Bittanti, D. boyd, B. Herr-Stephenson, P. Lange, C. J. Pascoe, and L. Robinson. 2010. *Hanging Out, Messing Around, and Geeking Out: Kids Living and Learning with New Media*. Cambridge, MA: MIT Press.

Ito, Mizuko, Misa Matsuda, and Daisuke Okabe. 2005. *Personal, Portable, Pedestrian: Mobile Phones in Japanese Life*. Cambridge, MA: MIT Press.

Jackson, Linda A., Edward A. Witt, Alexander Ivan Games, Hiram E. Fitzgerald, Alexander von Eye, and Yong Zhao. 2012. "Information Technology Use and Creativity: Findings from the Children and Technology Project." *Computers in Human Behavior* 28: 370–376.

James, Jonathan. 2012. *The College Wage Premium*. Federal Reserve Bank of Cleveland.

Jencks, Christopher, and Meredith Phillips. 1998. *The Black-White Test Score Gap*. Washington, DC: Brookings Institution Press.

Jenkins, Henry. 2006. *Convergence Culture: Where Old and New Media Collide*. New York: New York University Press.

Jenkins, Henry et al. 2009. *Confronting the Challenges of Participatory Culture: Media Education for the 21st Century*. With Ravi Purushotma, Margaret Weigel, Katie Clinton, and Alice J. Robison. Cambridge, MA: MIT Press, 2009.

Jenkins, Henry, Sangita Shresthova, Liana Gamber Thompson, Neta Kligler Vilenchik, and Arely M. Zimmerman. 2016. *By Any Media Necessary: The New Youth Activism*. New York: New York University Press.

Johnson, Larry, Samantha Adams, and Michele Cummins. 2012. *NMC Horizon Report: 2012 K–12 Edition*. Austin, TX: New Media Consortium.

Johnson, Larry, Samantha Adams, and Keene Haywood. 2011. *NMC Horizon Report: 2011 K–12 Edition*. Austin, TX: New Media Consortium.

Jones, Janelle, and John Schmitt. 2014. *A College Degree Is No Guarantee*. Washington, DC: Center for Economic and Policy Research.

Jones, Troy, and Kristen Cuthrell. 2011. "YouTube: Educational Potentials and Pitfalls." *Computers in the Schools* 28: 75–85.

Kahne, Joseph, Ellen Middaugh, Chris Evans. 2009. The Civic Potential of Video Games. Cambridge, MA: MIT Press.

Kalmus, Veronika., Pille Runnel, and Andra Siibak. 2009. "Opportunities and Benefits Online." In *Kids Online: Opportunities and Risks for Children*, edited by S. Livingstone and L. Haddon. Portland, OR: Policy Press: 71–82.

Kantor, Harvey and David B.Tyack. 1982. *Work, Youth and Schooling: Historical Perspectives on Vocationalism in American Education*. Palo Alto, CA: Stanford University Press.

Katz, Bruce, and Julie Wagner. 2014. *The Rise of Innovation Districts: A New Geography of Innovation in America*. Washington, DC: Metropolitan Policy Program, Brookings Institution.

Katz, James E. 2006. *Magic in the Air: Mobile Communication and the Transformation of Social Life*. London: Transaction.

Katz, Vikki S. 2014. *Kids in the Middle: How Children of Immigrants Negotiate Community Interactions for Their Families*. New Brunswick, NJ: Rutgers University Press.

Kaushal, Neeraj, Katherine Magnuson, and Jane Waldfogel. 2011. "How Is Family Income Related to Investments in Children's Learning?" In *Whither Opportunity? Rising Inequality, Schools, and Children's Life Chances*, edited by Greg J. Duncan and Richard J. Murnane. New York: Russell Sage Foundation:187–206.

Kelley, Kevin. 2012. "Better Than Human: Why Robots Will—and Must—Take Our Jobs." *Wired*, December.

Kelley, Robin D. G. 1997. *Yo' Mama's Disfunktional! Fighting the Culture Wars in Urban America*. Boston: Beacon Press.

Kena, Grace et al. 2016. *The Condition of Education 2016* (NCES 2016-144). U.S. Department of Education, National Center for Education Statistics. Washington, DC.

Kneebone, Elizabeth, and Alan Berube. 2013. *Confronting Suburban Poverty in America*. Washington, DC: Brookings Institution Press.

Kolb, Liz. 2008. *Toys to Tools: Connecting Student Cell Phones to Education*. International Society for Technology in Education. Eugene: Oregon.

Kress, Gunther. 2003. *Literacy in the New Media Age*. London: Routledge.

Krogstad, Jens Manuel, and Richard Fry. 2014. *More Hispanics, Blacks Enrolling in College, but Lag in Bachelor's Degrees*. Washington, DC: Pew Research Center.

Kutner, Lawrence, and Cheryl Olson. 2008. *Grand Theft Childhood: The Surprising Truth about Violent Video Games and What Parents Can Do*. New York: Simon & Schuster.

Labuhn, Andju Sara, Barry J. Zimmerman, and Marcus Hasselhorn. 2010. "Enhancing Students' Self-Regulation and Mathematics Performance: The Influence of Feedback and Self-Evaluative Standards." *Metacognition and Learning* 5 (2): 173–194.

Langdon, David, George McKittrick, David Beede, Beethika Khan, and Mark Doms. 2011. STEM: Good Jobs Now and for the Future.

Lange, Patricia G., and Mizuko Ito. 2010. "Creative Productions." In *Hanging Out, Messing Around, and Geeking Out: Kids Living and Learning with New Media*, edited by Mizuko Ito et al., 243–294. Cambridge, MA: MIT Press.

Lankshear, Colin, and Michele Knobel. 2008. *Digital Literacies: Concepts, Policies and Practices*. New York: Peter Lang.

Lareau, Annette. 2000. *Home Advantage: Social Class and Parental Intervention in Elementary Education*. Lanham, MD: Rowman & Littlefield Publishers.

———. 2003. *Unequal Childhoods: Class, Race, and Family Life*. Berkeley: University of California Press.

Lavin, Talia. 2016. "A Feminist Edit-a-Thon Seeks to Reshape Wikipedia." *New Yorker*. http://www.newyorker.com/tech/elements/a-feminist-edit-a-thon-seeks-to-reshape-wikipedia.

Lenhart, Amanda. 2009. *Teens and Mobile Phones over the Past Five Years: Pew Internet Looks Back*. Washington, DC: Pew Research Center

———. 2015. *Teens, Social Media & Technology Overview 2015*. Washington, DC: Pew Research Center.

Lenhart, Amanda, Sousan Arafeh, Aaron Smith, and Alexandra Rankin Macgill. 2008. *Writing, Technology, and Teens*. Washington, DC: Pew Research Center.

Lenhart, Amanda, Richard Ling, Scott Campbell, and Kristen Purcell. 2010. *Teens and Mobile Phones*. Washington, DC: Pew Research Center.

Lessig, Lawrence. 2008. *Remix: Making Art and Commerce Thrive in a Hybrid Economy*. New York: Penguin Group.

Levy, Frank, and Richard J. Murnane. 2004. *The New Division of Labor: How Computers Are Creating the Next Job Market*. Princeton, NJ: Princeton University Press.

———. 2013. *Dancing with Robots: Human Skills for Computerized Work*. NEXT Report. http://content.thirdway.org/publications/714/Dancing-With-Robots.pdf.

Levy, Pierre. 2000. *Collective Intelligence: Man's Emerging World in Cyberspace*. New York: Perseus.

Lin, Nan. 1999. "Social Network and Status Attainment." *Annual Review of Sociology* 25: 467–487.

———. 2001. *Social Capital: A Theory of Social Structure and Action*. New York: Oxford University Press.Ling, Richard. 2004. *The Mobile Connection: The Cell Phone's Impact on Society*. San Francisco: Morgan Kaufmann.

———. 2008. "Mobile Communication and Teen Emancipation." In *Mobile Technologies: From Telecommunications to Media*, edited by Gerard Goggin and Larissa Hjorth. London: Routledge.

Ling, Richard, Naomi Baron, Amanda Lenhart, and Scott Campbell. 2014. "'Girls Text Really Weird': Gender, Texting and Identity among Teens." *Journal of Children and Media* 8 (4): 423–439.

Ling, Richard, and Troels Bertel. 2013. "Mobile Communication Culture among Children and Adolescents." In *The Routledge International Handbook of Children, Adolescents and Media*, edited by Dafna Lemish. London: Routledge:127–133.

Livingstone, Sonia. 2009. *Children and the Internet*. Malden, MA: Policy Press.

Long, Joshua. 2010. *Weird City: Sense of Place and Creative Resistance in Austin, Texas*. Austin: University of Texas Press.

Lopez, Mark Hugo, Ana Gonzalez-Barrera, and Eileen Patten. 2013. *Closing the Digital Divide: Latinos and Technology Adoption*. Washington, DC: Pew Research Center.

Lucas, Samuel Roundfield. 1999. *Tracking Inequality: Stratification and Mobility in American High Schools*. New York: Teachers College Press.

Madden, Mary, Amanda Lenhart, Sandra Cortesi, Urs Gasser, Maeve Duggan, Aaron Smith, and Meredith Beaton. 2013. *Teens, Social Media, and Privacy*. Washington, DC: Pew Research Center.

Madden, Mary, Amanda Lenhart, Maeve Duggan, Sandra Cortesi, and Urs Gasser. 2013. *Teens and Technology 2013*. Washington, DC: Pew Research Center.

Mahoney, Joseph L., and Robert B. Cairns. 1997. "Do Extracurricular Activities Protect Against Early School Dropout?" *Developmental Psychology* 33: 241–253.

Margolis, Jane, et al. 2008. *Stuck in the Shallow End: Education, Race, and Computing*. Cambridge, MA: MIT Press.

Marsh, Herbert W. 1992. "Extracurricular Activities: Beneficial Extension of the Traditional Curriculum or Subversion of Academic Goals?" *Journal of Education Psychology* 84: 553–562.

Marsh, Herbert W., and Sabina Kleitman. 2002. "Extracurricular School Activities: The Good, the Bad, and the Nonlinear." *Harvard Educational Review* 72 (4): 464–514.

Marwick, Alice E. 2008. "To Catch a Predator? The MySpace Moral Panic." *First Monday* 13 (6). http://firstmonday.org/htbin/cgiwrap/bin/ojs/index.php/fm/article/view /2152/196.

Massey, Douglas S., and Nancy A. Denton. 1993. *American Apartheid: Segregation and the Making of the Underclass*. Cambridge, MA: Harvard University Press.

McFarland, Joel, Bill Hussar, Cristobal de Brey, Tom Snyder, Xiaolei Wang, Sidney Wilkinson-Flicker, Semhar Gebrekristos, Jijun Zhang, Amy Rathbun, Amy Barmer, Farrah Bullock Mann, and Serena Hinz. 2017. *The Condition of Education 2017.* NCES 2017-144. U.S. Department of Education. Washington, DC: National Center for Education Statistics. https://nces.ed.gov/pubsearch/pubsinfo.asp?pubid=2017144.

McKinsey & Company. 2017. *Jobs Lost, Jobs Gained: Workforce Transitions in a Time of Automation*. December.

Mellnik, Ted, and Carol Morello. 2013. "Washington: A World Apart." *Washington Post*, November 9. www.washingtonpost.com/sf/local/2013/11/09/washington-a-world -apart/?utm_term=.baed0913d540.

Merton, Robert K. 1968. "The Matthew Effect in Science." *Science* 159 (3810): 56–63.

Moretti, Enroci. 2012. *The New Geography of Jobs*. New York: Houghton Mifflin Harcourt.

Morrissette, Rhonda. 2008. "What Do They Know? A Strategy for Assessing Critical Literacy." *Knowledge Quest* 35 (5):14–17.

Murphy, Janet, and Robert Lebans. 2008. "Unexpected Outcomes: Web 2.0 in the Secondary School Classroom." *International Journal of Technology in Teaching and Learning* 4 (2): 134–147.

Musu-Gillette, Lauren et al. 2016. Status and Trends in the Education of Racial and Ethnic Groups 2016 (NCES 2016-007). U.S. Department of Education, National Center for Education Statistics. Washington, DC.

National Education Association. 1990. *Academic Tracking: Report of the NEA Executive Committee Subcommittee on Academic Tracking*. Washington, DC: National Education Association, Instruction and Professional Development, July.

National Employment Law Project. 2014. *An Unbalanced Recovery: Real Wage and Job Growth Trends*. Data Brief.

National Student Clearinghouse. 2016. *High School Benchmarks 2016: National College Progression Rates*. Herndon, VA: National Student Clearinghouse Research Center.

Neff, Gina. 2012. *Venture Labor: Work and the Burden of Risk in Innovative Industries*. Cambridge, MA: MIT Press.

Nielsen Media Research. 2013. "Smells Like Teen Spirit: How Teens Are Using Entertainment." Newswire, September 4. www.nielsen.com/us/en/insights/news/2013 /smells-like-teen-spirit—how-teens-are-using-entertainment.html.

Oakes, Jeannie. 2005. *Keeping Track: How Schools Structure Inequality*. New Haven, CT: Yale University Press.

O'Brien, Morgan. 2009. "The Tactics of Mobile Phone Use in the School-Based Practices of Young People." *Anthropology in Action* 16 (1): 30–40.

Omi, Michael, and Howard Winant. 2015. *Racial Formation in the United States.* 3rd ed. New York: Routledge.

Pacione, Chris. 2010. "Evolution of the Mind: A Case for Design Literacy." *Interactions* 17, no. 12 (March/April): 6–11.

Papastergiou, Marina. 2008. "Are Computer Science and Information Technology Still Masculine Fields? High School Students' Perceptions and Career Choices." *Computers & Education* 51 (2): 594–608.

Parker, Jessica K. 2010. *Teaching Tech-Savvy Kids.* Thousand Oaks, CA: Corwin.

Partnership for 21st Century Skills. 2008. *21st Century Skills, Education & Competitiveness: A Resource and Policy Guide.* Tucson, AZ: Partnership for 21st Century Skills. www.p21.org/storage/documents/21st_century_skills_education_and _competitiveness_guide.pdf.

Pew Latino Center. 2009. *Between Two Worlds: How Young Latinos Come of Age in America.* Washington, DC: Pew Latino Center. www.pewLatino.org/2009/12/11/ between-two-worlds-how-young-latinos-come-of-age-in-america/.

Pew Research Center. 2015. The Smartphone Difference. Washington, DC: Pew Research Center, http://www.pewinternet.org/2015/04/01/us-smartphone-use-in-2015/.

Pilloton, Emily. 2010. Teaching Design for Change. TEDGlobal 2010. https://www.ted .com/talks/emily_pilloton_teaching_design_for_change.

Pintrich, Paul R., and Akane Zusho (Edited by) Allan Wigfield and Jacquelynne S. Eccles. 2002. "The Development of Academic Self-Regulation: The Role of Cognitive and Motivational Factors." In *Development of Achievement Motivation,* edited by A. Wigfield and J. Eccles, 249–284. San Diego, CA: Academic Press.

Pope, Denise Clark. 2001. *Doing School: How We Are Creating a Generation of Stressed Out, Materialistic, and Miseducated Students.* New Haven, CT: Yale University Press.

Portes, Alejandro. 1998. "Social Capital: Its Origins and Applications in Modern Sociology." *Annual Review of Sociology* 24: 1–24.

President's Council of Advisors on Science and Technology. 2010. *Prepare and Inspire: K–12 Education in Science, Technology, Engineering and Math (STEM) for America's Future.* Washington, DC: President's Council of Advisors on Science and Technology.

Ramey, Garey, and Valerie Ramey. 2010. "The Rug Rat Race." In *Brookings Papers on Economic Activity: Spring 2010,* edited by David H. Romer and Justin Wolfers. Washington, DC: Brookings Institution Press.

Rheingold, H. 2012. *NetSmart.* Cambridge, MA: MIT Press.

Rideout, Vicky. 2015. Common Sense Census: Media Use by Tweens and Teens. San Francisco, CA: Common Sense.

Rideout, Victoria J., Ulla G. Foehr, and Donald F. Roberts. 2010. *Generation M2: Media in the Lives of 8- to 18-Year-Olds.* Menlo Park, CA: Henry J. Kaiser Family Foundation.

Rideout, Vicky and S. Craig Watkins. (Forthcoming). Millennials, Social Media, and Political Participation.

Rifkin, Jeremy. 1996. *The End of Work: The Decline of the Global Labor Force and the Dawn of the Post-Market Era.* New York: Tarcher/Putnam.

Roberts, Donald F., Ulla G. Foehr, and Victoria J. Rideout. 2005. *Generation M: Media in the Lives of 8–18 Year-Olds.* Menlo Park, CA: Henry J. Kaiser Family Foundation.

Roberts, Donald F., Ulla G. Foehr, Victoria J. Rideout, and Mollyann Brodie. 1999. *Kids & Media @ the New Millennium.* Menlo Park, CA: Henry J. Kaiser Family Foundation.

Robinson, Ken, and Lou Aronica. 2015. *Creative Schools: The Grassroots Revolution That's Transforming Education.* New York: Penguin Books.

Rodriguez, Carlos, Rita Kirshstein, Lauren Banks Amos, Wehmah Jones, Lorelle Espinosa, and David Watnick. 2012. *Broadening Participation in STEM: A Call to Action.* Report, NSF Grant No. HRD-1059774. Washington, DC: American Institutes for Research.

Rogers, Everett M. 1995. *Diffusion of Innovation.* 4th ed. New York: Free Press.

Ross, Andrew. 2009. *Nice Work If You Can Get It: Life and Labor in Precarious Times.* New York: New York University Press.

Rothstein, Richard. 2004. *Class and Schools: Using Social, Economic, and Educational Reform to Close the Black-White Achievement Gap.* New York: Teachers College Press, Columbia University.

———. 2017. *The Color of Law: A Forgotten History of How Our Government Segregated America.* New York: W. W. Norton.

Rothwell, Jonathan. 2013. *The Hidden Stem Economy.* Washington, D.C.: Brookings Institution.

Salen, Katie, and Eric Zimmerman. 2003. *The Rules of Play: Game Design Fundamentals.* Cambridge, MA: MIT Press.

Schell, Jesse. 2015. *The Art of Game Design: A Book of Lenses.* 2nd ed. London: CRC Press.

Schofield, Janet Ward, and Ann Locke Davidson. 2002. *Bringing the Internet to School: Lessons from an Urban District.* San Francisco: Jossey-Bass.

Seely-Brown, John. 2012. "Cultivating the Entrepreneurial Learner in the 21st Century." Keynote Speech, Digital Media and Learning Conference, San Francisco, CA.

Shapiro, Thomas. 2017. *Toxic Inequality: How America's Wealth Gap Destroys Mobility, Deepens the Racial Divide, and Threatens Our Future.* New York: Basic Books.

Sisario, Ben. 2014. "YouTube Music Key Is Introduced as New Rival in Streaming." *New York Times,* November 12.

Smith, Aaron. 2012. *Cell Internet Use 2012.* Washington, DC: Pew Research Center's Internet & American Life Project.

Smith, Morgan. 2014. "With Climbing Graduation Rates Come Renewed Doubts." *New York Times,* September 25.

Sormunen, Eero, Leeni Lehtiö, and Jannica Heinström. 2011. "Writing for Wikipedia as a Learning Task in the School's Information Literacy Instruction." Presented at the ISSSOME Conference, Finland.

Spradley, James P. 1980. *Participant Observation*. New York: Holt, Rinehart and Winston.

Stack, Carol. 1974. *All Our Kin: Strategies for Survival in a Black Community*. New York: Basic Books.

Stanton-Salazar, Ricardo D., and Sanford M. Dornbusch. 1995. "Social Capital and the Reproduction of Inequality: Information Networks among Mexican-Origin High School Students." *Sociology of Education* 68 (2): 116–135.

Stern, Shayla Thiel. 2007. *Instant Identity: Adolescent Girls and the World of Instant Messaging*. New York: Peter Lang Publishing.

Stiglitz, Joseph E. 2012. *The Price of Inequality: How Today's Divided Society Endangers Our Future*. New York: W. W. Norton.

Straubhaar, Joseph, Jeremiah Spence, Zeynep Tufekci, and Roberta G. Lentz, eds. 2012. *Inequity in the Technopolis: Race, Class, Gender, and the Digital Divide in Austin*. Austin: University of Texas Press.

Sum, Andrew et al. 2009. *The Consequences of Dropping Out of High School*. Boston: Center for Labor Market Studies.

Sum, Andrew et al. 2014. *The Plummeting Labor Market Fortunes of Teens and Young Adults*. Washington, DC: Brookings Institution: Metropolitan Policy Program. www.brookings.edu/interactives/the-plummeting-labor-market-fortunes-of-teens -and-young-adults/.

Susskind, Richard, and Daniel Susskind. 2015. *The Future of the Professions: How Technology Will Transform the Work of Human Experts*. New York: Oxford University Press.

Tang, Eric. 2014. *Outlier: The Case of Austin's Declining African-American Population*. Institute of Urban Poverty Research and Analysis, Issues Brief, May. www.utexas.edu /cola/insts/iupra/_files/pdf/Austin%20AA%20pop%20policy%20brief_FINAL.pdf.

Taylor, A. 2005. "Phone Talk." In *Mobile Communication: Re-Negotiation of the Social Sphere*, edited by R. Ling and P. E. Pedersen. London: Springer-Verlag.

Taylor, Paul, Rick Fry, and Russ Oates. 2014. *The Rising Cost of Not Going to College*. Washington, DC: Pew Research Center.

Texas Education Agency. 2008. "Glossary of Terms, 2007-08." Division of Research and Analysis. https://rptsvr1.tea.texas.gov/acctres/glosso708.html.

———. 2012. Chapter 126. Texas Essential Knowledge and Skills for Technology Applications Subchapter C. High School. §126.38. Game Programming and Design. Austin, TX: Texas Education Agency.

———. 2014. News release.

———. 2015. *Glossary: 2014-15 Texas Academic Performance Report*. Austin, TX: Texas Education Agency. https://rptsvr1.tea.texas.gov/perfreport/tapr/2015/glossary.pdf.

Thompson, Clive. 2008. "Brave New World of Digital Intimacy." *New York Times*, September 5.

Thornton, Sarah. 1996. *Club Cultures: Music, Media, and Subcultural Capital*. Hanover, MA: University Press of New England.

Tyner, Kathleen. 1998. *Literacy in a Digital World: Teaching and Learning in the Age of Information*. New York: Routledge.

Tyson, Karolyn. 2011. *Integration Interrupted: Tracking, Black Students, and Acting White after Brown*. New York: Oxford University Press.

U.S. Bureau of Labor Statistics. 2017. *Employment Projections—2016-2026*. Washington, DC: U.S. Department of Labor.

U.S. Department of Commerce. 1999. *Falling Through the Net: Defining the Digital Divide*. A Report on the Telecommunications and Information Technology Gap in America. Washington, DC. National Telecommunications and Information Administration.

———. 2014. *Exploring the Digital Nation: Embracing the Mobile Internet*. Washington, DC: National Telecommunications and Information Administration.

U.S. Department of Education. 2013. "Closing the Broadband Gap for Students and Teachers." https://blog.ed.gov/2013/06/closing-the-broadband-gap-for-students-and -teachers/.

U.S. Department of Education Office of Civil Rights. 2014. *Civil Rights Data Collection. Data Snapshot: School Discipline*. Washington, DC: U.S. Department of Education.

van 't Hooft, Mark. 2007. "Schools, Children, and Digital Technology: Building Better Relationships for a Better Tomorrow." *Innovate* 3 (4): Article 2: https://nsuworks. nova.edu/innovate/vol3/iss4/2/.

Venkatesh, Sudhir Alladi. 2006. *Off the Books: The Underground Economy of the Urban Poor*. Cambridge, MA: Harvard University Press.

Ventura, Matthew, Valerie Shute, and Weinan Zhao. 2013. "The Relationship between Video Game Use and a Performance-Based Measure of Persistence." *Computers & Education* 60: 52–58.

Vickery, Jacqueline Ryan. 2012. *Worth the Risk: The Role of Regulations and Norms in Shaping Teens' Digital Media Practices*. Austin: University of Texas at Austin. http:// repositories.lib.utexas.edu/bitstream/handle/2152/ETD-UT-2012-08-6246/VICKERY -DISSERTATION.pdf?sequence=1.

———. 2017. *Worried about the Wrong Things: Youth, Risk, and Opportunity in the Digital World*. Cambridge, MA: MIT Press.

Wacquant, Loic, and William Julius Wilson. 1989. "The Costs of Racial and Class Exclusion in the Inner City." *Annals of the Academy of Political and Social Science* 501: 8–25.

Warschauer, Mark. 2003. *Technology and Social Inclusion: Rethinking the Digital Divide*. Cambridge, MA: MIT Press.

Watkins, S. Craig. 2005. *Hip Hop Matters: Politics, Pop Culture and the Struggle for the Soul of a Movement*. Boston: Beacon Press.

———. 2009. *The Young and the Digital: What the Migration to Social Network Sites, Games, and Anytime, Anywhere Media Means for Our Future*. Boston: Beacon Press.

———. 2012. "Digital Divide: Navigating the Digital Edge." *International Journal of Learning and Media* 3 (2): 1–12.

———. 2014. "Future Cities: Diversifying Tech Talent." http://theyoungandthedigital. com/2014/07/09/future-cities-diversifying-tech-talent/.

———2017. "The Evolution of 'Black Twitter.'" In *Signs of Life in the U.S.A.: Readings on Popular Culture for Writers*, edited by Sonia Maasik and Jack Solomon, 9th ed. New York: Bedford/St. Martin's.

Watkins, S. Craig, and Krishnan Vasudevan. 2017. *The Diversity Crisis in Tech: Mapping the Challenges and Finding Solutions*. Irvine, CA: Digital Media and Learning Hub.

Wells, John, and Laurie Lewis. 2006. *Internet Access in U.S. Public Schools and Classrooms: 1994–2005*. NCES 2007-020. U.S. Department of Education. Washington, DC: National Center for Education Statistics.

Wheelock, Anne, and Massachusetts Advocacy Center. 1992. *Crossing the Tracks: How "Untracking" Can Save America's Schools*. New York: New Press.

Xue, Yi., and Richard C. Larson. 2015. "STEM Crisis or STEM Surplus? Yes and Yes." *Monthly Labor Review*, May. https://www.bls.gov/opub/mlr/2015/article/stem-crisis-or-stem-surplusyes-and-yes.htm.

Yee, Nick. 2007. Motivations of Play in Online Games. Journal of CyberPsychology and Behavior, 9:772-775.

Yeung, Wei-Jun Jean, and Kathryn M. Pfeiffer. 2009. "The Black-White Test Score Gap and Early Home Environment." *Social Science Research* 38: 412–437.

Zubrzycki, Jackie. 2016. "States Could Allow Students to Learn Coding Instead of Foreign Languages." *Education Week's Curriculum Matters*, June, 2. http://blogs.edweek. org/edweek/curriculum/2016/06/should_students_be_able_to_rep.html.

Zumbrunn, Sharon, Jose Tadlock, and Elizabeth Danielle Roberts. 2011. *Encouraging Self-Regulated Learning in the Classroom: A Review of the Literature. Metropolitan Educational Research Consortium (MERC)*: https://scholarscompass.vcu.edu/cgi /viewcontent.cgi?referer=https://www.google.com/&httpsredir=1&article=1017&con text=merc_pubs.

Index

About the Authors

S. Craig Watkins is a Professor in the Moody College of Communication at the University of Texas at Austin. He is the author of three previous books, *The Young and the Digital: What the Migration to Social Network Sites, Games, and Anytime, Anywhere Media Means for Our Future* (2009); *Hip Hop Matters: Politics, Pop Culture, and the Struggle for the Soul of a Movement* (2005); and *Representing: Hip Hop Culture and the Production of Black Cinema* (1998). His forthcoming book, *Don't Knock the Hustle: Young Creatives, Tech Ingenuity, and the Making of a New Innovation Economy,* will be published in 2019.

Alexander Cho is a digital media anthropologist who studies how young people use social media. He is a Postdoctoral Scholar at the University of California Humanities Research Institute.

Andres Lombana-Bermudez is a researcher, designer, and digital strategist working at the intersection of digital technology, youth, citizenship, and learning. He is a fellow at Harvard University's Berkman Center for Internet and Society and a Research Associate with the Connected Learning Research Network.

Vivian Shaw is a Doctoral Student in Sociology at the University of Texas at Austin.

Jacqueline Ryan Vickery is Assistant Professor in the department of Media Arts at the University of North Texas. She is the author of *Worried about the Wrong Things: Youth, Risk, and Opportunity in the Digital World* (2017).

Lauren Weinzimmer is a PhD Candidate with a concentration in Critical Media Studies in the department of Communication at the University of Minnesota.